DATE DUE

NOV 0 1 1982	
NOV 2 2 1982	
ILL 10 – 13 – 93	
FEB. 2 1994	

Spoken Word Recognition

COGNITION Special Issues

The titles in this series are paperback, readily accessible editions of the Special Issues of *COGNITION: An International Journal of Cognitive Science,* edited by Jacques Mehler and produced by special agreement with Elsevier Science Publishers B.V.

VISUAL COGNITION, Steven Pinker, guest editor

THE ONSET OF LITERACY: Cognitive Processes in Reading Acquisition, Paul Bertelson, guest editor

SPOKEN WORD RECOGNITION, Uli H. Frauenfelder and Lorraine Komisarjevsky Tyler, guest editors

Spoken Word Recognition

edited by
Uli H. Frauenfelder and
Lorraine Komisarjevsky Tyler

A Bradford Book
The MIT Press
Cambridge, Massachusetts
London, England

First MIT Press edition, 1987

Reprinted from *Cognition: International Journal of Cognitive Science,* Volume 25 (1987). The MIT Press has exclusive license to sell this English-language book edition throughout the world.

Library of Congress Cataloging-in-Publication Data

Spoken word recognition.

(Cognition special issues)
"A Bradford book."
Includes bibliographies and index.
1. Speech perception.   2. Word recognition.
I. Frauenfelder, Uli.   II. Tyler, Lorraine K.
(Lorraine Komisarjevsky), 1945–   .   III. Series.
BF463.S64S66   1987   153.6   87-2932
ISBN 0-262-56039-9 (pbk.)

Contents

The process of spoken word recognition: An introduction

LORRAINE KOMISARJEVSKY TYLER
University of Cambridge

ULI H. FRAUENFELDER*
Max-Planck-Institut für Psycholinguistik, Nijmegen

Abstract

This introduction sets the stage for the papers making up this special issue. Its focus is on two major problems in the study of lexical processing—determining the phases involved in recognising a spoken word and identifying the nature of different types of contextual influences on these phases. An attempt is made to decompose the process of recognising a word into phases which have both theoretical and empirical consequences. A similar analytic approach is taken in the discussion of the problem of context effects by distinguishing qualitatively different types of context (lexical, intra-lexical, syntactic, semantic, and inter-pretative). We argue that such an approach is necessary to make explicit the relationship between a particular type of contextual information and the phase(s) of processing at which it has its impact.

1. Introduction

Until recently, *spoken* word recognition has been a neglected area of study. Psychological research has focused on the *written* word, and generally has assumed that the processes involved in this modality were also those involved in the auditory modality. Thus, early models of word recognition (e.g., Becker & Killion, 1977; Forster, 1976; Morton, 1969) were developed on the basis of data obtained in reading tasks, although they were assumed to pro-

*Both authors contributed equally to this Introduction and to the Special Issue. Reprint requests should be sent to Uli Frauenfelder, Max-Planck-Institut für Psycholinguistik, Postbus 310, 6500AH Nijmegen, The Netherlands.

vide a general description of word recognition processes which was not modality-specific. More recently, there has been increased emphasis on developing models which are intended to account specifically for data on spoken language processing (e.g., Cole & Jakimik, 1980; Elman & McClelland, 1984; Marslen-Wilson, 1987, this issue; Marslen-Wilson & Tyler, 1980; Marslen-Wilson & Welsh, 1978) and to evaluate the relationship between processing in the two modalities (e.g., Bradley & Forster, 1987, this issue).

Apart from these developments in psycholinguistics, there have also been advances in speech perception, automatic speech recognition, linguistic theory and parsing that are all relevant to the problem of auditory word recognition.

In the area of speech perception, for example, there is growing awareness that the processing of the acoustic-phonetic input must be studied within the context of the lexical processing system, rather than merely within the phonetic domain (Nooteboom, 1979; Pisoni & Luce, 1987, this issue). In the field of automatic speech recognition, attempts to represent phonetic and phonological information formally and to develop algorithms for using this information in the analysis of the acoustic signal (e.g., Church, 1987, this issue) complement the efforts by psycholinguists to make mental structure and process explicit in models of lexical processing.

To capture structural regularities at different linguistic levels, phonological theory is moving away from the use of linear representations towards more hierarchical ones. Psycholinguists are taking increasing interest in such representations and are beginning to explore the possibility that listeners use phonological and prosodic knowledge to parse the sensory input during word recognition (cf. Frazier, 1987, this issue; Grosjean & Gee, 1987, this issue). The study of morphology has resulted in new theories of the structure and organisation of lexical entries that have provided important hypotheses for psycholinguistic research (e.g., Aronoff, 1976; Bybee, 1985; Selkirk, 1984), as has the development of grammatical theories which attribute considerable structural information to the lexicon (e.g., Bresnan, 1978). Finally, recent research in parsing has focused on specifying the informational content of lexical entries necessary to develop parsers which can use lexical representations for a word-by-word construction of higher-level representations (e.g., Ford, Bresnan & Kaplan, 1982).

Such a multi-disciplinary approach is necessary to understand the lexical processing system and the way in which it relates sound to meaning. Although not all of the work in these various disciplines is explicitly formulated as investigating psychological issues, it does, nevertheless, represent a body of knowledge which is invaluable in the development of psychological models of word recognition.

2. Lexical processing

In the following sections we will first outline what we consider to be the major phases involved in lexical processing and indicate how different theoretical positions have dealt with each of them. Then we will present a brief overview of the way in which context effects of different types have been assumed to intervene in these phases of lexical processing. Throughout this introduction we will raise some of the issues that continue to dominate research in lexical representation and process.

One of our objectives is to confront the terminological confusion plaguing word recognition research. Indeed, it is clear, even from the contributions to this volume, that we are still far from a terminological consensus. Basic terms like "word recognition" and "lexical access" are often used to refer to very different processes (cf. Tanenhaus & Lucas, 1987, this issue). We will attempt to identify in as theoretically neutral a fashion as possible the major aspects of lexical processing in an effort to develop a terminology which is consistent with various theoretical frameworks.

2.1. Initial lexical contact

The process of recognising a spoken word begins when the sensory input—or, more precisely, some representation computed from this input—makes initial contact with the lexicon. In this *initial contact phase*, the listener takes the speech wave as input and generates the representation(s) which contact the internally stored form-based representations associated with each lexical entry. A major question concerns the nature of the representation which makes contact with the lexicon. This representation has important consequences not only for *which* lexical entries are initially contacted but also for *when* they are contacted.

2.1.1. Contact representations

Many different *contact representations* have been proposed to mediate this initial phase—ranging from temporally defined spectral templates (e.g., Klatt, 1980) to abstract linguistic units like phonemes (e.g., Pisoni & Luce, 1987, this issue) or syllables (e.g., Mehler, 1981). The properties of these representations have potential consequences for the size of the initially contacted subset of the lexicon. The richer or more discriminative the information in the contact representation, the smaller the number of lexical entries initially contacted. To illustrate this point, we can contrast the effect of a phoneme-based representation with that of a robust feature representation (cf. Shipman & Zue, 1982) in which only six classes of phonemes are distinguished. In the former case, because the description of the input is much richer, it is more discriminative, and the size of the initially contacted set is smaller than in the latter case.

2.1.2. When initial contact occurs

The amount of speech required to compute the contact representation determines the moment at which initial contact can occur. Clearly, the longer the stretch of speech signal that the system needs to accumulate to construct this representation, the more the initial contact is delayed. We can contrast models with potentially immediate contact such as the LAFS model (Klatt, 1980) in which the first 10 ms spectral template initiates a path to a lexical entry, with models in which there is a much longer "dead period" during which no contact is possible. Consistent with the latter type of proposal, it has been suggested that the first syllable of a word (Bradley & Forster, 1987, this issue) or the first 150 ms of a word (Marslen-Wilson, 1984; Salasoo & Pisoni, 1985; Tyler, 1984) needs to be analysed before contact can be made.

In some models the first contact with lexical entries is based upon some initial portion of a word (Cole & Jakimik, 1980, Marslen-Wilson & Welsh, 1978). In the "cohort model", for example, the "word-initial cohort" contains all of the words in a language matching some beginning portion of the input (Marslen-Wilson & Tyler, 1980; Marslen-Wilson & Welsh, 1978). This view, in which priority is given to *temporally early* information, can be contrasted with approaches in which information which is physically *more salient*—irrespective of its temporal location—is used to contact the lexicon. For instance, Grosjean and Gee (1987, this issue) claim that stretches of the signal that are particularly reliable (such as stressed syllables) establish the initially contacted subset of the lexicon. These approaches all share the assumption that there is a discrete stage of initial contact which delimits a subset of the lexicon.

2.1.3. Advantages and disadvantages of discrete initial contact

The obvious advantage of discrete initial contact is that not all the entries in the lexicon need to be considered in subsequent phases of analysis. However, there are problems associated with the assumption that lexical entries are only ever considered if they are included in the initial subset of words matching the contact representation. For example, the intended word will never be located when the contact representation is misperceived. In order to reduce the risk of such unsuccesful initial contact, the contact representation has to be constrained. It has to be broad enough to ensure that the intended word is contacted, and yet specific enough so that only a minimal number of entries is contacted.

The contact representation must also be segmented correctly; it should correspond exactly to that portion of the stored lexical representation with which it is to be matched. If, for instance, a stretch of speech not corresponding to the initial part of a word is used to make contact with the beginnings of stored lexical representations, an inappropriate subset of the lexicon will be contacted, and the intended word will not be recognised (Frauenfelder, 1985). Positional or segmentation information, either in the contact representation itself or in the preceding context, must be available to ensure that proper initial contact takes place.

Models which do not assume a unique contact for each word avoid these potential problems. For example, the Trace model (Elman & McClelland, 1984) allows each activated phoneme to define a new subset of lexical entries containing this phoneme. The set of activated lexical entries constantly changes as old members drop out and new members are added. This avoids the problem of excluding the intended word from the pool of activated candidates, although it runs the risk of having too many activated words at each moment in time, making it more difficult to narrow in on and select the correct word. It remains an important—and unresolved—question whether or not word recognition does take the form of narrowing-down process of an initially established subset of the lexicon.

2.2. Activation

The lexical entries that match the contact representation to some criterial degree during the initial contact phase are assumed to change in state. In the absence of a theoretically neutral term for this change, we will refer to it as "activation". Theories differ in the claims they make concerning the factors that determine the relative status of activated words. For instance, the original version of the cohort theory proposed that all lexical entries matching the contact representation were equally activated and therefore had equal status. In the search model described by Bradley and Forster (1987, this issue), the relative status (the term "level of activation" is not appropriate for this model) of lexical entries at lexical contact depends upon properties of these entries themselves—in particular, upon their frequency of occurrence in the language. Lexical entries are ordered (within their respective subset or "bins") according to frequency. In other models, such as the current version of the cohort theory (Marslen-Wilson, 1987, this issue) and the Trace model, the degree of activation of a contacted lexical entry varies depending on both its goodness of fit with the contact representation(s) and its own internal specifications (e.g., frequency of occurrence).

2.3. Selection

After initial contact and activation of a subset of the lexicon, accumulating sensory input continues to map onto this subset until the intended lexical entry is eventually selected. This *selection phase* has been described in various ways: As a process of *differentiation* (McClelland & Rumelhart, 1986), *reduction* (Marslen-Wilson, 1984) or *search* (Forster, 1976). In the Trace model, the differential activation of lexical entries provides the basis for selection. Through processes of activation and inhibition, one entry eventually emerges as the most activated relative to all other entries. In contrast to this approach, the original formulation of the cohort theory saw this as an all-or-none process. The internal specifications of lexical entries were assessed against the sensory input and those which failed to match dropped out of the cohort. Thus, entries were either in or out of the cohort. A rather different approach is taken in the most recent version of the cohort theory (Marslen-Wilson, 1987, this issue) where lexical entries failing to match the input are not dropped from the cohort completely, but rather their level of activation starts to decay in the absence of further bottom-up support. In search models, the correct word is selected by a process which searches through the frequency-ordered set of lexical entries (Bradley & Forster, 1987, this issue).

2.4. Word recognition

We will reserve the term *word recognition* for the end-point of the selection phase when a listener has determined which lexical entry was actually heard. An important objective in approaches which emphasise the temporal nature of the recognition process, has been to determine the *word recognition point*, that is, the precise moment in time at which a word is recognised.

It is widely accepted that listeners generally recognize words, either in isolation or in context, before having heard them completely (Grosjean, 1980; Marslen-Wilson, 1984; Marslen-Wilson & Tyler, 1980). The exact recognition point of any given word depends upon a number of factors including its physical properties (e.g., length, stimulus quality), its intrinsic properties (frequency), the number and nature of other words in the lexicon that are physically similar to this word (i.e., its competitors or fellow cohort members) and the efficiency of the selection process. If the simplifying assumption is made that the acoustic signal is recognised sequentially, categorically and correctly as a sequence of discrete segments (e.g., phonemes or syllables) and that the selection process retains only those lexical entries matching this sequence, then it is possible to determine the recognition point for each word. In this case, a word's recognition point corresponds to its *uniqueness point—*

that is, the point at which a word's initial sequence of segments is common to that word and no other. If, however, the analysis of the input proceeds in a probabilistic rather than categorical fashion, then a word is not necessarily recognised at the uniqueness point, but rather later at the moment the sensory input matches one single lexical candidate better than all others by some criterial amount (Marcus & Frauenfelder, 1985).

2.5. Lexical access

The goal of lexical processing is to make available the stored knowledge associated with a word (cf. Johnson-Laird, 1987, this issue) so that this can be used to develop a meaningful interpretation of an utterance. We use the term *lexical access* to refer to the point at which the various properties of stored lexical representations—phonological, syntactic, semantic, pragmatic—become available. One central question is *when* does this lexical information become available to the rest of the language processing system?

Most theories agree that some form-based information must be available in the initial contact phase of lexical processing—otherwise there would be no basis for a match with the sensory input. There is disagreement, however, on the point at which other types of stored lexical knowledge become available. The range of different views is exemplified by the contrast between the cohort and search models. In the cohort model, all stored information is activated simultaneously upon initial contact (Marslen-Wilson & Tyler, 1980). In the search model, although some form-based description must be made available early in the process (upon initial contact), stored syntactic and semantic information does not become available until a word is accessed and recognised (Forster, 1976, 1979). This is because such information is stored centrally in a master file which is not entered until the word has been recognised (a process which takes place in the access "bin").

The assumed relationship between lexical access and word recognition varies depending upon the theory. In models like that of Bradley and Forster (1987, this issue), lexical access and word recognition, as defined here, are indistinguishable (although the authors themselves introduce another theoretical distinction between the two) since lexical information becomes available (lexical access) only when a single lexical entry has been found (word recognition). In models like the cohort model, there is a clear difference in that lexical access precedes word recognition.

Up to now we have only discussed the phases involved in recognising words and accessing stored lexical information. What remains to be considered now is how higher-order context influences spoken word recognition.

3. Context effects

An ubiquitous finding in the literature is that context plays an important role in spoken word recognition (e.g., Blank & Foss, 1978; Foss, 1982; Cairns & Hsu, 1980; Marslen-Wilson & Tyler, 1980, Salasoo & Pisoni, 1985). To explain the ease and rapidity with which listeners recognise words, psycholinguistics often appeal to context. Their general claim is that lexical processing depends on two broad classes of information—representations computed from the sensory input, and those constructed from the previous context using higher sources of knowledge (e.g., lexical, syntactic, semantic, and pragmatic). To understand the nature of these contextual influences we need to specify the answers to at least three related questions: (1) *which* types of context affect lexical processing? (2) *when* do these contexts influence specific processes involved in recognising a word? and (3) *how* do these types of context have their effects? The answers to these questions have important implications for the general structure of the language processing system.

3.1. Autonomy versus interaction

There are currently two strongly opposing views concerning the structure of the language processing system—the autonomous and the interactive views. Each provides different answers to questions about the way in which information can flow through the language processing system. According to autonomous theories, there are strong constraints on the way in which contextual information can affect the bottom-up analysis. Context *cannot* have its effect prior to the completion of the phases of lexical processing leading up to word recognition. It only contributes to the evaluation and integration of the output of lexical processing, but not to the generation of this output (e.g., Forster, 1979; Norris, 1986; Tanenhaus, Carlson & Seidenberg, 1984; Tanenhaus & Lucas, 1987, this issue). However, such models permit "lateral" flow of information *within* a given processing level (e.g., between words within the lexicon).

Interactive models, in contrast, allow different kinds of information to interact with each other. However, the extent to which contextual information is allowed to intervene in any of the phases of lexical processing varies considerably in different theories. In certain interactive models (e.g., Morton, 1969), expectations generated from higher-level representations actually intervene directly in the earliest phases of lexical processing by altering the activation of lexical elements. In others, context only operates on a subset of elements selected on the basis of the sensory input (e.g., Marslen-Wilson & Welsh, 1978).

At first glance, the predictions of these two classes of theories appear to be clear-cut, and choosing between them straightforward. In reality, however, differentiating between the models is extremely difficult. A major problem is that the distinction between autonomous and interactive models is not dichotomous but continuous. Models are autonomous or interactive to varying degrees. Consequently, there are relatively large differences between models *within* the autonomous or interactive class, and very small differences *between* some autonomous and interactive models (cf. Tyler & Marslen-Wilson, 1982).

For example, autonomous models vary in the extent to which the principle of autonomy constrains the system's operations. This is reflected in differences in the size and number of postulated autonomous modules. In Forster's model (1979), for example, there are several autonomous processing modules, each corresponding to a putative linguistic level (lexical, syntactic, and semantic). These modules are configured serially so that each module only receives and processes the output of the immediately lower level; any information derived from higher processing modules cannot affect processing operations at the lower level. In contrast, there is only a single module (the language processing module) in Fodor's (1983) model. Information can flow freely between the different subcomponents of the language processing module, but information coming from outside the language processor (knowledge of the world), cannot alter the course of its operations. In this model, then, the principle of autonomy applies only to the language processing module as a whole and does not constrain the intermediate levels of analysis, as in Forster's model.

Interactive models are just as varied as autonomous models. They primarily differ as a function of how (or how much) contextual information is permitted to affect the sensory analysis. On interactive accounts, both contextual and sensory information contribute to lexical processing. Context can propose lexical candidates for consideration even before any sensory input has been received (Morton, 1969). Other views, in which the flow of information is more highly constrained, allow context only to dispose of candidates and not to propose them (e.g., Marslen-Wilson, 1987, this issue). Lexical candidates which are contextually appropriate are integrated into the higher-level representation. Those which are contextually inappropriate are either completely eliminated from contention during the selection phase (Marslen-Wilson & Welsh, 1978), or their activation levels gradually decay (Marslen-Wilson, 1987, this issue).

Because there is no standard autonomous or interactive theory, it is often difficult in practice to distinguish between these two classes of models. Results that have been taken to favour interactive models can be explained by autonomous models making slightly different assumptions. For example, certain context effects can be accounted for by an autonomous model in which multiple, rather than single, outputs are passed on to higher-level modules (e.g., Norris, 1982, 1986). These outputs are then evaluated against the context in a parallel fashion. The lexical candidates that best match contextual requirements are recognised even in the absence of sufficient sensory input to uniquely specify the word. The process of word recognition is thus claimed to be unaffected by context, and the autonomy hypothesis remains unscathed. However, as Tyler and Marslen-Wilson (1982) point out, the assumptions of autonomy are so weakened in such a model that it essentially becomes indistinguishable empirically from an interactive model.

Most autonomous models do, however, make predictions about the nature of context effects which are empirically distinguishable from those proposed by interactionist models. The major difference between the models lies in the claims each makes about the *moment* at which context has its effect. For context to exert its influence *before* or *during* the selection phase constitutes evidence against a strong autonomy view and in favour of certain types of interactionist view.

Morton (1969) and Grosjean (1980), among others, have advanced strong interactionist positions by claiming that context can have an effect on lexical processing even before any sensory input is heard. This is achieved in Morton's model by allowing context to increase the level of activation of individual logogens even before the sensory input makes contact with the lexicon. As a result, less sensory input is needed to reach threshold and to recognise a contextually appropriate compared to a contextually inappropriate word. For Grosjean, rather than affecting threshold levels, context narrows down the set of words which are matched against the sensory input to those which are contextually appropriate. It is not made clear in either of these models how context can function in advance of any sensory input. Unless context effects operate via spreading activation, they can help select contextually appropriate lexical entries only if the syntactic and semantic properties of these lexical entries are already available for contextual evaluation. But how can they be when no sensory input corresponding to any lexical entry has yet entered the system? For such a system to work without spreading activation requires the stored semantic and syntactic information of *all* entries in the entire lexicon to always be available to be assessed against the context.

In most other interactionist models, context effects occur at a later phase of the process—when the sensory input has made initial contact with the lexicon. These models claim that this is the earliest moment in time at which context can exert its influence on lexical processing because this is when the stored properties of words first become available. It is on the basis of these stored representations that a word can be evaluated for its contextual appropriateness. So, for example, in the original version of the cohort theory, it was at the point of initial contact that word candidates were first evaluated for their contextual appropriateness. Candidates whose internal specifications were incompatible with the context dropped out of the activated subset. This process facilitated the selection of a single candidate from amongst the initially contacted set by reducing the set to only those words which were contextually appropriate. This resulted in earlier recognition for a word in context than in isolation. Word recognition in this model, then, was seen as involving both autonomous and interactive processes. The initial process of contacting the lexicon was autonomous, but the selection process was interactive.

Autonomy theorists in contrast, claim that it is only *after* a word emerges as the single best fit with the sensory input that context can begin to have an effect. For example, Forster (1976) claims that when the sensory input uniquely specifies a word, the pointer for this word contacts the appropriate entry in the master file. It is in the master file that a word's internal properties are stored and, therefore, it is only at this point that the syntactic and semantic properties of the word are evaluated against the specifications of the context. The role of context, therefore, is restricted to the post-access phase of lexical processing (e.g., Seidenberg, Tanenhaus, Leiman, & Bienkowski, 1982; Swinney, 1979).

To evaluate these various theoretical predictions, it is essential to establish the precise moment in processing at which context produces its effect. The recent development of on-line techniques has provided psycholinguists with increased power to resolve the temporal properties of word recognition necessary to determine the loci of context effects. Nonetheless, the use of these experimental techniques introduces new problems that make data interpretation difficult. In the first flush of enthusiasm over these techniques, any on-line task was thought to be as good as any other. The possibility that different tasks might tap different phases of lexical processing was largely ignored. However, individual tasks are now coming under greater scrutiny. This can be seen in the current debate over the appropriate use of naming and lexical decision tasks. The lexical decision task appears to be sensitive to late decision processes (e.g., Forster, 1979; Jakimik, Cole & Rudnicky, 1985; Seidenberg, Waters, Sanders & Langer, 1984) and is not, therefore, appropriate for assessing the role of context in the early phases of lexical processing. Naming, in contrast, seems to reflect earlier phases of lexical processing and therefore promises to be a more useful task with which to determine the locus of context effects.

3.2. Different types of context effects

The proper characterisation of context effects is a delicate task. Nonetheless, since context undeniably does affect lexical processing at some point, it is essential to determine the specific nature of this influence if we are to arrive at a complete understanding of the language processing system. In the following sections, we will distinguish between different types of context and examine the ways in which each has been argued to affect various phases of lexical processing. We will draw a broad distinction between two types of context which we will call *structural* and *non-structural*.

We can define structural context as that which results from constraints on the ways in which elements can be combined into higher-level units. This type of constraint can apply at the phoneme, morpheme, phrase, utterance and discourse levels. So, for example, the rules determining the legal combination of morphemes into polymorphemic words constitute one type of structural constraint. In principle, this is similar to the constraints governing the set of elements which can combine to form, for example, a noun phrase or a prepositional phrase. In each case, although the system of rules differs, the nature of the constraint is similar. That is, the rules determine which elements can legally combine to form structural units. Papers in this issue by Tanenhaus and Lucas and by Frazier discuss some of these different types of structural relations and their implications for the processes involved in spoken word recognition.

This type of structural context can be contrasted with contexts in which the relationship between elements does not result in some higher-level representation. One example of non-structural context is the associative relationship illustrated by the words *doctor* and *nurse*. These words are semantically related but they are not structurally related in the sense of forming a higher-level representation.

The distinction between structural and non-structural context effects is critical for certain autonomous models of lexical processing (e.g., Forster, 1981). To the extent that non-structural context effects can be explained in terms of relations holding between items within a *single* level of the processing system, they do not violate the autonomy hypothesis. In contrast, structural context effects involve *multiple* levels of the system and a top-down flow of information, and therefore are not consistent with strong versions of the autonomy view.

3.3. Non-structural context: Intra-lexical effects

The recognition of one word can have an impact upon the processing of another word which bears some relationship to the first. The relationship can be phonological, morphological, syntactic or semantic—but it does *not* involve the construction of a higher-level representation.

The intra-lexical context effects which are found for associatively related words provide a good example of non-structural context effect (Meyer & Schvaneveldt, 1971; Seidenberg et al., 1982). For example, the semantic properties of a word like *teacher* are assumed to prime or facilitate the processing of a semantically associated word such as *school*. Such priming effects have generally been interpreted within the framework of models like the Collins and Loftus (1975) spreading activation model of semantic networks. When the first word is presented, activation spreads to neighboring words or, rather, concepts with which it is linked. This activation translates into faster recognition of the related word.

Theorists like Forster and Fodor would argue that this type of "hardwired connection" between words is the only type of semantic context which can have an effect on any of the phases of word recognition. At issue then is the extent to which this type of context actually generalises to the recognition of words in utterance contexts, or whether it only operates when words appear in non-structured lists. Thus, the exact contribution of this type of context on lexical processing remains to be determined.

3.4. Structural context effects

3.4.1. Lexical context effects

Lexical effects refer to the influence that lexical representations are assumed to have upon acoustic-phonetic processing. Early evidence for such effects was furnished by Ganong (1980) who presented subjects with ambiguous phonemes (situated along a VOT continuum, e.g., k ↔ g continuum) in two different contexts. In one context, the first phoneme reading of the stimuli (e.g., /k/ in the context __iss) led to a word, whereas the other reading (/g/ in same context) produced a nonword (giss). Subjects gave more word phoneme responses than nonword responses, leading Ganong to argue that the lexical context within which phonemes are embedded influences the processing of these phonemes.

Two important questions must be answered in trying to characterise this effect: *how* and *when* are the two information sources brought into contact (cf. Segui & Frauenfelder, 1986)? With respect to the former question, we can distinguish two ways in which the higher level might affect the lower. Either it could contribute information to the lower level directly, or it could simply help in the evaluation of an autonomously constructed output.

In the Trace model (Elman & McClelland, 1984), lexical effects operate by modifying the analysis of the sensory input. This interactive activation model contains several levels of representation, each consisting of a set of interconnected nodes representing distinctive features, phonemes and words. These discrete, yet interactive, processing levels continuously exchange information. Incoming sensory input provides bottom-up excitation of the distinctive feature nodes which in turn activate phoneme nodes. As the phoneme nodes become excited, they can alter the level of activation of word nodes. Critically, the word nodes provide lexical feedback to lower level phoneme nodes, thereby increasing the level of activation of the phoneme node. As a consequence, phoneme processing and recognition depends not only on the bottom-up activation from the feature level but also on top-down influences from the lexical level. This view can be contrasted with an autonomous view in which the lexical level serves only to indicate the presence of a mismatch between its analysis and that of the lower level, and to suggest that a *revision* (or re-evaluation) of the analysis of the sensory input may be required.

In selecting further between these two alternative frameworks, we need to establish the temporal properties of lexical effects. First, we must determine the temporal locus of lexical effects with respect to: (a) the *phonetic categorisation* of the sensory input, and (b) *word recognition* (before or after a single lexical entry has been selected). Thus, it must be determined whether the lexicon influences phonetic decisions *before* or *after* phonetic categorisation is completed. Clearly, if a decision on the identity of a phonetic segment has already been made, lexical context can no longer have any effect upon the decision process itself, but only upon the process of evaluating the output of this process.

A complete account of the locus (or loci) of lexical effects must make reference not only to the temporal properties of acoustic-phonetic processing but also to those of lexical processing. In principle, the lexical level could exert its influence upon phonetic decisions either *after* word recognition (when a single lexical candidate has been selected) or *before* (when several lexical candidates are still active). Clearly, the contribution of the lexical level to phonetic processing is more valuable in the latter case. Indeed, only if the lexical level has its effect *during* the selection process of word recognition, can it really contribute to the process of recognising a word. If lexical context operates after word recognition, then its contribution is limited to serving other purposes—for example, identifying word boundaries.

Research into lexical effects has not yet provided adequate answers to the questions raised above. Nonetheless, despite the complexities of evaluating the contribution of lexical context to phonetic processing, the appropriate methodological tools appear to be within our grasp for addressing these questions empirically.

3.4.2. Syntactic context effects

A listener processing the syntactic structure of an utterance has information available that constrains the syntactic properties of upcoming words and their constituent structure. *How* and *when* does this syntactic information influence lexical processing? Theory (Frazier, 1987, this issue) and data (Tyler & Wessels, 1983; Tanenhaus et al., 1979) converge in attributing to syntactic context only a very limited capacity to intervene in the phases of lexical processing leading to word recognition.

This is not surprising since syntactic structure can impose only weak constraints on the form-class and morphological structure of lexical items. Although there is considerable cross-linguistic variation, in languages like English, it is only rarely possible to predict with absolute certainty the form-class of any given lexical item because each syntactic constituent has optional members. So, in most instances, a listener hearing the beginning of a noun phrase (e.g., having heard a determiner) cannot be certain of the form-class of the following item since it could be an adjective, adverb or noun.

However, there are rare cases where syntactic constraints do fix the form-class of a lexical entry. But, even in these cases their contribution still remains limited given the large number of words in each of the open class categories (e.g. adjectives, nouns, verbs). Moreover, in many instances the form-class of words is determined by their suffixes, or more precisely, their heads (Williams, 1981). Frazier (1987, this issue) argues that the fact that the rightmost derivational suffix generally determines a word's form-class limits the predictive power of the syntactic constraints. Listeners cannot confirm predictions based on preceding syntactic context until they correctly identify the element carrying the form-class information which often comes well after the stem has been heard. Some experimental evidence suggests that syntactic context can have an effect upon the recognition of suffixes. In a study examining the effects of different types of context on the recognition of polymorphemic words, Tyler and Marslen-Wilson (1986) found that syntactic constraints facilitate recognition of suffixes while semantic constraints facilitate recognition of stems. What this means is that the appropriate syntactic constraints can speed up the recognition of polymorphemic words, by facilitating recognition of suffixes. In these circumstances, a polymorphemic word may be recognised at the point at which its stem is recognised since the syntactic context can predict the suffixes.

3.4.3. Meaning-based context effects

We use the terms "semantic context" and "interpretative context" in order to highlight the distinction between a variety of types of contextual information which we believe ought to be distinguished, but rarely are. The term "semantic context" usually refers to any type of context which is meaningful—whether that meaning is based on such wildly differing types of meaning relations as semantic associations or pragmatic inference. In the interests of perspicuity, we propose that the term "semantic context" be reserved for the representation of an utterance which derives from the combination of those aspects of meaning which one wants to claim are based upon word meanings, together with the syntactic structure of the utterance. "Semantic context", then, would explicitly *not* involve pragmatic inferences, the discourse context and knowledge of the world. "Interpretative context" could then be used to refer to the more highly elaborated representation which incorporates these seemingly less tangible aspects of meaning (Marslen-Wilson & Tyler, 1980).

Semantic context. Unlike the effect of syntactic context, there is considerable evidence that semantic context affects lexical processing. Words which are semantically appropriate for the context are responded to faster and the identification of those which are contextually inappropriate are slowed down (Marslen-Wilson, 1984; Marslen-Wilson & Tyler, 1980; Morton & Long, 1976 (but see Foss & Gernsbacher, 1983); Tyler & Wessels, 1983). These facilitatory and inhibitory effects have been demonstrated using a variety of "on-line" tasks, for example, phoneme monitoring, lexical decision, mispronunciation detection, shadowing, naming, word monitoring and gating. There are two important issues in this research. First, there is the issue of the nature of semantic context effects. Second, there is the issue of where, in the various phases of lexical processing, these effects are to be located. Whenever we observe semantic context effects, we must determine whether they result from some type of higher-order structural representation of the words in an utterance or whether they can simply be explained in terms of intra-lexical associations. Because most researchers are neither explicit nor systematic about the type of meaning context they manipulate experimentally, the interpretation of their data is frequently difficult.

The difference between these two types of semantic context is critical for some autonomous models like that of Forster. While such models can accommodate intra-lexical semantic effects (because these can be located within a single level of the language system), they do not allow semantic context effects which are attributable to higher-level *structural* representations.

Undoubtedly, context effects of this latter type do exist, but what remains unresolved is exactly when they have their influence on lexical processing. If semantic context effects can be located in the early phases of lexical processing—as, for example, Grosjean (1980), Marslen-Wilson and Tyler (1980) and Morton (1969) would claim—they would be problematic for those autonomy models which confine structural information to a post-access role in lexical processing (Forster, 1979). Autonomy assumptions are not violated by such semantic context effects in Fodor's model because they can be located within the language module. It is only interpretative contextual effects which cannot be located within the language module and which involve the central processor (e.g., effects involving knowledge of the world) which violate autonomy assumptions.

Interpretative context. "Interpretative context" effects are certainly controversial for all versions of the autonomy thesis because such effects are outside the domain of an autonomous language processing system. If interpretative context can be shown to affect any of the phases of lexical processing prior to the point at which a single word is selected, then the autonomy assumption is violated. Such context effects are only consistent with the autonomy assumption if they operate after a single candidate has been selected.

Given the theoretical importance of this issue, we need to be able to demonstrate convincingly whether or not interpretative context does facilitate the processes involved in recognising spoken words. Much of the burden here is methodological. In addition to teasing apart the different types of meaning contexts distinguished above, we need to be able to specify what aspects of the word recognition process are reflected by different tasks. And we need to use tasks which are able, in principle, to tap the very *early* processes involved in word recognition. Otherwise there will be continuous dispute as to whether a particular task taps the appropriate phase of the process to allow us to make definitive claims about where context effects are to be located. As mentioned above, an attempt in this direction has been made recently with respect to lexical decision and naming tasks. Whether or not the current analyses of these tasks turn out to be correct, the enterprise is surely necessary.

4. Conclusions

We have focused in this short introduction on two major problems in the study of lexical processing—the phases involved in recognising a spoken word and the nature of different types of contextual influences on these phases. What we have attempted to do is to decompose the process of recognising a word into phases which have both theoretical and empirical consequences. There are necessarily pitfalls associated with such an enterprise. Although we found it necessary to break down lexical processing into its component phases, this does not mean that we assume that each phase is necessarily discrete. The extent to which the phases we differentiate are independent is still very much of an empirical issue. A related problem is terminological in nature; the terms we use to label these phases (like selection and lexical access) are ambiguous since they can refer either to a process or to the product of this process. A similar decompositional approach has been taken in our discussion of context effects. Here, we have attempted to distinguish qualitatively different types of context (lexical, intra-lexical, syntactic, semantic, and interpretative). This is necessary to make explicit the relationship between a particular type of top-down information and the phase(s) of processing at which it has its impact. Despite the problems inherent in the analytic approach taken here in this introduction, we consider it to be the most appropriate way to study lexical processing.

References

Aronoff, M. (1976). Word formation in generative grammar. *Linguistic Inquiry Monograph 1*. Cambridge, Mass.: MIT Press.

Becker, C.A., & Killion, T.H. (1977). Interaction of visual and cognitive effects in word recognition. *Journal of Experimental Psychology: Human Perception and Performance, 3*, 389–401.

Blank, M., & Foss D.J. (1978). Semantic facilitation and lexical access during sentence processing. *Memory and Cognition, 6*, 644–652.

Bradley, D.C., & Forster, K.I. (1987). A reader's view of listening. *Cognition, 25*, 103–134, this issue.

Bresnan, J. (1978). A realistic transformational grammar. In J. Bresnan, M. Halle & E. Miller (Eds.), *Linguistic theory and psychological reality*. Cambridge, Mass.: MIT Press.

Bybee, J. (1985). *Morphology. A study of the relation between meaning and form*. Amsterdam: Benjamins.

Cairns, H.S., & Hsu, J.R. (1980). Effects of prior context upon lexical access during sentence comprehension: A replication and reinterpretation. *Journal of Psycholinguistic Research, 9*, 319–326.

Church, K.W. (1987). Phonological parsing and lexical retrieval. *Cognition, 25*, 53–69, this issue.

Cole, R., & Jakimik, J. (1980). A model of speech perception. In R.A. Cole (Ed.), *Perception and production of fluent speech*. Hillsdale, N.J.: Erlbaum.

Collins, A., & Loftus, E. (1975). A spreading activation theory of semantic processing. *Psychological Review, 82*, 407–428.

Elman, J.L., & McClelland, J.L. (1984). Speech perception as a cognitive process: The interactive activation model. In N. Lass (Ed.), *Speech and Language, Vol. 10*. New York: Academic Press.

Fodor, J.A. (1983). *The modularity of mind: An essay on faculty psychology*. Cambridge, Mass.: MIT Press.

Ford, M., Bresnan, J., & Kaplan, R. (1982). A competence-based theory of syntactic closure. In J. Bresnan (Ed.), *The mental representation of grammatical relations*. Cambridge, Mass.: MIT Press.

Forster, K.I. (1976). Accessing the mental lexicon. In R.J. Wales & E. Walker (Eds.), *New approaches to language mechanisms*. Amsterdam: North-Holland.

Forster, K.I. (1979). Levels of processing and the structure of the language processor. In W.E. Cooper & E. Walker (Eds.), *Sentence processing: Psycholinguistic studies presented to Merrill Garrett*. Hillsdale, N.J.: Erlbaum.

Forster, K.I. (1981). Priming and the effects of sentence and lexical contexts on naming time: evidence for autonomous lexical processing. *Quarterly Journal of Experimental Psychology, 33A*, 465–495.

Foss, D.J. (1982). A discourse on semantic priming. *Cognitive Psychology, 14*, 590–607.

Foss, D.J., & Gernsbacher, M.A. (1983). Cracking the dual code: Toward a unitary model of phoneme identification. *Journal of Verbal Learning and Verbal Behavior, 22*, 609–632.

Fraunfelder, U.H. (1985). Cross-linguistic approaches to lexical segmentation. *Linguistics, 23*, 669–687.

Frazier, L. (1987). Structure in auditory word recognition. *Cognition, 25*, 157–187, this issue.

Ganong, W.F. (1980). Phonetic categorization in auditory word perception. *Journal of Experimental Psychology: Human Perception and Performance, 6*, 110–125.

Grosjean, F. (1980). Spoken word recognition processes and the gating paradigm. *Perception and Psychophysics, 28*, 267–283.

Grosjean, F., & Gee, J.P. (1987). Prosodic structure and spoken word recognition. *Cognition, 25*, 135–155, this issue.

Jakimik, J., Cole, R.A., & Rudnicky, A.I. (1985). Sound and spelling in spoken word recognition. *Journal of Memory and Language, 24*, 165–178.

Johnson-Laird, P.N. (1987). The mental representation of the meaning of words. *Cognition, 25*, 189–211, this issue.

Klatt, D.H. (1980). Speech perception: A model of acoustic-phonetic analysis and lexical access. In R.A. Cole (Ed.), *Perception and production of fluent speech*. Hillsdale, N.J.: Erlbaum.

Marcus, S.M., & Frauenfelder, U.H. (1985). Word recognition – uniqueness or deviation? A theoretical note. *Language and Cognitive Processes, 1–2*, 163–169.

Marslen-Wilson, W.D. (1973). Linguistic structure and speech shadowing at very short latencies. *Nature, 244*, 522–523.

Marslen-Wilson, W.D. (1984). Function and process in spoken word-recognition. In H. Bouma and D.G. Bouwhuis (Eds.), *Attention and Performance X: Control of language processes*. Hillsdale, N.J.: Erlbaum.

Marslen-Wilson, W.D. (1987). Functional parallelism in spoken word-recognition. *Cognition, 25*, 71–102, this issue.

Marslen-Wilson, W.D., & Tyler, L.K. (1980). The temporal structure of spoken language understanding. *Cognition, 8*, 1–71.

Marslen-Wilson, W.D., & Welsh, A. (1978). Processing interactions during word-recognition in continuous speech. *Cognitive Psychology, 10*, 29–63.

McClelland, J.L., & Rumelhart, D.E. (Eds.) (1986). *Parallel distributed processing: Explorations in the microstructure of cognition*. Cambridge, Mass.: Bradford Books.

Mehler, J. (1981). The role of syllables in speech processing: Infant and adult data. *Philosophical Transactions of the Royal Society, B 295*, 333–352.

Meyer, D., & Schvaneveldt, R. (1971). Facilitation in recognising pairs of words: Evidence of a dependence between retrieval operations. *Journal of Experimental Psychology, 90*, 227–234.

Morton, J. (1969). Interaction of information in word recognition. *Psychological Review, 76*, 165–178.

Morton, J., & Long, J. (1976). Effect of word transitional probability on phoneme identification. *Journal of Verbal Learning and Verbal Behavior, 15*, 43–52.

Nooteboom, S. (1979). More attention for words in speech communication research. In B. Lindblom & S. Ohman (Eds.), *Frontiers of speech communication research*. London: Academic Press.

Norris, D.G. (1982). Autonomous processes in comprehension: A reply to Marslen-Wilson and Tyler. *Cognition, 11*, 97–101.

Norris, D.G. (1986). Word recognition: Context effects without priming. *Cognition, 22*, 93–136.

Pisoni, D.B., & Luce, P.A. (1987). Acoustic-phonetic representations in word recognition. *Cognition, 25*, 21–52, this issue.

Salasoo, A., & Pisoni, D.B. (1985). Interaction of knowledge sources in spoken word identification. *Journal of Memory and Language, 24*, 210–231.

Segui, J., & Frauenfelder, U.H. (1986). The effects of lexical constraints upon speech perception. In F. Klix & H. Hagendorf (Eds.) *Human memory and cognitive capabilities: Symposium in memoriam Hermann Ebbinghaus*, Amsterdam: North-Holland.

Seidenberg, M.S., Waters, G., Sanders, M., & Langer, P.S. (1984). Pre- and postlexical loci of contextual effects on word recognition. *Memory and Cognition, 12 (4)*, 315–328.

Seidenberg, M.S., Tanenhaus, M.K., Leiman, J.M., & Bienkowski, M. (1982). Automatic access of the meanings of ambiguous words in context: Some limitations of knowledge-based processing. *Cognitive Psychology, 14*, 489–537.

Selkirk, E. (1984). *Phonology and syntax: The relation between sound and structure.* Cambridge, Mass.: MIT Press.

Shipman, D.W., & Zue, V.W. (1982). Properties of large lexicons: Implications for advanced isolated word recognition systems. *Proceedings of the 1982 IEEE International Conference on Acoustics, Speech and Signal Processing*, Paris, France, April.

Swinney, D. (1979). Lexical access during sentence comprehension: (Re)consideration of context effects. *Journal of Verbal Learning and Verbal Behavior, 14*, 645–660.

Tanenhaus, M., Carlson, G., & Seidenberg, M. (1984). Do listeners compute linguistic representation? In D. Dowty, L. Karttunen & A. Zwicky (Eds.) *Natural language parsing.* Cambridge: Cambridge University Press.

Tanenhaus, M., Leiman, J., & Seidenberg, M. (1979). Evidence for multiple stages in the processing of ambiguous words in syntactic contexts. *Journal of Verbal Learning and Verbal Behavior, 18*, 427–441.

Tanenhaus, M.K., & Lucas, M.M. (1987). Context effects in lexical processing. *Cognition, 25*, 213–234, this issue.

Tyler, L.K. (1984). The structure of the initial cohort: evidence from gating. *Perception and Psychophysics, 26*, 417–427.

Tyler, L.K., & Marslen-Wilson, W.D. (1982). Conjectures and refutations: A reply to Norris. *Cognition, 11*, 103–107.

Tyler, L.K., & Marslen-Wilson, W.D. (1986). The effects of context on the recognition of multimorphemic words. *Journal of Memory and Language, 25*, 741–752.

Tyler, L.K., & Wessels, J. (1983). Quantifying contextual contributions to word-recognition processes. *Perception and Psychophysics, 34*, 409–420.

Tyler, L.K., & Wessels, J. (1985). Is gating an on-line task? Evidence from naming latency data. *Perception and Psychophysics, 38 (3)*, 217–222.

Williams, E. (1981). On the notions of "lexically related" and "head of a word". *Linguistic Inquiry, 12*, 245–274.

Résumé

Cette introduction a pour but d'élaborer le cadre général auquel appartiennent les articles rassemblés ci-dessous. Elle s'adresse à deux problèmes importants dans l'étude du traitement lexical: l'identification des différentes étapes dans la reconnaissance de mots et la caractérisation des divers types d'influences contextuelles sur ces étapes. Nous essayons de décomposer les processus de reconnaissance de mots en plusieurs étapes ayant des conséquences aux niveaux théorique et empirique. Nous adoptons également une approche analytique en traitant des influences dues au contexte, en distinguant plusieurs types de contexte (lexical, intra-lexical, syntaxique, sémantique et interprétatif). Une telle démarche est nécessaire si nous voulons rendre explicite le rapport entre tel ou tel type d'information contextuelle et l'étape où s'exerce son influence.

2

Acoustic-phonetic representations in word recognition*

DAVID B. PISONI

PAUL A. LUCE

Indiana University

Abstract

This paper reviews what is currently known about the sensory and perceptual input that is made available to the word recognition system by processes typically assumed to be related to speech sound perception. In the first section, we discuss several of the major problems that speech researchers have tried to deal with over the last thirty years. In the second section, we consider one attempt to conceptualize the speech perception process within a theoretical framework that equates processing stages with levels of linguistic analysis. This framework assumes that speech is processed through a series of analytic stages ranging from peripheral auditory processing, acoustic-phonetic and phonological analysis, to word recognition and lexical access.

Finally, in the last section, we consider several recent approaches to spoken word recognition and lexical access. We examine a number of claims surrounding the nature of the bottom-up input assumed by these models, postulated perceptual units, and the interaction of different knowledge sources in auditory word recognition. An additional goal of this paper was to establish the need to employ segmental representations in spoken word recognition.

1. Introduction

Although the problems of word recognition and the nature of lexical representations have been long-standing concerns of cognitive psychologists, these topics have not been studied extensively by investigators working in the main-

*Preparation of this paper was supported, in part, by NIH research grant NS-12179, a contract with the Air Force Office of Scientific Research, Air Force Systems Command and a fellowship from the James McKeen Cattell Fund to the first author. We thank Howard Nusbaum, Beth Greene and Robert Remez for their comments and suggestions. We also thank the reviewers for many useful suggestions on an earlier draft of this paper. Reprint requests should be sent to David B. Pisoni, Department of Psychology, Indiana University, Bloomington, IN 47405, U.S.A.

stream of speech perception research. For many years, these two lines of research have remained quite distinct from each other. There are several reasons for this state of affairs. First, the bulk of research on word recognition has been concerned with investigating visual word recognition in reading, with little, if any, concern for the problems of spoken word recognition. Second, most of the interest and research effort in speech perception has been concerned with issues related to feature and phoneme perception in highly controlled environments using nonsense syllables. Such an approach is appropriate for studying "low-level" auditory and acoustic-phonetic analysis of speech, but it is not as useful in dealing with questions surrounding how words are recognized in isolation or in context or how various sources of information are used by the listener to recover the talker's intended message.

It is now clear that many interesting and potentially quite important problems in the field of speech perception involve the interface between acoustic-phonetic processes and the processes of word recognition and lexical access. These problems deal with the nature of the acoustic cues that listeners extract from the speech signal, the processes used to integrate these cues, and the various types of perceptual units that are computed by the speech processing system (Liberman, Cooper, Shankweiler, & Studdert-Kennedy, 1967; Stevens & House, 1972; Studdert-Kennedy, 1974). For example, it is of considerable interest to specify precisely the kinds of representations that exist in the mental lexicon and the intermediate representations that are computed by the listener in converting the speech waveform into a symbolic representation. Are words, morphemes, phonemes or sequences of spectral templates the correct way to characterize the representations of lexical entries in spoken language understanding? Is a word accessed in the lexicon on the basis of an acoustic, phonetic or phonological code? Why are high frequency words recognized so rapidly? And, how is context used to support word recognition and facilitate access to the meaning of a word? These are a few of the questions that will need to be answered before a complete understanding of spoken word recognition will be possible.

In this paper, we consider the nature of the sensory and perceptual input that is made available to the word recognition system by processes typically assumed to be related to speech sound perception. In the first section, we summarize several of the fundamental problems that speech researchers have attempted to deal with over the last thirty-five years. We focus our discussion on the long-standing problems of invariance, linearity, and segmentation of the speech signal in order to illustrate the complex relations that exist between the speech waveform and units of linguistic description. We also consider the problems associated with identifying the basic units of perceptual analysis and the types of representations that are computed by the speech perception system. In the second section, we consider one attempt to conceptualize the speech perception process within a theoretical framework that equates levels of linguistic analysis with processing stages. Finally, in the last section, we consider several recent approaches to spoken word recognition and lexical access. Here we examine claims surrounding the nature of the bottom-up input assumed by these models, the perceptual units, and the potential interaction of different sources of information in word recognition.

2. Fundamental problems in speech perception

The fundamental problems in speech perception today are the same problems that have eluded definitive solution for more than thirty-five years (Fant, 1973; Joos, 1948). Although the intractability of these long-standing problems has led to a voluminous body of literature on the production and perception of speech, researchers are still hard-pressed to explain precisely how the human listener converts the continuously varying speech waveform into discrete linguistic units and how these units are employed to extract the linguistic message intended by the talker. Indeed, not only are we still unsure about the exact nature of the linguistic units arrived at in perceptual processing of speech, little attention has yet been paid to the problem of how the sensory and perceptual analysis of the speech waveform makes contact with representations of words in the lexicon or how these representations are used to support language understanding.

Many, if not all, of the problems in speech perception stem from the manner in which speech is produced. Phonemes are rarely, if ever, realized in the speech waveform as a linearly-ordered sequence of discrete acoustic events. This is due primarily to the fact that speakers coarticulate adjacent phonemes, so that articulation of one phoneme is affected by articulation of neighboring phonemes. It has been extremely difficult to identify the acoustic features in the speech waveform that uniquely match the perceived phonemes independently of surrounding context (see Stevens & Blumstein, 1981). The acoustic consequences of coarticulation and other sources of contextually conditioned variability result in the failure of the acoustic signal to meet two important formal conditions, invariance and linearity, which in turn give rise to the problem of segmentation.

2.1. Linearity of the speech signal

The linearity condition states that for each phoneme there must be a corresponding stretch of sound in the utterance (Chomsky & Miller, 1963). Furthermore, if phoneme X is followed by phoneme Y in the phonemic representation, the stretch of sound corresponding to phoneme X must precede the stretch of sound corresponding to phoneme Y in the physical signal. The linearity condition is clearly not met in the acoustic signal. Because of coarticulation and other contextual effects, acoustic features for adjacent phonemes are often "smeared" across phonemes in the speech waveform. Although segmentation is possible according to strictly acoustic criteria (see Fant, 1962), the number of acoustic segments is typically greater than the number of phonemes in the utterance. Moreover, no *simple* invariant mapping has been found between these purely acoustic attributes or features and perceived phonemes. This smearing, or parallel transmission of acoustic features, results in stretches of the speech waveform in which acoustic features of more than one phoneme are present (Liberman et al., 1967). Therefore, not only is there rarely a particular stretch of sound that corresponds uniquely to a given phoneme, it is also rare that the acoustic features of one phoneme always precede or follow the acoustic features of adjacent phonemes in the physical signal. For this reason, Liberman et al. (1967) have argued that speech is not a simple cipher or alphabet, but is, instead, a complex code in which "speech sounds represent a very considerable restructuring of the phonemic 'message' " (p. 4). Therefore, one of the central concerns in the field of speech perception has focused on the transformation of the continuously varying speech signal into a sequence of discrete linguistic units such as phonemes, phones, or allophones.

2.2. Acoustic-phonetic invariance

Another condition that the speech signal fails to satisfy is the principle of invariance (Chomsky & Miller, 1963). This condition states that for each phoneme X, there must be a specific set of criterial acoustic attributes or features associated with it in all contexts. These features must be present whenever X or some variant of X occurs, and they must be absent whenever some other phoneme occurs in the representation. Because of coarticulatory effects, the acoustic features of a given speech sound frequently vary as a function of the phonetic environment in which it is produced. For example, the formant transitions for syllable-initial stop consonants, which cue place of articulation (e.g., /b/ vs. /d/ vs. /g/), vary considerably depending on the following vowel (Liberman, Delattre, Cooper, & Gerstman, 1954). The formant transitions for stop consonants in syllable-initial positions, then, do not uniquely specify place of articulation across all vowels. If formant transitions are the primary cues to place of articulation for stop consonants, they must be highly context-dependent and not invariant across different phonetic contexts. In short, the problem of invariance is one of explaining perceptual constancy for speech sounds in spite of the absence of reliable acoustic correlates in the speech waveform (Stevens & Blumstein, 1981; Studdert-Kennedy, 1974).

2.3. Segmentation into higher-order units

The context-conditioned variability in the correspondence between the speech signal and phoneme also presents enormous problems for segmentation of the speech waveform into higher-order units of linguistic analysis such as syllables and words. Because of the failure to meet the linearity and invariance conditions noted above, the speech signal cannot be segmented into acoustically defined units that are independent of adjacent segments or are free from the conditioning effects of sentence-level contexts. For example, it has been difficult to determine strictly by simple physical criteria where one word ends and another begins, especially in connected speech. However, word segmentation may be possible by taking into account the systematic internal structure of words, an issue we will return to below.

2.4. Units of perceptual analysis

In addition to the problems of linearity, invariance, and segmentation, there is one other troublesome problem that arises from the coarticulation of speech. This problem involves the relationship between units of perceptual analysis and the units assumed from linguistic analysis. It has been suggested that limitations on channel capacity in the auditory system require that raw sensory information must be recoded into some abstract representation that can be used for subsequent analysis (Liberman et al., 1967). However, what constitutes these abstract units of analysis has been a topic of long-standing debate in the field of speech research. Many investigators have argued for the primacy of the phonetic feature, the phoneme, and the word in the perceptual processing of speech. Other researchers have even proposed units as large as the clause or sentence (Bever, Lackner, & Kirk, 1969; Miller, 1962). In our view, much of the debate over the choice of a basic perceptual unit in language processing is somewhat misguided, for as the level of linguistic processing changes, so do the units of perceptual analysis. The question of whether there is *one* basic or primary unit is to a large extent the wrong question to ask, in our view, because there are, in fact, many units used by the speech processing mechanism. If anything, it is the interaction among the various units that presents a challenge to the perceptual theorist, not the identification or delineation of the one basic unit of perceptual analysis. For some purposes, abstract units such as phonemes are sufficient to capture important distinctions and generalizations within and across constraint domains (Allen, 1985). For other purposes, more parametric representations of the speech waveform may be more appropriate.

A crucial question remains, however, concerning what units are *obligatory* or necessary in the perceptual processing of speech and what the nature of these units may be. Although no one unit may be primary, it is still necessary to specify what units are employed at all in speech perception, word recognition, and lexical access. This problem has arisen primarily in attempts to specify the initial acoustic-phonetic representation of speech. Because of the highly encoded nature of phonemes in the speech waveform resulting from coarticulation (Fischer-Jorgensen, 1954; Liberman et al., 1967), a number of researchers have abandoned the notion that a segmental representation is actually perceived by the listener during speech processing. Alternative accounts, to name a few, have proposed syllables (Cole & Scott, 1974a,b; Massaro & Oden, 1980; Studdert-Kennedy, 1974, 1980), context-sensitive allophones (Wickelgren, 1969, 1976), and context-sensitive spectra (Klatt, 1980) as the minimal units of encoding the speech signal. These approaches have generally attempted to circumvent the problem of specifying how a phonemic segmental representation is constructed from the speech waveform in which the conditions of linearity and invariance are not met (see, however, Studdert-Kennedy, 1974). Although one or more of these approaches to the problem of the unit of analysis may be correct in some form, we believe that there is still considerable evidence that can be marshalled to support the claim that at initial stages of speech processing, some type of segmental representation is derived (see below). The question remains, however, concerning what the initial unit of speech encoding is and how it is computed by the processing system. For purposes of the present discussion, it is sufficient simply to note here that this issue has not been resolved satisfactorily even among researchers in the field. Nevertheless, research has continued despite the ambiguity and disagreements over the basic processing units in speech perception. It is our feeling that units like phonemes which are defined within linguistic theory are probably not good candidates for processing units in the real-time analysis of speech. However, units like phones, allophones or context-sensitive diphones may be more appropriate to capture important generalizations about speech and to serve as perceptual units during the earliest stages of speech perception.

3. Perceptual processing of speech

Speech perception has commonly been viewed as a process encompassing various stages of analysis in the transformation of the speech signal to the intended message (Studdert-Kennedy, 1974, 1976). This componential analysis of speech perception has proven very useful in establishing a conceptual framework from which to approach the study of spoken language understanding. Although the exact nature of each of the postulated stages and the interactions among the stages are still tentative, they are nevertheless theoretically justifiable on linguistic grounds. Studdert-Kennedy (1974) was the first to advocate this approach. He proposed four conceptual stages of analysis: (1) auditory, (2) phonetic, (3) phonological, and (4) lexical, syntactic, and semantic. In our discussion of the stages of perceptual processing of speech, we have added a fifth stage of processing—peripheral auditory analysis—to emphasize several recent approaches to speech perception that focus on the earliest transformations of the speech signal by the peripheral auditory system. Conceptually, this stage of processing actually constitutes a subcomponent of the stage of auditory analysis proposed by Studdert-Kennedy.

3.1. Peripheral auditory analysis

Over the last three or four years, a great deal of new research has been reported in the literature on how the peripheral auditory system encodes speech signals (see Carlson & Granstrom, 1982). Research on the peripheral processing of speech signals comes from two different directions. First, a number of important physiological studies using animals have been carried out to describe, in fairly precise terms, how speech signals are coded in the peripheral auditory system (Delgutte, 1980, 1982). These studies have examined auditory-nerve activity in response to simple speech signals such as steady-state vowels and stop consonants in consonant-vowel syllables. The goal of this work has been to identify reliable and salient properties in the discharge patterns of auditory-nerve fibers that correspond, in some direct way, to the important acoustic properties or attributes of speech sounds (Sachs & Young, 1979).

Pursuing a second approach to the peripheral processing of speech, several researchers have begun to develop psychophysically-based models of speech processing (Klatt, 1982). These models explicitly incorporate well-known psychoacoustic data in their descriptions of the filtering that is carried out by the peripheral auditory system (Searle, Jacobson, & Rayment, 1979; Zwicker, Terhardt, & Paulus, 1979). The goal of this line of research is to develop representations of the speech signal that take into account known psychophysical facts about hearing such as critical bands, upward spread of masking, and the growth of loudness (Klatt, 1982).

Searle et al. (1979) have addressed questions related to the appropriate bandwidth of the filters used by human listeners to process speech stimuli. Reviewing evidence from psychophysical and physiological studies, Searle et al. propose that the human peripheral auditory system analyzes auditory stimuli with approximately a $\frac{1}{3}$-octave frequency resolution. The choice of $\frac{1}{3}$-octave bandwidths is motivated not only by the psychophysical and physiological data, but also by the properties of human speech. Because bandwidth is proportional to frequency, $\frac{1}{3}$-octave bandwidths allow spectral resolution of low frequencies as well as temporal resolution at high frequencies. Spectral resolution of low frequencies enables separation of the first and second formants while temporal resolution of high frequencies provides accurate timing information for rapid onsets of bursts. Reasoning from known filtering properties of the human peripheral auditory system, Searle et al. were able to construct a phoneme recognizer with quite high levels of accuracy at discriminating initial stop consonants in consonant-vowel syllables, thereby demonstrating the degree to which speech recognition may be improved once psychologically reasonable transformations of the speech signal are incorporated in peripheral representations of speech.

The recent interest and extensive research efforts in developing new and presumably more appropriate and valid representations of speech signals derives, in part, from the assumption that a more detailed examination of these auditory representations should, in principle, provide researchers with a great deal more relevant information about the distinctive perceptual dimensions that underlie speech sounds (Stevens, 1980). It has been further assumed that information contained in these so-called neuroacoustic and psychoacoustic representations will contribute in important ways to finally resolving the acoustic-phonetic invariance problem in speech (Goldhor, 1983). Although new and important findings will no doubt come from continued research on how speech signals are processed in the auditory periphery, one should not be misled into believing that these new research efforts on the processing of speech by the auditory nerve will provide all the needed solutions in the field of speech processing. On the contrary, a great deal more research is still needed on questions concerning the central auditory mechanisms used in pattern recognition and higher level sources of information in speech perception (Klatt, 1982).

3.2. Central auditory analysis

Following the initial transformation of the speech signal by the peripheral auditory system, acoustic information about spectral structure, fundamental frequency, changes in source function, overall intensity, and duration of the signal, as well as amplitude onsets and offsets is extracted and coded by the auditory system (Stevens, 1980). These spectral and temporal patterns of the speech signal are assumed to be preserved in sensory memory for a brief period of time during which acoustic feature analysis is carried out (see Pisoni & Sawusch, 1975). The results of auditory analysis provide "speech cues"; that is, auditory-based representations of the speech signal that are subsequently used for phonetic classification.

A great deal of research over the last thirty-five years has been devoted to the description of acoustic cues to phonetic segments. (Reviews may be found in Darwin, 1976; Pisoni, 1978; Studdert-Kennedy, 1974, 1980.) Typically, many acoustic cues map onto a single phonetic feature. For example, Lisker (1978) has listed sixteen possible cues to voicing of intervocalic stop consonants. In general, however, a few basic cues can be listed that serve to signal place, manner, and voicing of consonants and frontness-backness and height of vowels. For example, for stop consonants (/b/, /d/, /g/, /p/, /t/, /k/), place of articulation may be signalled by the direction and extent of formant transitions, by the gross spectral shape of the release burst at onset, by the frequency of the spectral maximum at the burst, and by the bandwidth of the burst (see Cole & Scott, 1974a,b; Delattre, Liberman, & Cooper, 1955; Dorman, Studdert-Kennedy, & Raphael, 1977; Liberman, Delattre, & Cooper, 1952; Liberman, Delattre, Cooper, & Gerstman, 1954; Stevens & Blumstein, 1978).

Voicing of initial stops may be signalled by voice-onset time, frequency of the first formant transition, and amplitude of the burst (see Abramson & Lisker, 1965; Lisker & Abramson, 1964; Stevens & Klatt, 1974; Summerfield & Haggard, 1974). Among the many cues signalling voicing of post-vocalic stops are closure duration (in post-stressed syllable-medial position), duration of the preceding vowel, extent of formant transitions, and voicing into closure (Denes, 1955; Fitch, 1981; House, 1961; Lisker, 1957, 1978; Port, 1977, 1979; Raphael, 1972; Raphael & Dorman, 1980). For any given phonetic contrast, then, it is clear that multiple acoustic events are involved in signalling the contrast, and it is at the stage of auditory analysis that such cues are extracted.

3.3. Acoustic-phonetic analysis

The acoustic-phonetic level, the first level at which linguistic processing is accomplished, is assumed to be the next stage of perceptual analysis. Here the speech cues from the previous level of analysis are mapped onto distinctive phonetic features. Phonetic features may be thought of as abstract perceptual and memory codes that stand for combinations of both specific acoustic attributes on the one hand, and their articulatory antecedents on the other hand. In the phonetic and phonological literature, it has been convenient to describe these features in terms of articulatory descriptions and labels primarily because this notation captures linguistically relevant distinctions at the phonetic and phonological levels. One description of speech at this level consists of a phonetic matrix in which the columns represent discrete phonetic segments and the rows indicate the phonetic feature composition of each segment (Chomsky & Halle, 1968).

The acoustic-phonetic level of analysis has received a great deal of attention in connection with the hypothesis that specialized phonetic feature detectors may be operative at this stage of speech processing (Abbs & Sussman, 1971; Eimas & Corbit, 1973; see Diehl, 1981, for a review). The notion of feature detectors in speech perception was originally proposed by Eimas and Corbit (1973) on the basis of two sources of evidence. The first line of evidence came from research on infant speech perception that demonstrated that 1- and 4-month-old infants discriminate certain speech and non-speech stimuli in much the same way that adults do (Eimas, Siqueland, Jusczyk, & Vigorito, 1971). Infants discriminated speech contrasts in a categorical-like manner, such that between-category stimuli (e.g., /bae/ and /dae/) were discriminated better than within-category stimuli (e.g., two different tokens of /bae/). Infant discrimination of comparable non-speech stimuli, however, was not demonstrably superior for between-category stimuli than within-category stimuli (Eimas, 1974). Because of the striking similarity of the infants' and adults' performance on both the speech and nonspeech stimuli, Eimas (1974) proposed that infants are equipped at birth with feature detectors specialized for processing speech stimuli. (See Aslin, Pisoni, & Jusczyk, 1983, for further discussions of these and related issues in infant speech perception.)

A second line of evidence for the feature detector hypothesis comes from studies on the selective adaptation of speech, the first of which was conducted by Eimas and Corbit (1973). For reviews see Cooper (1975) and Eimas and Miller (1978). Eimas and Corbit (1973) interpreted their demonstration of selective adaptation of speech as evidence for the operation of specialized phonetic feature detectors. They reasoned that the repeated presentation of an endpoint stimulus fatigued detectors tuned to the phonetic features of the stimulus. Fatigue of the detector sensitive to the voicing feature causes a shift in the identification function toward either the voiced or voiceless end of the continuum, depending on the adaptor used. Eimas and Corbit concluded that the results from the infant data as well as the demonstration of selective adaptation for speech supported the notion of specialized feature detectors at the level of phonetic analysis.

The Eimas et al. (1971) and Eimas and Corbit (1973) studies inspired a large number of studies on both infant perception and selective adaptation, a review of which is well beyond the scope of the present discussion (see the references cited above for reviews). Suffice it to note here that the notion of specialized phonetic feature detectors has been abandoned. Studies on both infant perception and selective adaptation have since shown that the previously demonstrated effects lie not at the level of phonetic analysis, but rather at an earlier stage or stages of auditory feature analysis (Eimas & Miller, 1978; Ganong, 1978; Sawusch, 1977a,b; see also Remez, 1979). In an elegant study by Sawusch and Jusczyk (1981), the locus of selective adaptation effects at the auditory level was clearly identified. Sawusch and Jusczyk found that adaptation followed the spectral characteristics of the adaptor and not the perceived phonetic identity, thus clearly placing the effects of selective adaptation at the level of auditory analysis.

3.4. Phonological analysis

At the level of phonological analysis, the phonetic features and segments from the previous level are converted into phonological segments. The phonological component provides information about the sound structure of a given language that is imposed on the phonetic matrix to derive a phonological matrix (Chomsky & Halle, 1968). Thus, the phonological rules that are applied to the phonetic input at this level determine the extent to which the phonetic segments function as distinctive elements in the language and the extent to which these attributes may be predicted from either language-specific rules or language universal principles. Thus, predictable and redundant phonetic details can be accounted for systematically at this level. Allophonic variations present at the phonetic level are also eliminated and only phonologically distinctive information is coded for subsequent processing.

Historically, the output of the phonological component was believed by linguists to be a linearly-ordered sequence of phonemes in which syllables played no role in phonological organization (Chomsky & Halle, 1968). Recently, however, some phonologists (Clements & Keyser, 1983; Halle & Vergnaud, 1980; Kahn, 1976; Selkirk, 1980) have postulated a hierarchical representation of the internal structure of the syllable in which the major constituents are an *onset*—an optional initial consonant or consonant cluster—and a *rime*—the rest of the syllable excluding inflectional endings. Some preliminary behavioral evidence (Treiman, 1983) indicates that such constituents may be psychologically real. It may be, then, that both phonemic and syllabic tiers of organization are computed at this stage of analysis (see Halle, 1985, for a similar proposal).

Two aspects of the phonological level in this processing scheme are worthy of mention here. The first concerns the suggestion, already alluded to above, that a segmental representation is computed by listeners in the on-line processing of speech. As we mentioned earlier, several researchers have abandoned the notion of a distinct phonemic level of representation in speech perception, primarily due to the difficulties encountered in identifying linearly-ordered, invariant acoustic segments in the waveform that correspond to phonemes (e.g., Klatt, 1979, 1980; Massaro & Oden, 1980; Wicklegren, 1969, 1976). If sufficient evidence for a phonetic level of representation cannot be rallied, it would be superfluous to postulate a phonological level of analysis in any conceptual framework for speech perception. However, we believe that a number of compelling arguments can be made to demonstrate the need for an abstract segmental representation at some level of the speech perception process (see also Studdert-Kennedy, 1976, 1980). Because the assumption of segmental representations has played such an important role in linguistics and especially in speech perception and word recognition over the last thirty-five years, below we present a brief defense of the existence of segmental representations in speech processing.

3.5. Higher-order analysis of speech

Beyond the level of phonological analysis, several additional levels of "higher-order" analysis are carried out on the recoded speech signal. First, we assume that word recognition and lexical access accept as input some segmental representation of the speech signal. This representation could consist of phones, allophones or context-sensitive phoneme-like units. In word recognition, patterns from lower levels of analysis are then matched to representations of words residing in long-term memory. Lexical access takes place when the meanings of words are contacted in long-term semantic memory (see other papers in this issue).

Second, a word's functional, semantic, and syntactic roles are also derived from some segmental representation of the speech signal in order to parse and interpret the utterance. Prosodic information is interpreted as well in order to organize the utterance in short-term memory, to identify syntactic boundaries, to predict upcoming stress patterns, and to evaluate certain pragmatic aspects of the conversational situation. In short, a great deal of analysis subsequent to the phonological level is necessary to recover the speaker's intended message.

The precise roles of these higher levels of analysis in guiding the earlier levels of processing is a topic of considerable interest among researchers. Some of the questions currently under examination concern the degree to which higher levels of processing interact with the initial acoustic-phonetic and phonological analyses, the role of higher level sources of information in predicting upcoming speech input, and the degree to which other sources of information can compensate for misperceptions and impoverished acoustic-phonetic information in the signal. Although many of these issues were formerly believed to be beyond the immediate concern of researchers in speech perception, a growing number of theorists are realizing the need to specify the contributions of higher levels of analysis in order to understand more fully the speech perception process. Perhaps more important, there is a real need to establish a point of contact in language comprehension between the early sensory-based acoustic-phonetic input and the language processing system itself. The primary locus of this interface appears to lie at the level of processing corresponding to word recognition and lexical access (see Marslen-Wilson & Tyler, 1980; Marslen-Wilson & Welsh, 1978).

4. Segmental representations in speech perception

For a number of years there has been a continuing debate concerning the role of segmental representations in speech perception and spoken word recognition. Several theorists have totally abandoned an intermediate segmental level of representation in favor of direct access models. In these models, words are recognized without an intermediate analysis of their "internal structure" into units like allophones, phonemes, diphones or demisyllables. Proponents of this view have argued that their recognition models do not require the postulation or use of these intermediate representations and that human listeners do not actually employ these units in the real-time analysis of spoken language. In this section, we argue against this position and summarize evidence from several different areas supporting the existence of these processing units in speech perception and spoken word recognition. While some theorists have attempted to ignore or even to deny the existence of these units, we suggest that they are, in fact, *tacitly* assumed by all contemporary models of word recognition. Without this assumption, it would not be possible to recover the internal structure of words and access their meanings. Based on several sources of evidence, we argue that the output from the speech perception system consists of some form of segmental representation. Furthermore, it is this representation that forms the input to processes involved in word recognition and lexical access.

The first general line of evidence we offer in support of segmental representations in speech perception comes from linguistics. One of the fundamental assumptions of linguistic analysis is that the continuously varying speech waveform can be represented as a sequence of discrete units such as features, phones, allophones, phonemes, and morphemes. This assumption is central to our current conceptions of language as a system of rules that governs the sound patterns and sequences used to encode meanings (Chomsky & Halle, 1968). The very existence of phonological phenomena such as alternation, systematic regularity, and diachronic and synchronic sound changes require, ipso facto, that some type of segmental level be postulated in order to capture significant linguistic generalizations. In describing the sound structure of a given language, then, a level of segmental representation is required in order to account for the idiosyncratic and predictable regularities in the sound pattern of that language (see Kenstowicz & Kisseberth, 1979). Whether these segmental units are actually used by human listeners in the real-time analysis of spoken language is, however, another matter.

The second general line of evidence in support of segmental representations in speech perception is more psychological in nature. Psychological evidence for the hypothesis of a segmental level of representation in speech perception comes from a number of diverse sources. One source of evidence comes from observations of speakers of languages with no orthography who are attempting to develop writing systems. In his well-known article "The psychological reality of phonemes," Sapir (1963) cites several examples of cases in which the orthographic choices of an illiterate speaker revealed a conscious awareness of the phonological structure of his language. More recently, Read (1971) has described a number of examples of children who have invented their own orthographies spontaneously. The children's initial encounters with print show a systematic awareness of the segmental structure of language, thereby demonstrating an ability to analyze spoken language into representations of discrete segments such as phones, allophones, or phonemes. Indeed, it has been recently suggested (Liberman, Shankweiler, Fischer, & Carter, 1974; Rozin & Gleitman, 1977; Treiman, 1980) that young children's ability to learn to read an alphabetic writing system like English orthography is highly dependent on the development of phonemic analysis skills, that is, skills that permit the child to consciously analyze speech into segmental units.

The existence of language games based on insertion of a sound sequence at specifiable points in a word, the movement of a sound or sound sequence from one point to another in a word, or the deletion of a sound or sound sequence all provide additional support for the existence of segmental representations of the internal structure of words (see Treiman, 1983, 1985). The existence of rhymes and the metrical structure of poetry also entail the awareness, in one way or another, that words have an internal structure and organization to them and that this structure can be represented as a linear sequence of discrete units distributed in time.

An examination of errors in speech production provides additional evidence that words are represented in the lexicon in terms of some sort of segmental representation. The high frequency of single segment speech errors such as substitutions and exchanges provide evidence of the phonological structure of the language (Fromkin, 1973, 1980; Garrett, 1976, 1980; Shattuck-Hufnagel & Klatt, 1979; Stemberger, 1982). It has been difficult, if not impossible, to explain these kinds of errors without assuming some kind of segmental representation in the organization of the lexicon used for speech production.

Over the years there have been many perceptual findings that can be interpreted as support for an analysis of speech into segmental representations. Perhaps the most compelling data have come from numerous experiments involving an analysis of errors and confusions in short-term memory and of the errors produced in listening to words and nonsense syllables presented in noise (Conrad, 1964; Klatt, 1968; Miller & Nicely, 1955; Wang & Bilger, 1973; Wickelgren, 1965, 1966). While some of these findings were originally interpreted as support for various types of feature systems, they also provide strong evidence for the claim that the listener carries out an analysis of the internal structure of the stimulus input into dimensions used for encoding and storage in memory. While these findings can be interpreted as support for segmental analysis of spoken input, they have also been subject to alternative interpretations because of the specific tasks involved. As we noted earlier, the size of the perceptual unit changes as the level of analysis shifts according to the experimental task and instructions to subjects. If perceptual and short-term memory data were the only findings that could be cited in support of segmental representations, one might be less inclined to accept a segmental level of representation in speech perception and spoken word recognition. However, there are other converging sources of evidence from perceptual studies that provide additional support for this view.

For example, there have been numerous reports describing the phoneme restoration effect (Samuel, 1981a,b; Warren, 1970), a phenomenon demonstrating the on-line synthesis of the segmental properties of fluent speech by the listener. Numerous studies have also been carried out using the phoneme monitoring task in which subjects are required to detect the presence of a specified target phoneme while listening to sentences or short utterances (see Foss, Harwood, & Blank, 1980). Although some earlier findings (Foss & Swinney, 1973; Morton & Long, 1976) suggested that listeners first recognize the word and then carry out an analysis of the segments within the word, other more recent findings (Foss & Blank, 1980) indicate that subjects can detect phonemes in nonwords that are not present in the lexicon (see also Foss & Gernsbacher, 1983). Thus, subjects can detect phonemes based on two sources of knowledge, information from the sensory input and information developed from their knowledge of the phonological structure of the language (Dell & Newman, 1980).

A large body of data has also been collected on the detection of mispronunciations in fluent speech (see, for example, Cole, 1973; Cole & Jakimik, 1978, 1980). While these findings have been interpreted as support for the primacy of word recognition in speech perception (Cole, 1973), these results can just as easily be used to support the claim that listeners can gain access to the internal structure of words in terms of their segmental representations, and that they can do this while listening to continuous speech.

Finally, in terms of perceptual data, there is a small body of data on misperceptions of fluent speech (Bond & Garnes, 1980; Bond & Robey, 1983). The errors collected in these studies suggest that a very large portion of the misperceptions involve segments rather than whole words.

Having considered several sources of evidence for positing a phonological level of analysis, we now briefly consider what types of analyses are performed at this level. We have argued that at the level of phonological analysis, a segmental representation is derived based on the acoustic-phonetic features computed at the previous level of analysis. That is, the phonetic segment is converted into an abstract, systematic segmental representation (Chomsky & Halle, 1968). The process of converting information at the phonetic level into systematic segmental representations is complex, in that these representations are abstract entities that may be realized in any number of ways at the phonetic level. For example in fluent speech, the word "and" may be produced as [ænd], [æn], or [ən] (Oshika, Zue, Weeks, Neu, & Aurbach, 1975).

At the phonological level of analysis, the listener applies his knowledge of the phonological rules of the language in mapping phonetic representations onto more abstract segmental representations. Much of the variability at the phonetic level is inherently rule-governed, so that the listener may greatly simplify the task of deriving abstract representations from the acoustic-phonetic waveform by employing his knowledge of phonology and morphology. Oshika et al. (1975) have proposed a general class of phonological rules that attempt to describe this systematic pronunciation variation in order to illustrate the role that knowledge of phonological rules may play in speech processing. Among the rules proposed by Oshika et al. are (1) vowel reduction, (2) alveolar flapping, (3) palatalization, (4) homorganic stop deletion, and (5) geminate reduction. Each of these rules describes general phenomena found in continuous speech. For example, the vowel reduction rule describes the tendency for unstressed vowels to be realized as [ə]. Thus, although "and" may frequently be realized as [ən] at the phonetic level of analysis, the listener may "recover" the underlying representation by employing his knowledge of the phonological rule governing vowel reduction. Likewise, a listener's knowledge of the circumstances under which obstruent alveolars palatalize may allow him to recover the representation "did you" from its phonetic realization as [dɪ̆yu]. In this way, much of the task of translating acoustic-phonetic information into some type of segmental representation is simplified by knowledge of a few general rules that account for much of the variability at the phonetic level (see Church, 1987, this issue).

5. Spoken word recognition and lexical access

Among the most important recent trends in the field of speech perception has been the increased interest in theories of auditory word recognition and lexical access. Although much basic work is still being conducted on fundamental problems in acoustic-phonetics, many researchers have begun to expand their domain of inquiry to include the processes by which spoken words are recognized and meanings are retrieved from long-term memory. In our view, speech perception is not synonymous with phoneme perception, although much of the early work emphasized this orientation. There can be little doubt in anyone's mind that speech perception is an extremely complex process involving many levels of processing from phonetic perception to semantic interpretation. To isolate one level of processing for investigation, while ignoring the possible contributions of and interaction with other levels, is, in our view, somewhat myopic, and may lead to grossly incorrect theories. What we learn about word recognition, for example, may inform our theories of phonetic perception, and vice versa. Of course, analysis of the speech perception process is made much easier by the division of our domain of inquiry into isolatable subcomponents. However, investigating one subcomponent (e.g., phonetic perception) to the exclusion of others (e.g., word recognition) would appear to limit our insights into the process as a whole, as well as lead us to postulate theories at one level that are clearly untenable or unparsimonious given what we know about processing at other levels of analysis.

A good deal of the work carried out over the last thirty-five years in speech perception has been concerned with the "primary recognition problem"; that is, how the *form* of a spoken utterance is recognized or identified from an analysis of the acoustic waveform (Fry, 1956). Conscious identification and awareness of all of the segments in a word is probably not necessary or even obligatory for word recognition to take place, although it is certainly possible under special circumstances when a listener's attention is directed specifically to the sound structure of an utterance. Under normal listening conditions, the human listener may not have to *identify* all of the phonetic input to recognize the words in an utterance. Context and other constraints can serve to narrow down the available choices so that only a small portion of the acoustic waveform need be identified for word recognition to take place successfully.

Although the theories of word recognition and lexical access that we discuss below are too vague to render any significant insights into the nature of speech sound perception at this time, they are indicative of a growing trend to consider speech perception in a broader framework of spoken language processing. In addition, these theories represent what might be called a "new" interest among some speech researchers, namely, the way in which acoustic-phonetic information is used to contact lexical items in long-term memory. In this final section, we briefly review five current approaches to word recognition and lexical access. Each of these accounts was proposed to deal with somewhat different empirical issues in word recognition and lexical access, but each addresses a current topic of some interest in word recognition, namely, the extent to which higher-level knowledge sources come to bear on the perception of spoken words. Another issue addressed, in part at least, by each of these theories is the means by which lexical items are activated in memory. Here we are interested in specifying the nature of the bottom-up input and the processing units assumed by each theory. More specifically, we are interested in the degree to which these models assume the existence of segmental representations either tacitly or explicitly in order to solve the primary recognition problem.

Throughout the following discussion, we make a distinction between word recognition and lexical access. When speaking of *word recognition*, we refer explicitly to those processes responsible for generating a pattern from the acoustic-phonetic information in the speech waveform and matching this pattern to patterns previously stored in memory (i.e., for words) or to patterns generated by rule (i.e., for pseudowords). Word recognition, in our view, is synonymous with the term *form perception* as discussed by Bradley and Forster (1987, this issue) and *phonetic perception* as discussed by Liberman et al. (1967) and Studdert-Kennedy (1974, 1980). When speaking of *lexical access*, we refer explicitly to those processes that are responsible for contacting the appropriate lexical information in memory once a pattern match has been accomplished. Lexical access, then, is that process by which information about words stored in the mental lexicon is retrieved. More detailed discussions of several of these models can be found in other contributions to this issue.

It should be clear from the distinction we have drawn between the process-es of word recognition and lexical access that most contemporary models of word recognition that claim to be concerned with lexical access are actually models of word recognition. Little, if any, work has been devoted to describ-ing the structure and organization of the mental lexicon (see however Johnson-Laird, 1975; Miller & Johnson-Laird, 1976). Moreover, it should also be obvious that assumptions about word recognition and the input to the lexicon are probably not independent from assumptions made about the struc-ture and organization of the lexicon itself (see Bradley & Forster, 1987, this issue; Luce, 1986). Indeed, it may be difficult or impossible to separate the pro-cesses of word recognition and lexical access from their products. To take one example, segmentation of the speech waveform into discrete linguistic units such as phonemes or words has always been a troublesome problem to deal with because of the continuous nature of the speech signal. However, segmenta-tion may very well be a natural by-product of the recognition process itself (Reddy, 1976). As we learn more about the sources of variability in speech, it is becoming clear that the variability in the speech waveform is extremely systematic and potentially quite useful to the recognition process (Church, 1983; Elman & McClelland, 1984). Indeed, the recent findings of Church have demonstrated how knowledge of allophonic variation can aid in phonological parsing and lexical retrieval and therefore reduce the search process in locating the correct lexical entry (see Church, 1987, this issue).

6. Models of word recognition

6.1. Logogen theory

In Morton's (1969, 1979, 1982) logogen theory, passive sensing devices called "logogens" represent each word in the mental lexicon. Each logogen contains all of the information about a given word, such as its meaning, its possible syntactic functions, and its phonetic and orthographic structure. A logogen monitors for relevant sensory and/or contextual information and, once such information is encountered, the activation level of the logogen is raised. Upon sufficient activation, a logogen crosses threshold, at which time the information about the word that the logogen represents is made available to the response system.

One important feature of the logogen theory is that logogens monitor all possible sources of information, including higher-level semantic and syntactic information as well as lower level sensory information. Thus, information from any level can combine to push a logogen over its threshold. In this way, logogen theory is a highly *interactive* model of word recognition. For example, a word of high frequency, which has a starting threshold lower than words of lower frequency, may require very little sensory input if syntactic and semantic sources of information strongly favor the word. Likewise, a word of low frequency with few associated higher-level expectations may require considerable sensory input for the activation level to reach threshold. Thus, it may not really matter what sort of information activates a logogen, so long as the threshold is exceeded.

According to logogen theory, word recognition is accomplished when the activation threshold of a logogen is reached. As we have seen, logogen theory portrays the word recognition process as highly interactive. Lexical access, in our terminology, is achieved when the information contained within the logogen is made available to the response system. Thus, lexical access is a fairly automatic process once the word has been recognized. It is of interest to note that not only are interactive knowledge sources at play at the level of word recognition, but word frequency is handled at this stage as well. Words of higher frequency have lower activation thresholds than those of lower frequency (see, however, Luce, 1986).

The specific details of logogen theory have changed somewhat over the years, although the basic mechanisms have remained unchanged. For example, Morton (1982) has recently broken the logogen system into separate visual and auditory subsystems. Nevertheless, the fundamental notion of a passive threshold device that monitors information from a variety of sources has remained. As it stands, logogen theory, like many of the theories we will discuss, is extremely vague. At best, the theory helps to conceptualize how an interactive system may work and how word frequency and contextual effects in word recognition may be accounted for. However, the theory says very little, if anything, about precisely how acoustic-phonetic and higher-level sources of information are integrated, the time-course of word recognition, the nature of the perceptual units, or the role of the lexicon in word recognition.

6.2. Cohort theory

Marslen-Wilson's (Marslen-Wilson & Tyler, 1980; Marslen-Wilson & Welsh, 1978) cohort theory posits two stages in the word recognition process, one autonomous and one interactive. In the first, autonomous stage of word recognition, acoustic-phonetic information at the beginning of an input word activates all words in memory that share this word-initial information. For example, if the word "slave" is presented to the system, all words beginning with /s/ are activated, such as "sight," "save," "sling," and so on. The words activated on the basis of word-initial information comprise the "cohort." Activation of the cohort is an autonomous process in the sense that *only* acoustic-phonetic information can serve to specify the members of a cohort. At this stage of the model, then, word recognition is a completely data-driven or bottom-up process.

The key to this approach is the notion of a set of "word initial cohorts" or recognition candidates which are defined by the acoustic-phonetic commonality of the initial sound sequences of words. A particular word is "recognized" at that point—the "critical recognition point"—where the word is *uniquely* distinguished from any other word in the language beginning with the same *initial sound sequence*. The theory accounts for the facilitatory effects of context in word recognition by assuming, as in Morton's logogen model, that context influences the recognition of a particular word. However, unlike the logogen model, context is used to deactivate candidate words and therefore reduce the size of a word initial cohort set that is active at any time. The interaction of context with the sensory input is assumed to occur at the level of word recognition (see Marslen-Wilson & Welsh, 1978). Processing at early sensory levels is assumed to occur automatically and is not influenced by other higher-order sources of information. In cohort theory, the set of word initial cohorts that is activated is defined, in principle, by the internal segmental structure of the linear arrangement of speech sounds. To say, as Marslen-Wilson has done, that his theory makes no claim about the structure of the input to the word recognition system in terms of segmental representations is simply to deny the existence of a prima facie assumption that is central to the organization of his word initial cohort set. The theory, as currently formulated, would never work if the internal structure of words could not be described formally as a sequence of segment-like units.

Once a cohort structure is activated, all possible sources of information may come to bear on selection of the appropriate word from the cohort. Thus, further acoustic-phonetic information may eliminate "sight" and "save" from the cohort, leaving only words that begin with /sl/, such as "sling" and "slave." Note that word recognition based on acoustic-phonetic information is assumed to operate in a strictly left-to-right fashion. At this stage of word recognition, however, higher-level sources of information may also come into play to eliminate candidates from the set of hypothesized word cohorts. Thus, if "sling" is inconsistent with the presently available semantic or syntactic information, it will be eliminated from the cohort. At this second stage of word recognition, the theory is highly interactive. Upon isolation of a single word in the cohort, word recognition is accomplished.

Marslen-Wilson's cohort theory has attracted a considerable amount of attention in the last few years, presumably because of its relatively precise description of the word recognition process, its novel claim that all words in the mental lexicon sharing initial acoustic-phonetic information with the input word are activated in the initial stage of the word recognition process, and because of the priority it affords to the beginnings of words, a popular notion in the literature (see also Cole & Jakimik, 1980).

The theory is not without its shortcomings, however. For example, the original version of cohort theory incorporates no mechanism by which word frequency can be accounted for (see, however, Marslen-Wilson, 1987, this issue). Do high frequency words have higher activation levels in the cohort structure or are high frequency words simply more likely to be selected as candidates for a cohort than low frequency words? This last possibility seems unlikely, for the system would then be hard pressed to account for recognition of low frequency words that may be excluded a priori from the cohort structure. Perhaps associating various activation levels with word candidates would be more appropriate, but the theory as it stands has no means of accounting for differential activation levels.

Another problem with cohort theory is error recovery. For example, if "foundation" is perceived as "thoundation," due to a mispronunciation or misperception, the word-initial cohort will not contain the word candidate "foundation." Marslen-Wilson allows for some *residual* activation of acoustically similar word candidates in the cohort structure so a second pass through the cohort structure may be possible to attempt a best match, but as it currently stands the theory does not specify how such off-line error recovery may be accomplished.

6.3. Forster's autonomous search model

In contrast to Morton's logogen theory and Marslen-Wilson's cohort theory, Forster's (1976, 1979) theory of word recognition and lexical access is autonomous in the strictest sense. Whereas Morton and Marslen-Wilson allow parallel processing of information at some stage, in Forster's theory, linguistic processing is completely serial. Forster's theory posits three separate linguistic processors: a lexical processor, a syntactic processor, and a message processor. In addition, the latest version of Forster's theory incorporates a third, non-linguistic processor, the General Processing System (GPS).

In the first stage of Forster's model, information from peripheral perceptual systems is submitted to the lexical processor. The lexical processor then attempts to locate an entry in three peripheral access files: an orthographic file (for visual input), a phonetic file (for auditory input), and syntactic-semantic file (for both visual and auditory input). Search of the peripheral access files is assumed to proceed by frequency, with higher frequency words being searched prior to lower frequency words. Once an entry is located in the peripheral access files, a pointer is retrieved by which the entry is located in the master lexicon. Thus, word recognition is accomplished at the level of the peripheral access files. Once an entry is located in the peripheral files, lexical access is accomplished by locating the entry in the master lexicon.

Upon location of an item in the master lexicon, information regarding the location of that item in the master list is passed on to the syntactic processor, which attempts to build a syntactic structure. From the syntactic processor information is passed to the message processor which attempts to build a conceptual structure for the intended message. Each of the three processors— the lexical processor, the syntactic processor, and the message processor—can pass information to the GPS. However, the GPS cannot influence processing in any of the three dedicated linguistic processors. The GPS serves to incorporate general conceptual knowledge with the output of the information from the linguistic processors in making a decision (or response).

Forster's theory is autonomous in two senses. First, the lexical processor is independent of the syntactic and message processors, and the syntactic processor is independent of the message processor. Second, the entire linguistic system is independent of the general cognitive system. This strictly serial and autonomous characterization of language processing means that word recognition and lexical access are in no way influenced by higher-level knowledge sources and are exclusively bottom-up or data-driven processes. Forster's model is attractive because of its relative specificity and the apparently testable claims it makes regarding the autonomy of its processors. Forster's model also attempts to describe word recognition and lexical access in the context of sentence processing. In addition, the model incorporates a specific explanation of the word frequency effect, namely that entries in the peripheral access files are organized according to frequency and that search proceeds from high to low frequency entries.

6.4. Elman and McClelland's interactive-activation theory

Elman and McClelland's (1984, 1986) model is based on a system of simple processing units called "nodes." Nodes may stand for features, phonemes, or words. However, nodes at each level are alike in that each has an activation level representing the degree to which the input is consistent with the unit the node stands for. In addition, each node has a resting level and a threshold. In the presence of confirmatory evidence, the activation level of a node rises toward its threshold; in the absence of such evidence, activation decays toward the resting level of the node (see also McClelland & Rumelhart, 1981).

Nodes within this system are highly interconnected and when a given node reaches threshold, it may then influence other nodes to which it is connected. Connections *between* nodes are of two types: excitatory and inhibitory. Thus, a node that has reached threshold may raise the activation of some of the nodes to which it is connected while lowering the activation of other nodes. Connections between levels are exclusively excitatory and are bidirectional. Thus, phoneme nodes may excite word nodes and word nodes may in turn excite phoneme nodes. For example, the phoneme nodes corresponding to /l/ and /e/ may excite the word node "lake," and the word node "lake" may then excite the phoneme nodes /l/, /e/, and /k/. Connections *within* levels are inhibitory and bidirectional. Thus, activation of the phoneme node /l/ may inhibit activation of the phoneme node /b/, lowering the probability that the word node "bake" will raise its activation level.

The Elman and McClelland model illustrates how a highly interactive system may be conceptualized (see also McClelland & Elman, 1986). In addition, it incorporates notions of excitation *and* inhibition. By so doing, it directly incorporates a mechanism that reduces the possibility that nodes inconsistent with the evidence will be activated while at the same time allowing for positive evidence at one level to influence activation of nodes at another. Although Elman and McClelland's model is very interactive, it is not without constraints. Namely, connections between levels are only excitatory and within levels only inhibitory.

Elman and McClelland's model explicitly assumes a segmental representation for speech. The entire organization of the network is based on the existence of different processing units at each level corresponding to acoustic-phonetic features or cues, segmental phonemes and finally words. Because of the architecture of the system, words have a much more complex structure than other elements. Thus, word nodes not only reflect activation of the word as a whole but also activation of each of the constituent phonemes of the word and their component features.

There are two interesting features of this model that are worth noting here. First, although coarticulation effects and contextual variability have been considered by theorists as "noise" that is imposed on an ideal discrete phonetic transcription of speech by the speech production apparatus, Elman and McClelland's model treats this variability, what they call "lawful variability," as a source of useful information and provides a "graceful" way to account for the effects of context in speech perception (Elman & McClelland, 1984). Second, there is no explicit segmentation of the input speech waveform at any time during processing in their model. The segmentation into phones or allophones simply falls out naturally as a result of the labeling process itself. Thus, the problem of dealing with segmentation directly is avoided by permitting the activation of all feature and phoneme nodes and simply observing the consequences at the word level.

6.5. Klatt's LAFS model

Whereas Elman and McClelland's model allows for interaction between and within levels of nodes, Klatt's *L*exical *A*ccess *F*rom *S*pectra (LAFS) model assumes direct, noninteractive access of lexical entries based on context-sensitive spectral sections (Klatt, 1980). Klatt's model assumes that adult listeners have a dictionary of all lawful diphone sequences in long-term memory. Associated with each diphone sequence is a prototypical spectral representation. Klatt proposes spectral representations of diphone sequences to overcome the contextual variability of individual segments. To a certain extent, then, Klatt tries to overcome the problem of the lack of acoustic-phonetic invariance in speech by precompiling coarticulatory effects directly into the representations residing in memory.

In Klatt's LAFS model, the listener computes spectral representations of an input word and compares these representations to the prototypes in memory. Word recognition is accomplished when a best match is found between the input spectra and the diphone representations. In this portion of the model, word recognition is accomplished directly on the basis of spectral representations of the sensory input. There is a means by which phonetic transcriptions can be obtained intermediate to lexical access (i.e., via the SCRIBER module), but in most circumstances access is direct, with no intermediate levels of computation corresponding to segments or phonemes.

One important aspect of Klatt's LAFS model is that it explicitly avoids any need to compute a distinct level of representation corresponding to discrete phonemic segments. Instead, LAFS uses a precompiled, acoustically-based lexicon of all possible words in a network of diphone power spectra. These spectral templates are assumed to be context-sensitive units much like "Wickelphones" because they are assumed to represent the acoustic correlates of phones in different phonetic environments (Wickelgren, 1969). Diphones in the LAFS system accomplish this by encoding the spectral characteristics of the segments themselves and the transitions from the middle of one segment to the middle of the next segment.

Klatt argues that diphone concatenation is sufficient to capture much of the context-dependent variability observed for phonetic segments in spoken words. Word recognition in this model is accomplished by computing a power spectrum of the input speech signal every 10 ms and then comparing this input spectrum to spectral templates stored in a precompiled network. The basic idea of LAFS, adapted from the Harpy system, is to find the path through the network that best represents the observed input spectra (Klatt, 1977). This single path is then assumed to represent the optimal phonetic transcription of the input signal.

Elman and McClelland's and Klatt's models fall on either end of a continuum of theories of word recognition and lexical access. Elman and McClelland's theory represents the class of theories that emphasize *interactive* systems in which many different levels of information play a role in word recognition and lexical access. In this sense, their model is closest to those of Morton and Marslen-Wilson, although Marslen-Wilson's cohort theory does incorporate an initial autonomous stage of processing. Klatt's model, on the other hand, represents the class of models in which lexical access is accomplished almost entirely on the basis of bottom-up acoustic-phonetic information. In this sense, Klatt's model resembles Forster's approach. However, Forster's model does posit intermediate levels of analysis in the word recognition process, unlike Klatt's LAFS, which assumes *direct* mapping of power spectra onto words in a precompiled network. One of the central questions to be addressed with regard to current theories of word recognition involves the extent to which word recognition involves interactive knowledge sources and the manner in which these processes interact with processes involved in speech sound perception (see other contributions to this issue).

7. Summary and conclusions

In this paper, we have attempted to review briefly what is currently known about the nature of the input to the word recognition system provided by mechanisms employed in speech sound perception. After considering several of the basic issues in speech perception such as linearity, invariance and segmentation, we described several stages of perceptual analysis within a conceptual framework. This framework assumed that speech is processed through a series of analytic stages ranging from peripheral auditory processing, acoustic-phonetic and phonological analysis to word recognition and lexical access. Finally, we examined several contemporary approaches to word recognition in order to make explicit some of the major assumptions regarding the nature of the input to the word recognition process. An additional goal of the paper was to establish the need for segmental phonemic representations in spoken word recognition. This is the point in spoken language processing that serves to interface the initial sensory information in the speech waveform with the representation of words in the lexicon. An examination of current models revealed the extent to which segmental representations are assumed either explicitly or tacitly in mediating word recognition and lexical access.

References

Abbs, J.H., & Sussman, H.M. (1971). Neurophysiological feature detectors and speech perception: A discussion of theoretical implications. *Journal of Speech and Hearing Research, 14*, 23–36.

Abramson, A.S., & Lisker, L. (1965). Voice onset time in stop consonants: Acoustic analysis and synthesis. *Proceedings of the 5th International Congress of Acoustics* (Liege).

Allen, J. (1985). A perspective on man-machine communication by speech. *Proceedings of the IEEE, 74* (11) 1541–1550.

Aslin, R.N., Pisoni, D.B., & Jusczyk, P.W. (1983). Auditory development and speech perception in infancy. In P. Mussen (Ed.), *Carmichael's manual of child psychology* (4th ed.) (Vol. 2) *Infancy and the biology of development* (Eds. M.M. Haith & J.J. Campos)(Vol. 2). New York: Wiley.

Bever, T.G., Lackner, J., & Kirk, R. (1969). The underlying structures of sentences are the primary units of immediate speech processing. *Perception & Psychophysics, 5*, 225–231.

Bond, Z.S., & Garnes, S. (1980). Misperceptions of fluent speech. In R.A. Cole (Ed.), *Perception and production of fluent speech.* Hillsdale, N.J.: Erlbaum.

Bond, Z.S., & Robey, R.R. (1983). The phonetic structure of errors in the perception of fluent speech. In N.J. Lass (Ed.), *Speech and language: Advances in basic research and practice* (Vol. 9). New York: Academic Press.

Bradley, D.C., & Forster, K.I. (1987). A reader's view of listening. *Cognition, 25*, this issue.

Carlson, R., & Granstrom, B. (Eds.) (1982). *The representation of speech in the peripheral auditory system.* New York: Elsevier Biomedical Press.

Chomsky, N., & Halle, M. (1968). *The sound pattern of English.* New York: Harper and Row.

Chomsky, N., & Miller, G.A. (1963). Introduction to formal analysis of natural languages. In R.D. Luce, R. Bush, & E. Galanter (Eds.), *Handbook of mathematical psychology* (Vol. 2). New York: Wiley.

Church, K.W. (1983). Phrase-structure parsing: A method for taking advantage of allophonic constraints. Bloomington, Ind.: Indiana University Linguistics Club.

Church, K.W. (1987). Phonological parsing and lexical retrieval. *Cognition, 25*, this issue.

Clements, G.N., & Keyser, S.J. (1983). *CV phonology: A generative theory of the syllable.* Cambridge, Mass.: MIT Press.

Cole, R.A. (1973). Listening for mispronunciations: a measure of what we hear during speech. *Perception & Psychophysics, 13*, 153–156.

Cole, R.A., & Jakimik, J. (1978). Understanding speech: How words are heard. In G. Underwood (Ed.), *Strategies of information processing.* New York: Academic Press.

Cole, R.A., & Jakimik, J. (1980). A model of speech perception. In R.A. Cole (Ed.), *Perception and production of fluent speech.* Hillsdale, N.J.: Erlbaum.

Cole, R.A., & Scott, B. (1974a). The phantom in the phoneme: Invariant cues for stop consonants. *Perception & Psychophysics, 15*, 101–107.

Cole, R.A., & Scott, B. (1974b). Toward a theory of speech perception. *Psychological Review, 81*, 348–374.

Conrad, R. (1964). Acoustic confusions in immediate memory. *British Journal of Psychology, 55*, 75–84.

Cooper, W.E. (1975). Selective adaptation to speech. In F. Restle, R.M. Shiffrin, N.J. Castellan, H.R. Lindman, & D.B. Pisoni (Eds.), *Cognitive theory* (Vol. 1). Hillsdale, N.J.: Erlbaum.

Darwin, D.J. (1976). The perception of speech. In E.C. Carterette & M.P. Friedman (Eds.), *Handbook of perception.* New York: Academic Press.

Delattre, P.C., Liberman, A.M., & Cooper, F.S. (1955). Acoustic loci and transitional cues for consonants. *Journal of the Acoustical Society of America, 27*, 769–773.

Delgutte, B. (1980). Representation of speech-like sounds in the discharge patterns of auditory-nerve fibers. *Journal of the Acoustical Society of America, 68*, 843–857.

Delgutte, B. (1982). Some correlates of phonetic distinctions at the level of the auditory nerve. In R. Carlson

& B. Granstrom (Eds.), *The representation of speech in the peripheral auditory system*. New York: Elsevier Biomedical Press.

Dell, G.S., & Newman, J.E. (1980). Detecting phonemes in fluent speech. *Journal of Verbal Learning and Verbal Behavior, 19,* 608–623.

Denes, P. (1955). Effect of duration on the perception of voicing. *Journal of the Acoustical Society of America, 27,* 761–764.

Diehl, R.L. (1981). Feature detectors for speech: A critical reappraisal. *Psychological Bulletin, 89,* 1–18.

Dorman, M., Studdert-Kennedy, M., & Raphael, L. (1977). Stop consonant recognition: Release bursts and formant transitions as functionally equivalent context-dependent cues. *Perception & Psychophysics, 22,* 109–122.

Eimas, P.D. (1974). Auditory and linguistic processing of cues for place of articulation by infants. *Perception & Psychophysics, 16,* 513–521.

Eimas, P.D., & Corbit, J.D. (1973). Selective adaptation of linguistic feature detectors. *Cognitive Psychology, 4,* 99–109.

Eimas, P.D., & Miller, J.L. (1978). Effects of selective adaptation on the perception of speech and visual patterns: Evidence for feature detectors. In H.L. Pick, & R.D. Walk (Eds.), *Perception and experience.* New York: Plenum.

Eimas, P.D., Siqueland, E.R, Jusczyk, P., & Vigorito, J. (1971). Speech perception in infants. *Science, 171,* 303–306.

Elman, J.L., & McClelland, J.L. (1986). Exploiting lawful variability in the speech waveform. In J.S. Perkell & D.H. Klatt (Eds.) *Invariance and variability in speech processes.* Hillsdale, N.J.: Erlbaum.

Elman, J.L. & McClelland, J.L. (1984). Speech perception as a cognitive process: The interactive activation model. In N.J. Lass (Ed.), *Speech and language: Advances in basic research and practice* (Vol. 10) (pp. 337–374) New York: Academic Press.

Fant, G. (1962). Descriptive analysis of the acoustic aspects of speech. *Logos, 5,* 3–17.

Fant, G. (1973). *Speech sounds and features.* Cambridge, Mass.: MIT Press.

Fischer-Jorgensen, E. (1954). Acoustic analysis of stop consonants. *Miscellanea Phonetica, 2,* 42–59.

Fitch, H.L. (1981). Distinguishing temporal information for speaking rate from temporal information for intervocalic stop consonant voicing. *Haskins Laboratories Status Report on Speech Research* SR-65 (pp. 1–32). New Haven: Haskins Laboratories.

Forster, K.I. (1976). Accessing the mental lexicon. In R.J. Wales, & E. Walker (Eds.), *New approaches to language mechanisms.* Amsterdam: North-Holland.

Forster, K.I. (1979). Levels of processing and the structure of the language processor. In W.E. Cooper, & E.C.T. Walker (Eds.), *Sentence processing: Psycholinguistic studies presented to Merrill Garrett.* Hillsdale, N.J.: Erlbaum.

Foss, D.J., & Blank, M.A. (1980). Identifying the speech codes. *Cognitive Psychology, 12,* 1–31.

Foss, D.J., & Gernsbacher, M.A. (1983). Cracking the dual code: Towards a unitary model of phoneme identification. *Journal of Verbal Learning and Verbal Behavior, 22,* 609–632.

Foss, D.J., Harwood, D.A., & Blank, M.A. (1980). Deciphering decoding decisions: Data and devices. In R.A. Cole (Ed.), *Perception and production of fluent speech.* Hillsdale, N.J.: Erlbaum.

Foss, D.J., & Swinney, D.A. (1973). On the psychological reality of the phoneme: Perception, identification, and consciousness. *Journal of Verbal Learning and Verbal Behavior, 12,* 246–257.

Fromkin, V. (1973). *Speech errors as linguistic evidence.* The Hague: Mouton.

Fromkin, V. (1980). *Errors in linguistic performance.* New York: Academic Press.

Fry, D.W. (1956). Perception and recognition. In M. Halle, H.G. Lunt, H. McClean, & C.H. van Schoonefeld (Eds.), *For Roman Jakobson.* The Hague: Mouton.

Ganong, W.F. (1978). The selective effects of burst-cued stops. *Perception & Psychophysics, 24,* 71–83.

Garrett, M.F. (1976). Syntactic processes in sentence production. In R.J. Wales, & E. Walker (Eds.), *New approaches to language mechanisms.* Amsterdam: North-Holland.

Garrett, M.F. (1980). Levels of processing in sentence production. In B. Butterworth (Ed.), *Language production* (Vol. 1). New York: Academic Press.

Goldhor, R. (1983). A speech signal processing system based on a peripheral auditory model. *Proceedings of IEEE, ICASSP-83*, 1368–1371.

Halle, M. (1985). Speculations about the representation of words in memory. In V. Fromkin (Ed.), *Linguistic phonetics: Papers presented to Peter Ladefoged*. New York: Academic Press.

Halle, M., & Vergnaud, J.-R. (1980). Three dimensional phonology. *Journal of Linguistic Research, 1*, 83–105.

House, A.S. (1961). On vowel duration. *Journal of the Acoustical Society of America, 33*, 1174–1178.

Johnson-Laird, P.N. (1975). Meaning and the mental lexicon. In A. Kennedy, & A. Wilkes (Eds.), *Studies in long-term memory* (pp. 123–142). London: Wiley.

Joos, M.A. (1948). Acoustic phonetics. *Language, 24* (Suppl.), 1–136.

Kahn, D. (1976). *Syllable-based generalizations in English phonology*. Bloomington, Ind.: Indiana University Linguistics Club.

Kenstowicz, M., & Kisseberth, C. (1979). *Generative phonology*. New York: Academic Press.

Klatt, D.H. (1968). Structure of confusions in short-term memory between English consonants. *Journal of the Acoustical Society of America, 44*, 401–407.

Klatt, D.H. (1977). Review of the ARPA speech understanding project. *Journal of the Acoustical Society of America, 62*, 1345–1366.

Klatt, D.H. (1979). Speech perception: A model of acoustic-phonetic analysis and lexical access. *Journal of Phonetics, 7*, 279–312.

Klatt, D.H. (1980). Speech perception: A model of acoustic-phonetic analysis and lexical access. In R.A. Cole (Ed.), *Perception and production of fluent speech*. Hillsdale, N.J.: Erlbaum.

Klatt, D.H. (1982). Speech processing strategies based on auditory models. In R. Carlson & B. Granstrom (Eds.), *The representation of speech in the peripheral auditory system*. New York: Elsevier Biomedical Press.

Liberman, A.M., Cooper, F.S., Shankweiler, D.P., & Studdert-Kennedy, M. (1967). Perception of the speech code. *Psychological Review, 74*, 431–461.

Liberman, A.M., Delattre, P.C., & Cooper, F.S. (1952). The role of selected stimulus variables in the perception of the unvoiced stop consonants. *American Journal of Psychology, 52*, 127–137.

Liberman, A.M., Delattre, P.C., Cooper, F.S., & Gerstman, L.H. (1954). The role of consonant-vowel transitions in the perception of the stop and nasal consonants. *Psychological Monographs, 68*, 1–13.

Liberman, I.Y., Shankweiler, D., Fischer, F.W., & Carter, B. (1974). Explicit syllable and phoneme segmentation in the young child. *Journal of Experimental Child Psychology, 18*, 201–212.

Lisker, L. (1957). Closure duration and the intervocalic voiced-voiceless distinction in English. *Language, 33*, 42–49.

Lisker, L. (1978). *Rapid* vs. *rabid*: A catalogue of acoustic features that may cue the distinction. *Haskins Laboratories Status Report on Speech Research* SR-65 (pp. 127–132). New Haven: Haskins Laboratories.

Lisker, L., & Abramson, A.S. (1964). A cross language study of voicing in initial stops: Acoustical measurements. *Word, 20*, 384–422.

Luce, P.A. (1986). Neighborhoods of words in the mental lexicon. *Research on Speech Perception, Technical Report No. 6*. Bloomington, Ind.: Department of Psychology, Speech Research Laboratory.

Marslen-Wilson, W.D. (1987). Parallel processing in spoken word recognition. *Cognition, 25*, this issue.

Marslen-Wilson, W.D., & Tyler, L.K. (1980). The temporal structure of spoken language understanding. *Cognition, 8*, 1–71.

Marslen-Wilson, W.D., & Welsh, A. (1978). Processing interactions and lexical access during word recognition in continuous speech. *Cognitive Psychology, 10*, 29–63.

Massaro, D.W., & Oden, G.C. (1980). Speech perception: A framework for research and theory. In N.J. Lass (Ed.), *Speech and language: Advances in basic research and practice* (Vol. 3) (pp. 129–165). New York: Academic Press.

McClelland, J.L. & Elman, J.L. (1986). The TRACE model of speech perception. *Cognitive Psychology, 18*, 1–86.

McClelland, J.L., & Rumelhart, D.E. (1981). An interactive-activation model of context effects in letter perception, Part I: An account of basic findings. *Psychological Review, 88*, 375–407.

Miller, G.A. (1962). Decision units in the perception of speech. *IRE Transactions on Information Theory, IT-8*, 81–83.

Miller, G.A., & Johnson-Laird, P.N. (1976). *Language and perception*. Cambridge, Mass.: Harvard University Press.

Miller, G.A., & Nicely, P.E. (1955). An analysis of perceptual confusions among some English consonants. *Journal of the Acoustical Society of America, 27*, 338–352.

Miller, M.I., & Sachs, M.B. (1983). Representation of stop consonants in the discharge patterns of auditory-nerve fibers. *Journal of the Acoustical Society of America, 74*, 502–517.

Morton, J. (1969). Interaction of information in word recognition. *Psychological Review, 76*, 165–178.

Morton, J. (1979). Word recognition. In J. Morton & J.D. Marshall (Eds.), *Psycholinguistics 2: Structures and processes* (pp. 107–156). Cambridge, Mass.: MIT Press.

Morton, J. (1982). Disintegrating the lexicon: An information processing approach. In J. Mehler, E. Walker, & M. Garrett (Eds.), *On mental representation*. Hillsdale, N.J.: Erlbaum.

Morton, J., & Long, J. (1976). Effect of word transitional probability on phoneme identification. *Journal of Verbal Learning and Verbal Behavior, 15*, 43–52.

Oshika, B.T., Zue, V.W., Weeks, R.V., Neu, H., & Aurbach, J. (1975). The role of phonological rules in speech understanding research. *IEEE Transactions on Acoustics, Speech, and Signal Processing, ASSP-23*, 104–112.

Pisoni, D.B. (1978). Speech perception. In W.K. Estes (Ed.), *Handbook of learning and cognitive processes* (Vol. 6). Hillsdale, N.J.: Erlbaum.

Pisoni, D.B. (1983). In defense of segmental representations in speech processing. *Journal of the Acoustical Society of America, 69*, S32.

Pisoni, D.B. (1985). Speech perception: Some new directions in research and theory. *Journal of the Acoustical Society of America, 78*, 381–388.

Pisoni, D.B., Nusbaum, H.C., Luce, P.A., & Slowiaczek, L.M. (1985). Speech perception, word recognition and the structure of the lexicon. *Speech Communication, 4*, 75–95.

Pisoni, D.B., & Sawusch, J.R. (1975). Some stages of processing in speech perception. In A. Cohen, & S. Nooteboom (Eds.), *Structure and process in speech perception* (pp. 16–34). Heidelberg: Springer-Verlag.

Port, R.F. (1977). *The influence of speaking tempo on the duration of stressed vowel and medial stop in English trochee words*. Bloomington, Ind.: Indiana University Linguistics Club.

Port, R.F. (1979). Influence of tempo on stop closure duration as a cue for voicing and place. *Journal of Phonetics, 7*, 45–56.

Raphael, L.J. (1972). Preceding vowel duration as a cue to the perception of the voicing characteristics of word-final consonants in American English. *Journal of the Acoustical Society of America, 51*, 1296–1303.

Raphael, L.J., & Dorman, M.F. (1980). Silence as a cue to the perception of syllable-initial and syllable-final stop consonants. *Journal of Phonetics, 8*, 269–275.

Read, C. (1971). Preschool children's knowledge of English phonology. *Harvard Educational Review, 41*, 1–34.

Reddy, D.R. (1976). Speech recognition by machine: A review. *Proceedings of the IEEE, 64*, 501–523.

Remez, R.E. (1979). Adaptation of the category boundary between speech and nonspeech: A case against feature detectors. *Cognitive Psychology, 11*, 38–57.

Rozin, P., & Gleitman, L.R. (1977). The structure and acquisition of reading II: The reading process and the acquisition of the alphabetic principle. In A.S. Reber, & D.L. Scarborough (Eds.), *Toward a psychology of reading*. Hillsdale, N.J.: Erlbaum.

Sachs, M.B., & Young, E.D. (1979). Encoding of steady-state vowels in the auditory nerve: Representation in terms of discharge rate. *Journal of the Acoustical Society of America, 66*, 470–479.

Samuel, A.G. (1981a). Phonemic restoration: Insights from a new methodology. *Journal of Experimental Psychology: General, 110*, 474–494.

Samuel, A.G. (1981b). The role of bottom-up confirmation in the phonemic restoration illusion. *Journal of Experimental Psychology: Human Perception and Performance, 7*, 1124–1131.

Sapir, E. (1963). The psychological reality of phonemes. In D. Mandelbaum (Ed.), *Selected writings of Edward Sapir*. Berkeley: University of California Press.

Sawusch, J.R. (1977a). Peripheral and central processes in selective adaptation of place of articulation in stop consonants. *Journal of the Acoustical Society of America, 62*, 738–750.

Sawusch, J.R. (1977b). Processing place information in stop consonants. *Perception & Psychophysics, 22*, 417–426.

Sawusch, J.R., & Jusczyk, P.W. (1981). Adaptation and contrast in the perception of voicing. *Journal of Experimental Psychology: Human Perception and Performance, 7*, 408–421.

Searle, C.L., Jacobson, J.F., & Rayment, S.G. (1979). Stop consonant discrimination based on human audition. *Journal of the Acoustical Society of America, 65*, 799–809.

Selkirk, E. (1980). The role of prosodic categories in English word stress. *Linguistic Inquiry, 11*, 563–603.

Shattuck-Hufnagel, S., & Klatt, D.H. (1979). The limited use of distinctive features and markedness in speech production: Evidence from speech error data. *Journal of Verbal Learning and Verbal Behavior, 18*, 41–45.

Stemberger, J.P. (1982). *The lexicon in a model of language production*. Unpublished doctoral dissertation, University of California, San Diego.

Stevens, K.N. (1980). Acoustic correlates of some phonetic categories. *Journal of the Acoustical Society of America, 68*, 836–842.

Stevens, K.N., & Blumstein, S.E. (1978). Invariant cues for place of articulation in stop consonants. *Journal of the Acoustical Society of America, 64*, 1358–1368.

Stevens, K.N., & Blumstein, S.E. (1981). The search for invariant acoustic correlates of phonetic features. In P.D. Eimas & J.L. Miller (Eds.), *Perspectives on the study of speech*. Hillsdale, N.J.: Erlbaum.

Stevens, K.N., & Klatt, D.H. (1974). Role of formant transitions in the voiced-voiceless distinction for stops. *Journal of the Acoustical Society of America, 55*, 653–659.

Stevens, K.N., & House, A.S. (1972). Speech perception. In J. Tobias (Ed.), *Foundations of modern auditory theory* (Vol. II). New York: Academic Press.

Studdert-Kennedy, M. (1974). The perception of speech. In T.A. Sebeok (Ed.), *Current trends in linguistics*. The Hague: Mouton.

Studdert-Kennedy, M. (1976). Speech perception. In N.J. Lass (Ed.), *Contemporary issues in experimental phonetics*. New York: Academic Press.

Studdert-Kennedy, M. (1980). Speech perception. *Language and Speech, 23*, 45–66.

Summerfield, Q., & Haggard, M.P. (1974). Perceptual processing of multiple cues and contexts: Effects of following vowel upon stop consonant voicing. *Journal of Phonetics, 2*, 279–295.

Treiman, R. (1980). *The phonemic analysis ability of preschool children*. Unpublished doctoral dissertation, University of Pennsylvania.

Treiman, R. (1983). The structure of spoken syllables: Evidence from novel word games. *Cognition, 15*, 49–74.

Treiman, R. (1985). Onsets and rimes as units of spoken syllables: Evidence from children. *Journal of Experimental Child Psychology, 39*, 161–181.

Wang, M.D., & Bilger, R.C. (1973). Consonant confusions in noise: A study of perceptual features. *Journal of the Acoustical Society of America, 54*, 1248–1266.

Warren, R.M. (1970). Perceptual restoration of missing speech sounds. *Science, 176*, 392–393.

Wickelgren, W.A. (1965). Acoustic similarity and retroactive interference in short-term memory. *Journal of Verbal Learning and Verbal Behavior, 4*, 53–61.

Wickelgren, W.A. (1966). Phonemic similarity and interference in short-term memory for single letters. *Journal of Experimental Psychology, 71*, 396–404.

Wickelgren, W.A. (1969). Context-sensitive coding, associative memory, and serial order in (speech) behavior. *Psychological Review, 76*, 1–15.

Wickelgren, W.A. (1976). Phonetic coding and serial order. In E.C. Carterette, & M.P. Friedman (Eds.), *Handbook of perception* (Vol. 7). New York: Academic Press.

Young, E.D., & Sachs, M.B. (1979). Representation of steady-state vowels in the temporal aspects of the discharge patterns of populations of auditory-nerve fibers. *Journal of the Acoustical Society of America, 66*, 1381–1403.

Zwicker, E., Terhardt, E., & Paulus, E. (1979). Automatic speech recognition using psychoacoustic models. *Journal of the Acoustical Society of America, 65*, 487–498.

Résumé

Cet article passe en revue quelques théories récentes qui rendent compte de la façon dont les informations sensorielles et perceptuelles sont transmises au système de reconnaissance de mots par les processus qui sous-tendent la perception de la parole. Dans la première partie, nous évoquons quelques problèmes que tentent de résoudre depuis une trentaine d'années les chercheurs du domaine. Dans la deuxième partie, nous examinons un cadre théorique de la perception de la parole où les étapes de traitement sont associés à des niveaux d'analyse linguistique. Dans ce cadre on part de l'hypothèse que la parole est traitée dans une série d'étapes analytiques allant du traitement auditif périphérique, de l'analyse phonétique acoustique et phonologique à la reconnaissance de mots et l'accès lexical.

Enfin, dans la dernière partie, diverses approches des problèmes de la reconnaissance de mots et de l'accès lexical sont évaluées. Nous examinons différentes propositions concernant l'analyse de "bas-en-haut", les unités perceptuelles postulées et l'interaction entre différents types d'information dans la reconnaissance de mots. Un objectif supplémentaire de ce travail consiste à établir l'importance des représentations segmentales dans la reconnaissance.

3

Phonological parsing and lexical retrieval*

KENNETH W. CHURCH**

Bell Telephone Laboratories

Abstract

Speech is a natural error-correcting code. The speech signal is full of rich sources of contextual redundancy at many levels of representation including allophonic variation, phonotactics, syllable structure, stress domains, morphology, syntax, semantics and pragmatics. The psycholinguistic literature has tended to concentrate heavily on high level constraints such as semantics and pragmatics and has generally overlooked the usefulness of lower level constraints such as allophonic variation. It has even been said that allophonic variation is a source of confusion or a kind of statistical noise that makes speech recognition that much harder than it already is. In contrast, I argue that aspiration, stop release, flapping, palatalization and other cues that vary systematically with syllabic context can be used to parse syllables and stress domains. These constituents can then constrain the lexical matching process, so that much less search will be required in order to retrieve the correct lexical entry. In this way, syllable structure and stress domains will be proposed as an intermediate level of representation between the phonetic description and the lexicon.

My argument is primarily a computational one and will include a discussion of a prototype phonetic parser which has been implemented using simple well-understood parsing mechanisms. No experimental results will be presented.

1. Allophonic variation is "noise"?

The lack of phonemic invariance has always been considered one of the classic hard problems for speech research. It is well known that phonemes

---

*This research was supported (in part) by the National Institutes of Health Grant No. 1 P01 LM 03374-01 and 03374-02 from the National Library of Medicine.

**I have received a considerable amount of help and support over the course of this project. Let me mention just a few of the people that I should thank: Jon Allen, Glenn Burke, Francine Chen, Scott Cyphers, Sarah Ferguson, Margaret Fleck, Osamu Fujimura, Dan Huttenlocher, Jay Keyser, Lori Lamel, Mark Liberman, Mitch Marcus, Ramesh Patil, Janet Pierrehumbert, Dave Shipman, Pete Szolovits, Meg Withgott and Victor Zue. Reprint requests should be sent to K.W. Church, office 2d454, Bell Telephone Laboratories, 600 Mountain Avenue, Murray Hill, NJ 07974, U.S.A.

have very different acoustic phonetic properties in different contexts. For instance, the phoneme /t/ in "Tom" will almost certainly be released and aspirated unlike the /t/'s in "càt", "butter", "atlas", etc. Moreover, it is also well known that different phonemes can be realized with almost the same allophone (phonetic variant). For example, /t/ and /d/ conflate in flapping contexts (e.g., "writer"/"rider"), vowels often neutralize to schwa when unstressed, /dy/ and /dǰ/ merge under palatalization ("did you"), and so forth. Thus the mapping between phonemes and their allophonic realization is highly variable and extremely ambiguous; there are many ways that a speaker might choose to realize a given phoneme and there are many ways that a listener might choose to interpret a given allophone. This uncertainty is generally considered to be problematic for practical applications of speech technology (e.g., speech synthesis and recognition) as well as scientific investigations of human production and perception.

The view of allophonic variation as problematic was commonly held during the time of the ARPA speech project; one can find support for this position from both the psychological (Cole & Jakimik, 1980) (CMU) and computational literatures (Jelinek, 1982) (IBM). This position was most clearly presented by Klatt (1974, 1977, 1980) (MIT), who argued that even if we had an ideal front-end that could produce an error-free phonetic transcription, it would still be very difficult to build a speech recognition device that could decode a phonetic transcription such as [dɪjəhɪʃɪʔtɬtam] into the sentence "Did you hit it to Tom," because the decoding device would have to account for at least five allophonic rules:

- Palatalization of /d/ before /y/ in "did you"
- Reduction of unstressed /u/ to schwa in "you"
- Flapping of intervocalic /t/ in "hit it"
- Reduction of schwa and devoicing of /u/ in "to Tom"
- Reduction of geminate t in "it to"

Klatt concluded that (1980, pp. 548–549):

> In most systems for sentence recognition, such modifications must be viewed as a kind of 'noise' that makes it more difficult to hypothesize lexical candidates given an input phonetic transcription. To see that this must be the case, we note that each phonological rule results in irreversible ambiguity—the phonological rule does not have a unique inverse that could be used to recover the underlying phonemic representation for a lexical item. For example, in a word like 'about' or the surface realization of almost any English vowel appearing in a sufficiently destressed word. The tongue flap [ʃ] could have come from a /t/ or a /d/.

2. Allophonic variation is useful

In contrast, I argue that allophonic variation is useful. When I find a flap, I know that it is foot internal (not initial in a stressed syllable); when I find a reduced vowel, I know that it has zero stress; and when I find an aspirated stop, I know it probably starts a syllable. These examples demonstrate the well-known fact that allophonic distribution determines, in part, the location of syllables and stress. Thus, *in principle*, there ought to be important information in the distribution of allophones, though admittedly, *in practice*, distributional information is often confusing to existing speech recognizers, as Klatt points out, because the existing technology doesn't know how to take advantage of it. We need a principled mechanism for extracting distributional information from the speech signal. I will propose that well-understood parsing technology is ideally suited to fill this gap. The next-generation recognizer ought to be able to parse a phonetic description of an utterance into a limited set of well-formed syllable structures and stress domains. These constituents will then be used to constrain the lexical matching process, so that much less search will be required in order to retrieve the correct lexical entry.

Let me illustrate the approach with Klatt's example (enhanced with allophonic diacritics to show aspiration and glottalization): [dɪdjəhɪʕɪ?tʰɪtʰam].[1] Using phonotactic and allophonic constraints on syllable structure such as:[1]

- /h/ is always syllable initial,
- [?] is always syllable final,
- [ʕ] is always syllable final, and
- [tʰ] is always syllable initial,

the parser can insert the following syllable boundaries:
[dɪjə # hɪʕ # ɪ? # tʰ ɪ # tʰam].

With most of the syllables correctly parsed, it is now relatively easy to match the constituents with words in the lexicon to find the sentence: "Did you hit it to Tom?".

---

[1]This formulation of the constraints is oversimplified for expository convenience (see Fujimura & Lovins, 1982; Kahn, 1976; Kiparsky, 1981, and references therein for discussion of the more subtle issues).

Parsed transcription		Decoding
[dɪdjə]	→	did you
[hɪʕ]	→	hit
[ɪʔ]	→	it
[tʰ]	→	to
[tʰam]	→	Tom

This example shows that allophonic variation should not be viewed as noise; even though allophonic rules are extremely difficult to invert, they can be very powerful cues for a syllable parser.

Thus far, the discussion has been assuming perfect input transcriptions, an idealization that is obviously unrealistic in practice. This idealization is convenient for exposition, and permits me to demonstrate the usefulness of allophonic constraints as parsing cues without having to discuss control and representation strategies (e.g., island driving) for dealing with errorful input. On the other hand, being an engineer, I really would like to expand upon these issues, and I have already begun to apply parsing techniques in limited practical problems such as the recognition of connected digit sequences. The parsing mechanisms have been extended to accept extremely ambiguous and errorful input, produced, in fact, by a statistical training procedure that generates a probability score for each allophone every 2 ms. Parsing these scores requires considerable engineering knowhow since straightforward methods would be too slow to deal with the extremely long input sentences of approximately 1000 speech frames. Let me resist the temptation to discuss these complex and interesting questions here, and simply continue to assume ideal (though unrealistic) input, for the remainder of this paper.

3. Syllable structure as an intermediate level of representation

The proposed solution to Klatt's puzzle demonstrated the role of syllables and other linguistically motivated constituents as an intermediate level of representation between the input transcription and the output word lattice. In this way, I have factored the lexical retrieval problem into two subtasks:

- *Parse* the segment lattice into the intermediate representation, and
- *Match* the intermediate constituent structure against the lexicon.

This parsing and matching approach differs from many psychological/computational models (e.g., the Cohort model, IBM's Markov model) which attempt a direct match between acoustic/phonetic segments and the lexicon, and do not assume an intermediate constituent structure.

Output from Lower Level Processing
↓
Segmentation Lattice
↓
Syllable Structure and Stress Domains
↓
Lattice of Lexical Hypotheses
↓
Input to Higher Level Processing

A few psycholinguists have noticed the usefulness of allophonic rules as parsing cues. Two examples will be cited here (Christie, 1974, p. 820):

> In evaluating these data, linguists will not be surprised that aspiration on a voiceless stop in English serves as a cue that that stop is in syllable initial position. Such a result would be expected to follow from the fact that in English aspirated stops appear only in initial position in a stressed syllable. One would like to suggest that allophones are more than excess baggage through which a listener must work his way, and that they actually can carry information about the structure of the message. Such a suggestion was made and discussed in Lehiste (1960). But ... By contrast, in the present experiment ... Lehiste's suggestion that the allophones can serve to carry information about the structure of the message is thus confirmed.

Nakatani (unpublished ms., p. 3) has also noted that so-called word boundary rules can be used as very powerful parsing cues:

> We see the fission and fusion processes fitting into a comprehensive model of speech perception in the following way. The prosodic stress and rhythm cues indicate when a word boundary is likely to occur, but they do not indicate precisely where the word boundary is. For example, a word boundary must occur somewhere between the syllabic nuclei of 'gray twine' since two consecutive stressed syllables cannot belong to a single English word. The precise location of the word boundary is indicated by the allophonic cues. In this example, the word boundary must fall before the /t/ because its strong aspiration is characteristic of word-initial allophones of voiceless stops. [In contrast, in 'great wine', the word boundary must fall after the /t/ because its realization is characteristic of word-final allophones.]

4. Review of phonotactic constraints

In addition to allophonic constraints, the parsing approach is also well suited to take advantage of phonotactics, the constraints on ordering (tactics) of phonemes. Most models of speech recognition and perception operate with an inadequate model of phonotactic constraints of the form

word → syllable*
syllable → initial-cluster vowel final-cluster

This model assumes a list of permissible initial and final clusters. How can I estimate the set of permissible clusters? It is widely assumed that the set of *syllable* initial clusters are identical to the set of *word* initial clusters, and that the set of *syllable* final clusters are identical to the set of *word* final clusters. But this is inadequate for two reasons. First, it will be necessary to add some more constraints (e.g., the maximal onset principle and stress resyllabification) so that words like "extra" are assigned just one syllabification /ek-stra/, not three: /ek-stra/, */eks-tra/ and */ekst-ra/. Secondly though, the set of syllable final clusters is far more constrained than the set of word final clusters. Note, for example, if any word final cluster could end a syllable then we might expect to find a word final cluster like /rnt/ to appear in word medial position followed by another syllable. But sequences of consonants like /rntstr/ are not found in word medial position. It will be argued that sequences of six consonants can be excluded for principled reasons. In practice, one rarely finds sequences with as many as four consonants within the same morpheme. Long sequences of consonants almost always cross a morpheme boundary (e.g., "iN-STRructive", "eX-PLanation", "thaNKS-Giving"). Phonotactic constraints such as this might improve the performance of a speech recognition device in many ways. In particular, these constraints could lead to more compact representation of lexical entries, and more efficient search procedures for matching portions of the utterance against the lexicon.

According to Kiparsky's review paper of developments in suprasegmental phonology (Kiparsky, 1981) there are three types of phonotactic constraints on syllable structure (excluding morpheme final syllables for the moment):

- *Length*: There are at most three consonants before the vowel and two afterward.
- *Sonority*: The relative prominence (vowel-likeness) must decrease from the nucleus towards the margins. More precisely, the sonority order (stops < fricatives < nasals < liquids < glides < vowels) must strictly decrease from the nucleus.
- *Idiosyncratic systematic gaps*: English happens not to allow certain possibilities, e.g., voiced stops after nasals and [u], even though these meet the previous two conditions.

In addition, there are also some well-known voicing and place assimilation and dissimilation facts.

4.1. The affix position

All of these constraints can be violated in morpheme final syllables.

- *Length*: wild, world, paint, exempt, lounge, texts
- *Sonority*: apse, axe, bets, width, depth, paths, laughs
- *Idiosyncratic systematic gaps*: bind, sand, mend, wood, hood, could, should
- *Place assimilation*: seemed, seems, sings, hanged

In order to account for these exceptions, many analyses introduce a morpheme final *affix* position. This position was originally intended to hold regular inflectional affixes (e.g., plural /s, z/ and past tense /t, d/), though it has been generalized to apply whenever there is an apparent violation of one of the phonotactic constraints mentioned above. Thus, for example, the /d/ is analyzed as an affix in both "fined" and "find,"[2] even though the latter /d/ is not a regular inflectional affix. The consonants in the affix position must be coronal and they must agree in voicing.

It also turns out that a number of phonotactic principles can be violated in certain other positions. For example, /s/ doesn't seem to to fit into the sonority hierarchy; it has to be less sonorous than a stop in "stress" but more sonorous in "most". One solution is to consider /st/, /sp/, /sk/ and other s-clusters to be a single "unit," and thereby exempt from the constraints. In addition, this move would permit the length constraint to be tightened so that onsets, as well as codas, would be limited to at most two "units".

4.2. The maximal onset principle and stress resyllabification

Phonotactic constraints are not sufficiently strong to produce a unique syllabification in all cases. For example, in words like "wesTern", "winTer", "waTer", "veTo", "diviniTy", and so forth, phonotactic constraints do not say which way the /t/ will attach. Most theories of syllable structure invoke "tie-breaking principles" for words such as these. Two very common "tie-breaking principles" are the *Maximize Onset Principle* and *Stress Resyllabification*. By the first principle, there is a preference toward assigning consonants to the onset of the following syllable rather than the coda of the previous syllable. Thus, for example, the /t/ in "reTire" will be assigned to the onset of the second syllable (i.e., "re-tire"), and not to the coda of the first syllable

---

[2]Note that "find" violates the length constraint because it has three post-vocalic consonants /ynd/. It also violates the prohibition in English against voiced obstruents after nasals.

(i.e., "*ret-ire"). By the second principle, there is a preference toward assigning consonants to a stressed syllable over an unstressed one. Thus, for example, the /k/ in "record" will be assigned to the first syllable when it is stressed (i.e., "REC-ord"), and to the second syllable when it is stressed (i.e., "re-CORD").

- *Maximize onsets*: When phonotactic and morphological constraints permit, maximize the number of consonants in onset position (e.g., "re-tire").
- *Stress resyllabification*: When phonotactic and morphological constraints permit, maximize the number of consonants in stressed syllables (e.g., "re-CORD" vs. "REC-ord").

The maximal onset principle is relatively uncontroversial. Stress resyllabification, on the other hand, has been the subject of considerable debate. Stress resyllabification is intended to adjust syllable boundaries so that it will be possible to account for stress dependent phonetic and phonemic facts at the level of syllable structure without direct reference to stress. Thus, in order to account for the phonetic and phonemic differences in a pair like "re-CORD"/"RECord", the stress resyllabification principle will syllabify the /k/ into the stressed syllable, and then define the phonetic and phonemic rules to predict the observed phonetic and phonemic differences from the different syllable structures. In a very similar fashion, Kahn and other proponents of ambisyllabicity, would assign two different syllable structures to "reCORD"/ "RECord" in order to account for the different phonetic and phonemic possibilities and then define the phonetic rules to run off each of these structures appropriately. Similarly, metrical phonology would account for the difference by assigning two different foot structures: re[cord] and [record], and then account for the phonetic difference by defining the phonetic rules to work differently when the /k/ is in foot initial (pre-stress) position than when it is in foot internal (post-stress) position. Other solutions are also possible.

In summary, although there is still room for considerable debate over many of the details, there is a fairly well established general consensus. Each of the elements of the syllable (i.e., onset, peak, coda, affix) are highly restricted in a number of ways (e.g., length, sonority, place and voicing assimilation). The boundary between syllables is somewhat less well understood, though it too is governed by well-studied principles (e.g., maximal onset and stress resyllabification). All of these constraints can be encoded into a phrase structure grammar so that the parser can take advantage of phonotactic constraints in order to restrict the set of possible syllable assignments.

5. Parser implementation

The parsing approach depends upon the hypothesis that the intermediate level of representation captures a large number of significant linguistic generalizations that are manifested by a large number of multiple (often redundant) low level cues: phonotactics, allophonics, suprasegmentals (e.g., duration, pitch, intensity), etc. This observation could be viewed as a form of a "constituency hypothesis." Just as syntacticians have argued for the constituent-hood of noun phrases, verb phrases and sentences on the grounds that these units seem to capture crucial linguistic generalizations (e.g., question formation, wh-movement), so too, I might argue (along with certain phonologists such as Kahn (1976)) that syllables, onsets, and rhymes are constituents because they also capture important allophonic and phonotactic generalizations. If this constituency hypothesis for phonology is correct, then it seems natural to propose a syllable parser for processing speech, by analogy with sentence parsers that have become standard practice in the natural language community for processing text.

A program has been implemented (Church, 1983) which parses a lattice of phonetic segments into a lattice of syllables and other phonological constituents. In many ways it is very much like a standard chart parser. Let me provide a quick review of context-free chart parsing. Recall that a context-free parser takes an input sentence such as *They are flying planes* and a grammar such as

$$
\begin{array}{lll}
N \rightarrow \text{they} & V \rightarrow \text{are} & N \rightarrow \text{flying} \\
A \rightarrow \text{flying} & V \rightarrow \text{flying} & N \rightarrow \text{planes} \\
S \rightarrow NP\ VP & VP \rightarrow V\ NP & VP \rightarrow V\ VP \\
NP \rightarrow N\ NP & NP \rightarrow AP\ NP & NP \rightarrow VP \\
AP \rightarrow A & VP \rightarrow V &
\end{array}
$$

and produces as output a set of parse trees such as:

For efficiency purposes, the set of parse trees is usually represented as a *chart* of *labeled phrases*. A labeled phrase is a sequence of words from the input sentence labeled with a part of speech, for example, [NP *flying planes*]. Formally, a labeled phrase is a triple $\langle i, j, c \rangle$ where i and j indicate where the phrase starts and ends and c is a category label (part of speech). Thus, [NP *flying planes*] would be represented as the triple $\langle 2, 4, NP \rangle$, indicating that the phrase spans from position 2 to position 4 and is labeled NP. Positions are numbered as following:

0 They 1 are 2 flying 3 planes 4

A chart is simply a set of triples. For the sentence *They are flying planes* and the above grammar, the parser would compute the following triples:

$\langle 0, 1, \text{they} \rangle$	$\langle 0, 1, NP \rangle$	$\langle 0, 2, S \rangle$
$\langle 1, 2, \text{are} \rangle$	$\langle 1, 2, VP \rangle$	$\langle 0, 3, S \rangle$
$\langle 2, 3, \text{flying} \rangle$	$\langle 2, 3, NP \rangle$	$\langle 0, 4, S \rangle$
$\langle 3, 4, \text{planes} \rangle$	$\langle 2, 3, VP \rangle$	
	$\langle 2, 3, AP \rangle$	
$\langle 0, 1, N \rangle$	$\langle 3, 4, NP \rangle$	
$\langle 1, 2, V \rangle$		
$\langle 2, 3, N \rangle$	$\langle 1, 3, VP \rangle$	
$\langle 2, 3, V \rangle$	$\langle 1, 4, VP \rangle$	
$\langle 2, 3, A \rangle$	$\langle 2, 4, VP \rangle$	
$\langle 3, 4, N \rangle$	$\langle 2, 4, NP \rangle$	

Various shorthand notations have been adopted for representing these triples. In the AI literature (e.g., Kaplan, 1973; Kay, 1973), the chart is often presented as a graph where each position is represented as a node and each triple $\langle i, j, c \rangle$ is represented as a labeled arc spanning from node i to node j with the label c. I prefer to present the chart as an i by j table:

	0	1	2	3	4
0	{}	{NP,N,they}	{S}	{S}	{S}
1	{}	{}	{VP,V,are}	{VP}	{VP}
2	{}	{}	{}	{NP,VP,AP,N,V,A,flying}	{NP,VP}
3	{}	{}	{}	{}	{NP,N,planes}
4	{}	{}	{}	{}	{}

where phrases with common i and j are factored together. This tabular notation is popular in the algorithms literature (e.g., Aho, 1972, p. 316).

There are many well-known parsing algorithms that produce a chart like
that above in time $O(n^3)$ (proportional to the cube of the number of words).
One such algorithm is outlined below. It finds a phrase between positions i
and j by picking a position k in between and testing whether there are two
phrases, one from i up to k and another from k to j, that can combine
according to the grammar. For example, the algorithm will determine the
triple $\langle 0, 4, S \rangle$ because there is an NP from 0 to 1 and there is a VP from 1
to 4 and the two phrases can combine according to the grammar rule S →
NP VP. The general entry in the chart is[3]

$$chart(i,j) = \bigcup_{i<k<j} chart(i,k) \cdot chart(k,j)$$

where multiplication combines sets of phrases according to the rules of the
grammar (e.g., {NP} · {VP} = {S}) and union combines alternative sets of
analyses (e.g., {NP} ∪ {VP} = {NP, VP}).

for $j := 1$ to n do

    $chart(j-1, j) := \{A | A$ derives the jth word$\}$

    for $i := j-2$ down to 0 do

        $chart(i,j) := \bigcup_{i<k<j} chart(i,k) \cdot chart(k,j)$

This algorithm can be performed in $O(n^3)$ time by choosing all combinations of i, j and k, each of which has n possible values. (The multiplication
step requires constant time, independent of the actual input words. It depends
only on the grammar and hence it is often known as the *grammar constant*.)

---

[3]This formulation assumes the phrases have one or two daughters, or more formally, that the grammar is
in Chomsky Normal Form. Let me not complicate the issues here by showing how this restriction can be
relaxed.

6. Chart parsing of phonetic transcriptions

The same chart parsing methods can be used to find syllable structure from an input transcription. Suppose that I was given an ideal error-free transcription [tɪtam] of the phrase "to Tom" and I was asked to recover the syllable structure. Recall that a parser takes a grammar and an input sentence. In this case, let's assume a highly oversimplified grammar:

onset → [t]|[m]   peak → [ɪ]|[a]
coda → [t]|[m]   syl → (onset) peak (coda)

The input sentence is the transcription (shown here with position numbers for the reader's convenience):

Input Sentence: 0 [t] 1 [ɪ] 2 [t] 3 [a] 4 [m] 5 (= to Tom)

Using the algorithm outlined above, the resulting chart is:

	0	1	2	3	4	5
0	{}	{[t],onset,coda}	{syl}	{syl}	{}	{}
1	{}	{}	{ɪ,peak, syl}	{syl}	{}	{}
2	{}	{}	{}	{[t],onset,coda}	{syl}	{syl}
3	{}	{}	{}	{}	{[a],peak,syl}	{syl}
4	{}	{}	{}	{}	{}	{[m],onset,coda}
5	{}	{}	{}	{}	{}	{}

From this chart, it is possible to determine that the input sentence is ambiguous and that there are two alternative parses: [tɪ][tam] and [tɪt][am]. But as suggested above, the parser ought to be able to rule out the second analysis by exploiting allophonic constraints. Recall that I argued that there must be a syllable boundary before the aspirated /t/ in "Tom" because (at least as a first approximation in American English), aspirated /t/'s are constrained to be in syllable initial position. This reasoning can be captured within the parsing framework by refining the grammar to express the aspiration constraint discussed above. The rules below account for the aspiration constraint by permitting aspiration in syllable initial position (under the onset node), but not in syllable final position (under the coda). And consequently, with this refined grammar, the parser no longer finds the spurious syllables from 0 to 3 and from 1 to 3.

Input Sentence: 0 [tʰ] 1 [ɪ] 2 [tʰ] 3 [a] 4 [m] 5 (= to Tom)

Grammar:

| syllable → (onset) peak (coda) |
| onset → tʰ\|kʰ\|pʰ\|... |
| coda → t⁻\|k⁻\|p⁻\|... |

Chart:

	0	1	2	3	4	5
0	{}	{[tʰ],onset,coda}	{syl}	{syl}	{}	{}
1	{}	{}	{ɪ,peak,syl}	{syl}	{}	{}
2	{}	{}	{}	{[tʰ],onset,coda}	{syl}	{syl}
3	{}	{}	{}	{}	{[a],peak,syl}	{syl}
4	{}	{}	{}	{}	{}	{[m],onset,coda}
5	{}	{}	{}	{}	{}	{}

Stating allophonic and phonotactic processes in this way allows the speech recognition device to exploit allophonic constraints on syllable structure and stress with very powerful and well understood parsing techniques.

7. Matching

Once the syllable structure has been established, the structure is then matched against the dictionary to find word hypotheses. Matching ought to be a subject of future research; I was primarily concerned in this work with the parser, and simply implemented enough of a matcher so that I could demonstrate a working system which inputs linguistic transcriptions and outputs lexical entries.

7.1. Dictionary lookup

The dictionary is stored in two levels along the lines suggested in Smith (1976); the first indexes words in terms of syllables, and the second indexes syllables in terms of its sub-constituents (sylparts). The matcher looks up every sylpart in the syllable dictionary, and then every syllable in the word dictionary. I should have added a third level of indexing at the level of foot structure. Thus, syllables would be indexed in terms of feet, and feet in terms of words. This was not implemented.

Noah uses two leves between the input level of segment-label hypotheses and the output level of word hypotheses, where POMOW [an earlier system based on Markov processes] uses one. There are 1) the *sylpart* level, consisting of parts of syllables—onsets (the initial non-nucleus part of syllables), vowels, and codas (the final non-nucleus part of syllables)—and 2) the syllable level, consisting of complete syllables (not syltypes as found in POMOW). Knowledge is stored in a *hierarchy-tree* representation. That is, between each pair of adjacent levels (segment-sylpart, sylpart-sylpart, and syllable-word level pairs) is a tree structure storing a sequence of lower level units to define a higher level unit. The last node of the sequence of lower level units points to the defined higher level unit. For example, the syllable-word tree stores sequences of syllables defining each word in the vocabulary. The tree between each pair of levels permits merging common initial parts of sequences to reduce storage costs and recognition time. Thus, the words "confide" and "confuse" share the first syllable node "con", in the tree, which then points to subnodes "fide", "fuse", etc. [Smith (1977)]

Smith achieved two bottom-line engineering advantages by adopting a hierarchical representation: both storage cost and recognition time are reduced due to sharing. For example, the tree stores the syllable "con" just once, not once for each word containing the prefix "con" (e.g., "confide", "confuse", and so forth). Furthermore, the hierarchical system will recognize the prefix "con" just once, not once for each word containing the prefix. Smith argues that his representation will reduce recognition costs by 41% over the HWIM design for the same 1000 word dictionary, at a 22% increase in storage due to pointer overhead [Smith, p. 40]. In addition, Smith found that savings increase approximately logarithmically with larger lexicons, and that accuracy improves with larger lexicons.

Smith rested most of his argument for hierarchical representation on the force of these engineering advantages. There are, though, some equally important linguistic advantages. A hierarchical representation allows the lexicon to be organized along lines that reflect natural linguistic generalizations. Thus, for example, the prefix /ri-/ ought to be shared in words like "retry" and "recycle" where it is a linguistically motivated constituent, but it should not be shared in words like "read" and "real" where /ri/ is merely a common subsequence of segments. In this respect, Smith's proposal fairs favorably to the Cohort model which would lump all words beginning with /ri/ into a single cohort, whether /ri/ forms a constituent or not.

If Smith had employed a phonetic parser, he might also have found that the /ri/ constituent will be realized with different allophones from the /ri/ which is not a constituent, and these differences could (often) be detected with the phonetic parser. Thus, representing the lexicon along linguistically motivated lines has the additional advantage that the matching process can take advantage of the constituent structure provided to it by the parsing process.

7.2. Canonicalization

Before constituents are looked up in the dictionary, a canonicalization process is applied which undoes postlexical (allophonic) rules. Canonicalization strips a phonetic segment of its so-called "non-distinctive" features (e.g., aspiration, flapping, glottalization) and leaves the segment with just its "distinctive" features (e.g., place, voice, manner). For example, canonicalization replaces both aspirated and glottalized variants of /t/ with the phoneme /t/. In some cases, canonicalization introduces nondeterminism by mapping a single allophone into two or more phonemes. Flaps, for instance, are mapped into both /t/ and /d/ (and also into /n/ in certain contexts). Canonicalization removes all variant phonetic detail, but does not sacrifice information, I hypothesize, because the information content of the allophonic constraints has already been milked by the parser. Thus, whatever information was encoded in the distribution of allophones has already been recoded into the syllable (and metrical) constituent structures.

In suggesting the canonicalization process, I am assuming along with linguists such as Kiparsky that the lexicon is represented solely in terms of phonological features and does not contain allophones. Kiparsky and other advocates of lexical phonology assume that allophones are generated solely by postlexical rules such as flapping and aspiration and that these rules apply outside the lexicon. Lexical phonology distinguishes postlexical rules from lexical rules such as trisyllabic laxing (e.g., *divīne* → *divīnity*) and /t/ → /s/ (e.g., *president* → *presidency*) which do not generate allophones. Advocates of lexical phonology point out that lexical rules must apply within the lexicon because they are subject to lexically marked exceptions and because they are sensitive to the internal morphological structure of words. In contrast, postlexical rules share neither of these properties; they apply without lexical exceptions and without regard for the internal morphological structure of words. Moreover, the fact that postlexical rules cross word boundaries (unlike lexical rules) suggests that postlexical rules do not operate on words, but rather on some other level of representation. For these reasons, I accept Kiparsky's conclusion that the lexicon is free of allophones and reject the hypothesis that allophonic rules are compiled into the lexicon, an alternative that was popular during the ARPA speech project (e.g., Oshika, Zue, Weeks, Nen, & Aurbach, 1975).

8. Conclusions

I have argued that lexical retrieval should be decomposed into two subproblems: parsing and matching. This model elegantly makes use of both contextually varying cues as well as contextually invariant cues. The parser is designed to take advantage of features that vary systematically with context, whereas the matcher performs optimally with invariant cues. This is no accident; it is hard to imagine how invariant cues could be used to parse the context or how variant cues could be used to match constituents.

Most previous models (e.g., the Cohort Model, Harpy) were unable to make much use of variant cues because they lacked a mechanism such as a parser for reasoning about context. These pure matching models were forced to depend entirely on invariant features because they had no principled way to take advantage of the rich contextual constraints imposed by allophonic variation and phonotactics.

References

Aho, A. (1972). The theory of parsing, translations and compiling. (Vol. I). Englewood Cliffs, NJ: Prentice-Hall.

Chomsky, N., & Halle, M. (1968). *The sound pattern of English.* New York: Harper & Row.

Christie, W. (1974). Some cues for syllable juncture perception in English. *Journal of the Acoustical Society of America, 55* (4), 819–821.

Church, K. (1983). *Phrase-structure parsing: A method for taking advantage of allophonic constraints.* Unpublished Doctoral Dissertation, Department of Electrical Engineering and Computer Science, MIT (also available from Indiana University Linguistics Club).

Cole, R., & Jakimik, J. (1980). A model of speech perception. Hillsdale, NJ: Erlbaum.

Earley, J. (1970). An efficient context-free parsing algorithm. Communications of the ACM, *13* (2) February.

Fry, D. (1955). Duration and intensity as physical correlates of linguistic stress. *Journal of the Acoustical Society of Amerika, 17* (4). Reprinted in I. Lehiste (Ed.) (1967). *Readings in acoustic phonetics.* Cambridge, MA: MIT Press.

Fujimura, O., & Lovins, J. (1982). Syllables as concatenative phonetic units. Indiana University Linguistics Club.

Jelinek, F. (1982). Course notes, MIT, 1982.

Kahn, D. (1976). Syllable-based generalizations in English phonology. Indiana University Linguistics Club.

Kaplan, R. (1973). A general syntactic processor. In R. Rustin (Ed.), *Natural language processing.* New York: Algorithmics Press.

Kay, M., (1973). The MIND system. In R. Rustin (Ed.), *Natural language processing.* New York: Algorithmics Press.

Kiparsky, P. (1981). Remarks on the metrical structure of the syllable. In W. Dressler (Ed.) *Phonologica 1980.* Proceedings of the Fourth International Phonology Meeting.

Klatt, D. (1974). Word verification in a speech understanding system. In R. Reddy (Ed.), *Speech Recognition* (Invited Papers Presented at the 1974 IEEE Symposium) (pp. 321–344). New York: Academic Press.

Klatt, D. (1977). Review of the ARPA Speech Understanding Project. *Journal of the Acoustical Society of America, 62* (6) December.

Klatt, D. (1980). Scriber and Lafs: Two new approaches to speech analysis. In W. Lea (Ed.), *Trends in speech recognition*. Englewood Cliffs, NJ: Prentice-Hall.

Nakatani, L. (no date). Fission and fusion processes in speech perception, Unpublished MS, Bell Laboratories, Murray Hill, New Jersey.

Oshika, B., Zue, V., Weeks, R., Neu, H., & Aurbach, J. (1975). The role of phonological rules in speech understanding research. *IEEE Transactions, Acoustical Speech and Signal Processing AASP-23* (1), 104–112.

Smith, A. (1976). Word hypothesization in the hearsay-II speech system. *Proceedings IEEE International Conference ASSP* (pp. 549–552).

Smith, A. (1977). Word hypothesization for large-vocabulary speech understanding systems, unpublished doctoral dissertation, CMU.

Résumé

La parole est un code naturel de correction d'erreurs. Le signal de la parole est riche en redondances contextuelles à de nombreux niveaux de représentation, qu'il s'agisse des variations allophoniques, de la phonotactique, de la structure syllabique, des domaines d'accentuation, de la morphologie, de la syntaxe, de la sémantique et de la pragmatique. Les recherches psycho-linguistiques ont eu tendance à insister sur des contraintes à des niveaux élevés comme la sémantique et la pragmatique et ont en général laissé de côté l'utilité de contraintes de niveau inférieur comme la variation allophonique. Il a même été dit que la variation allophonique est une source de confusion ou une sorte de bruit statistique qui rend la reconnaissance de la parole bien plus difficile qu'elle ne l'est déjà. Par opposition à ces idées, je soutiendrai que l'aspiration, le "flapping", la palatalisation et d'autres indices qui varient de manière systématique avec le contexte syllabique peuvent être utilisés pour analyser les syllabes et les domaines d'accentuation. Ces constituants peuvent ensuite limiter le processus d'identification lexicale, de sorte que l'identification de la bonne entrée lexicale demandera bien moins de travail. Je proposerai donc que la structure syllabique et les domaines d'accentuation constituent un niveau intermédiaire de représentation entre la description phonétique et le lexique.

Ma discussion est avant tout computationnelle et inclut la présentation d'un prototype de parseur phonétique qui a été implémenté en utilisant des mécanismes de parsing connus. Aucun résultat expérimental ne sera présenté.

4

Functional parallelism in spoken word-recognition

WILLIAM D. MARSLEN-WILSON*

Max-Planck-Institut für Psycholinguistik, Nijmegen, and MRC Applied Psychology Unit, Cambridge

Abstract

The process of spoken word-recognition breaks down into three basic functions, of access, selection and integration. Access concerns the mapping of the speech input onto the representations of lexical form, selection concerns the discrimination of the best-fitting match to this input, and integration covers the mapping of syntactic and semantic information at the lexical level onto higher levels of processing. This paper describes two versions of a "cohort"-based model of these processes, showing how it evolves from a partially interactive model, where access is strictly autonomous but selection is subject to top-down control, to a fully bottom-up model, where context plays no role in the processes of form-based access and selection. Context operates instead at the interface between higher-level representations and information generated on-line about the syntactic and semantic properties of members of the cohort. The new model retains intact the fundamental characteristics of a cohort-based word-recognition process. It embodies the concepts of multiple access and multiple assessment, allowing a maximally efficient recognition process, based on the principle of the contingency of perceptual choice.

1. Introduction

To understand spoken language is to relate sound to meaning. At the core of this process is the recognition of spoken words, since it is the knowledge representations in the mental lexicon that provide the actual bridge between sounds and meanings, linking the phonological properties of specific word-

*I thank Uli Frauenfelder and Lorraine Tyler for their forbearance as editors, and for their comments on the manuscript. I also thank Tom Bever and two anonymous reviewers for their stimulating criticism of previous drafts. The first version of this paper was written with the support of the Department of Experimental Psychology, University of Cambridge, which I gratefully acknowledge. Reprint requests should be sent to William Marslen-Wilson, MPI für Psycholinguistik, Wundtlaan 1, 6525 XD Nijmegen, The Netherlands forms to their syntactic and semantic attributes. This duality of lexical representation enables the word-recognition process to mediate between two radically distinct computational domains—the acoustic-phonetic analysis of the incoming speech signal, and the syntactic and semantic interpretation of the message being communicated. In this paper, I am concerned with the consequences of this duality of representation and of function for the organisation of the word-recognition process as an information-processing system.

The overall process of spoken word-recognition breaks down into three fundamental functions. These I will refer to as the *access*, the *selection*, and the *integration* functions. The first of these, the access function, concerns the relationship of the recognition process to the sensory input. The system must provide the basis for a mapping of the speech signal onto the representations of word-forms in the mental lexicon. Assuming some sort of acoustic-phonetic analysis of the speech input, it is a representation of the input in these terms that is projected onto the mental lexicon.

The integration function, conversely, concerns the relationship of the recognition process to the higher-level representation of the utterance. In order to complete the recognition process, the system must provide the basis for the integration, into this higher level of representation, of the syntactic and semantic information associated with the word that is being recognised.

Finally, and mediating between access and integration, there is the selection function. In addition to accessing word-forms from the sensory input, the system must also discriminate between them, selecting the word-form that best matches the available input.

These three functional requirements have to be realised in some way in any model of spoken word-recognition. They need to be translated into claims about the kinds of processes that subserve these functions, and about the processing relations between them during the recognition of a word. I will begin the discussion here by considering the way that the access and selection functions are realised, and their relationship to the integration function. How far do access, selection, and integration correspond to separate processing stages in the recognition of a spoken word, and to what extent do they operate in computational isolation from one another?

I will develop the argument here in its approximate historical sequence. In Section 2 I will argue that, while the accessing of the mental lexicon is a strictly autonomous, bottom-up process, there seems to be a close computational dependency between the process of selecting the word-form that best matches the sensory input and the process of integrating the syntactic and semantic properties of word-forms with their utterance context. The characteristics of the real-time transfer function of the system suggest that the selection phase of the recognition process cannot depend on bottom-up information alone, and that contextual constraints also affect its outcome. This, as I will show in Section 3, led to the first version of the cohort model: a parallel, interactive model of spoken word-recognition. In Section 4 I will examine the properties and predictions of this early model. In Section 5 I will show how this model now needs to be modified. In particular, I will argue that it needs to incorporate the concept of activation, and I will re-examine the role of top-down interaction in the on-line recognition process, suggesting a model where different information sources are integrated together to give the perceptual output of the system, but where they do not, in the conventional sense, interact. In particular, I argue for the autonomy of form-based selection, as well as for the autonomy of form-based access.

2. The earliness of spoken word-recognition

The crucial constraint on the functional properties of access and selection is the *earliness* of correct selection. This I define as the reliable identification of spoken words, in utterance contexts, *before* sufficient acoustic-phonetic information has become available to allow correct identification on that basis alone. If this can be demonstrated, then it places strong restrictions not only on how the selection process is organised, but also on the ways in which representations are initially accessed from the bottom-up.

To prove early selection, two things must be established. The first is how long it takes to recognise a given word. This reflects the timing with which the selection function is completed. The second is whether the acoustic-phonetic information available at this estimated selection-point is or is not sufficient, by itself, to support correct identification.

The major techniques for establishing the timing of on-line word-recognition—thereby answering the first of these two questions—involve fast reaction-time tasks. Typical examples are the shadowing and the identical monitoring tasks, where the listener responds directly to the words he hears—either by repeating them aloud, or by making a detection response to a word-target. The mean reaction-times in such tasks, measured from word-onset, can be used as a direct estimate of selection-time, subject to a correction factor to allow for the time it takes to execute the response.[1] Typical values obtained in these tasks (for one- and two-syllable content words heard

---

[1]The use of a correction factor compensates for the fact that a monitoring reaction-time of, for example, 250 ms, does not mean that the word was not identified until 250 ms of it had been heard. There is undoubtedly *some* lag between the internal decision process and the external evidence that this decision has been made. The correction factor reflects this.

in normal utterance contexts) are of the order of 250–275 ms, which, with a correction factor of 50–75 ms, gives a mean selection-time of around 200 ms (e.g., Marslen-Wilson, 1973, 1985; Marslen-Wilson & Tyler, 1975, 1980).

Similar values can be obtained, more indirectly, from reaction-time tasks where the listeners are asked to respond, not to the word itself, but to some property of the word whose accessibility for response depends on first identifying the word in question. Examples of this are the rhyme-monitoring results reported by Marslen-Wilson & Tyler (1975, 1980) and others (e.g., Seidenberg & Tanenhaus, 1979), and at least some research involving the phoneme-monitoring task (e.g., Marslen-Wilson, 1984; Morton & Long, 1976). By subtracting an additional constant from the response-times in these tasks, to take into account the extra phonological matching processes they involve, one again arrives at selection-times for words in context of the order of 200 ms from word-onset.

But these estimates are only half of the equation. It is also necessary to establish whether or not the acoustic-phonetic information available at these selection-points is sufficient for correct selection. For the research described above, this could only be done indirectly, by estimating the average number of phonemes that could be identified within 200 ms of word-onset, and then using that estimate to determine how many words would normally still be consistent with the input. If, as the available measurements suggest, 200 ms would only be enough to specify an initial two phonemes, then there would on average be more than 40 words still compatible with the available input (this estimate is based on the analysis of a 20,000-word phonetic dictionary of American English (Marslen-Wilson, 1984)). The limitation of this indirect inference to early selection is that it cannot take into account possible coarticulatory and prosodic effects. This could lead to an underestimate of the amount of sensory information actually available to the listener after 200 ms.

The second main technique allows a more direct measure of the sufficiency of the acoustic-phonetic input available at the estimated selection-point. This is the gating task, as developed by Grosjean (1980), and exploited by Tyler and others (e.g., Salasoo & Pisoni, 1985; Tyler & Wessels, 1983). Listeners are presented with successively longer fragments of a word, at increments ranging (in different experiments) from 20 to 50 ms, and at each increment they are asked to say what they think the word is, or is going to become. This tells us exactly how much acoustic-phonetic input the listener needs to hear to be able to reliably identify a word under various conditions. In the original study by Grosjean (1980), we find that subjects needed to hear an average of 199 ms of a word when it occurred in sentential context, as opposed to 333 ms for the same acoustic token presented in isolation.

Because of the unusual way the auditory input is presented in the gating task, there has been some criticism of its validity as a reflection of normal word-recognition processes. Since the listener hears the same fragments repeated many times in sequence, this might encourage abnormal response strategies. This objection is met by Cotton and Grosjean (1984) and Salasoo and Pisoni (1985), whose subjects heard only one fragment for any given word, and where the pattern of responses matched very closely the results for the same words when presented as complete sequences to each subject. It is also possible that responses are distorted by the effectively unlimited time—in comparison to normal listening—that listeners have available to think about what the word could be at each presentation. This objection is met by Tyler and Wessels (1985), in an experiment where subjects also heard only one fragment from each word, and where they responded by naming the word as quickly as possible. Mean naming latencies were 478 ms from fragment offset, and the response patterns again closely corresponded to those obtained without time-pressure.

In a recent study (Brown, Marslen-Wilson, & Tyler, unpublished) we have combined reaction-time measures for words heard normally with gating tests for the same words. This provides the most direct evidence presently available for early selection. In the first half of the experiment, subjects monitored pairs of sentences for word targets, with a mean reaction-time for words in normal contexts of 241 ms. This gives an estimated selection-time of 200 ms or less. In the second part of the experiment, the target-words were edited out of the stimulus tapes and presented, as isolated words, to a different set of subjects in a standard gating task. The mean identification-time estimated here was 301 ms, indicating that the words were being responded to in the monitoring task some 100 ms before sufficient acoustic-phonetic information could have accumulated to allow recognition on that basis alone.[2]

Given, then, that we have accurate and reliable estimates of the two variables in our equation, simple arithmetic tells us that content words, heard in utterance contexts, can usually be selected—and, indeed, recognised—earlier than would be possible if just the acoustic-phonetic input was being taken into account. Naturally, as Grosjean and Gee (1987, this issue) point out, some words—especially function words and short, infrequent content words—will often not be recognised early. In fact, under certain conditions of temporary ambiguity, as Grosjean (1985) has documented, "late" selection will occur, where the word is not only not recognised early, but may not even be identified until the word following it has been heard. These observations nonetheless do not change the significance of the fact that a large proportion

---

[2]There is still the problem here of factoring out the purely acoustic-phonetic effects of removing words from their contexts. We are investigating this in current research.

of words *are* selected early. A theory of lexical access has to be able to explain this, just as it has to deal with late selection as well. Late selection, however, places far weaker constraints on the properties of the recognition process than does early selection.[3]

A different type of objection is methodological in character. It is argued that none of the tasks used to establish early selection are measuring "real" word-recognition. Instead, by forcing subjects to respond unnaturally early, they elicit some form of sophisticated guessing behaviour. Forster (1981), for example, argues that when a subject responds before the end of the word, as in the shadowing task, he must in some way be guessing what the word will be, on the basis of fragmentary bottom-up cues plus knowledge of context.

Such objections, however, have little force. First, because the claim that subjects are responding "unnaturally early" does not have any independent empirical basis. There is no counter evidence, from "more natural" tasks, showing that under these conditions different estimates of recognition-time are obtained—nor is the notion "more natural task" itself easy to defend except in terms of subjective preference. Secondly, to distinguish under these conditions between "*perception* of the target word and *guessing*" (Forster, 1981, p. 490; emphases in original) is to assume, as a theoretical a priori, a particular answer to the fundamental questions at issue.

Forster apparently wants to rule out, as an instance of normal perception, cases where the listener responds before all of the sensory information potentially relevant to that response has become available. But this presupposes a theory of perception where there is a very straightforward dependency between the sensory input and the corresponding percept. The claims that I am trying to develop here allow for the possibility of a less direct causal relationship between the sensory input and the percept (see Marcel, 1983, for a discussion of some related issues). These claims may or may not prove to be correct. But one cannot settle the issue in advance by excluding evidence on the grounds that it conflicts with the theoretical assumptions whose validity one is trying to establish. If one is advancing the view that normal perception *is* just the outcome of the integration of partial bottom-up cues with contextual constraints, then it is not an argument against this view simply to assert that perception under these conditions is not perception.

---

[3] It should also be clear, contrary to Grosjean and others, that the phenomenon of "late selection", does not constitute a problem for theories, like the cohort model, which emphasise the real-time nature of the word-recognition process. Activation-based versions of the cohort model, as discussed in Section 5, and as modelled, for example, in the McClelland and Elman (1986) TRACE model, function equally well independent of whether the critical sensory information arrives before or after the word boundary (as classically defined).

3. Implications of early selection

Early selection means that the acoustic-phonetic and the contextual constraints on the identity of a word can be integrated together at a point in time
when each source of constraint is inadequate, by itself, to uniquely specify
the correct candidate. The sensory input can do no more than specify a class
of potential candidates, consisting of those entries in the mental lexicon that
are compatible with the available input. Similarly, the current utterance and
discourse context provides a set of acceptability criteria that also can do no
more than delimit a class of potentially appropriate candidates. It is only by
intersecting these two sets of constraints that the identity of the correct candidate can be derived at the observed selection-point. It is this that forces a
parallel model of access and selection, and that poses intractable difficulties
for any model which depends on an autonomous bottom-up selection process
to reliably identify the single correct candidate for submission to subsequent
processing stages (e.g., Forster, 1976, 1979, 1981).

To see this, consider the major functional requirements that early selection
places upon the spoken word-recognition system. These are the requirements
of *multiple access*, of *multiple assessment*, and of *real-time efficiency*. They
reflect the properties the recognition system needs to have if it is to integrate
sensory and contextual constraints to yield mean selection-times of the order
of 200 ms.

Multiple access is the accessing of multiple candidates in the original mapping of the acoustic-phonetic input onto lexical representations. The sensory
input defines a class of potential word-candidates, and, in principle, all of
these need to be made available, via a multiple access process, to the selection
phase of spoken word-recognition. The second requirement is the requirement for multiple assessment. If contextual constraints are to affect the selection phase at a point in time when many candidates are compatible with the
sensory input, then the system must provide a mechanism whereby each of
these candidates can be assessed for their syntactic and semantic appropriateness relative to the current context.

The final, and critical, requirement is for real-time efficiency. The system
must be organised to allow these access and assessment activities to take
place in real time, such that the correct candidate can be identified—and
begin to be integrated into an utterance-level representation—within about
200 ms of word-onset.

These requirements, taken together, cannot be met by a serial process
moving through the decision space one item at a time (cf. Fahlman, 1979).
They point, instead, to some form of parallel or distributed recognition model
(e.g., Hinton & Anderson, 1981). But they do not, however, uniquely deter-

mine the form of such a model. In particular, they do not unambiguously dictate the manner in which the word-recognition process is divided up into distinct processing stages. But they do place strong constraints on the functional properties of the recognition model. The strategy that I have followed, therefore, is to propose a model which rather literally embodies these constraints, and then to use this model as a heuristic starting-point for a detailed investigation of the properties of on-line speech processing. Accordingly, I will begin here by describing the first version of this model and the predictions it makes. In a later section, I will discuss the ways the model now needs to be expanded and modified.

The model in question, labelled an "active direct access model" in Marslen-Wilson and Welsh (1978), but now usually referred to as the "cohort model", evolved out of an analysis of Morton's logogen model (as stated in Morton, 1969) and of the Forster "bin" model (Forster, 1976). As originally stated, it meets the requirements of multiple access and multiple assessment by assuming a distributed, parallel processing system. In this system, each individual entry in the mental lexicon is assumed to correspond to a separate computationally active recognition unit. This unit represents a functional coordination of the acoustic-phonetic and of the syntactic and semantic specifications associated with a given lexical entry.

Given such an array of recognition elements, this leads to the characteristic "cohort" view of the recognition process, with its specific claims about the way this process develops over time. A lexical unit is assumed to become active when the sensory input matches the acoustic-phonetic pattern specified for that unit. The model prohibits top-down activation of these units in normal word-recognition, so that *only* the sensory input can activate a unit. There is no contextually driven pre-selection of candidates, so that words cannot become active as potential percepts without some bottom-up (sensory) input to the structures representing these words.

Early in the word, when only the first 100–150 ms have been heard, then the recognition devices corresponding to all of the words in the listener's mental lexicon that begin with this initial sequence will become active— thereby meeting the requirement for multiple access.[4] This subset of active elements, constituting the *word-initial cohort*, monitors both the continuing sensory input, and the compatibility of the words that the elements represent

---

[4]The notion of "activity" will be examined more closely in Section 5. What it means here is that each lexical recognition unit, as a computationally independent pattern-matching device, can respond to the presence of a match with the signal. All words that *could* match the input *are* matched by it, and this changes the state of the relevant pattern matching devices, thereby differentiating them from the other devices in the system, which do not match the current input.

with the available structural and interpretative context—which meets the requirement for multiple assessment. A mismatch with either source of constraint causes the elements to drop out of the pool of potential candidates. This means that there will be a sequential reduction over time in the initial set of candidates, until only one candidate is left. At this point, the correct word-candidate can be recognised, and the correct word-sense, with its structural consequences, is incorporated into the message-level representation of the utterance. This is a system that allows for optimal real-time efficiency, since each word will be recognised as soon as the accumulating acoustic-phonetic information permits, given the available contextual constraints.[5]

In terms of the issues raised earlier in this paper, the model treats the initial access phase as a functionally separable aspect of the recognition process. It does not do this by postulating an independent processing component which performs the access function—in the style, for example, of the peripheral access files proposed by Forster and others (e.g., Forster, 1976; Norris, 1981). It assumes, instead, that the processing mechanisms underlying word-recognition can only be engaged by a bottom-up input. It is the speech signal, and only the speech signal, that can activate perceptual structures in the recognition lexicon.[6] This has the effect of making access functionally autonomous, without having to make claims about additional levels and processes.

Once the word-initial cohort has been accessed, and the model has entered into the selection phase, then top-down factors begin to affect its behaviour. It is this that allows the model to account for early selection. When a word is heard as part of a normal utterance, then both sensory and contextual constraints contribute jointly to a process of mapping word senses onto

---

[5]The sequential cohort recognition process is sometimes treated as if it were equivalent to following a path down a "pronunciation tree". This is a branching structure, starting from a single phoneme (e.g., /t/), and branching at each subsequent phonetic choice point. By following the path to its terminal node one arrives at the correct word—*trespass, tress, trend*, or whatever. This captures in a limited sense the sequential decision process represented in the cohort model. Where it fails, however, is to capture the treatment of context in the cohort model. In a pronunciation tree, it is only when one reaches the terminal node that one can know what word one is hearing. It is only at this point, therefore, that the syntactic and semantic information associated with this word can be accessed, and made available for interaction with context. But the cohort model—and the evidence on which it is based—require context to be able to operate much earlier in the word, to help select the correct word even before the sensory input could have uniquely identified it. The pronunciation tree is neither an adequate model of human word-recognition nor an accurate depiction of the cohort model.

[6]It is not an argument against this claim to point out that one can often predict what someone is going to say before they say it. There is no doubt that this is true. But to be able to predict what someone will say is (i) not the same as having the percept that they have actually said it, nor (ii) is it evidence that this knowledge can penetrate, top-down, into the mental lexicon, and change the state of the basic recognition devices—and it is this that's at issue here.

higher-level representations. The way this is realised in the model is by allowing the semantic and syntactic appropriateness of word-candidates to directly affect their status in the current cohort, which causes the selection process to converge on a single candidate earlier than it would if only acoustic-phonetic constraints were being taken into consideration.

Even in this rough and ready form—that is, as stated in Marslen-Wilson and Welsh (1978) and Marslen-Wilson and Tyler (1980)—the model serves its heuristic purpose. It makes a number of strong predictions, which not only differentiate it from other models, but also, more importantly, raise novel and testable questions about the temporal microstructure of spoken word-recognition. In the next section of this paper I will summarise the research by myself and others into three of these major predictions: The model's claims about the concept of "recognition-point", about optimal real-time analysis, and about the early activation of multiple semantic codes.

4. Some predictions of the cohort model

4.1. The concept of recognition-point

The unique feature of the cohort model is its ability to make predictions about the precise timing of the selection and integration process for any individual word in the language. Other models have had essentially nothing to say about the recognition process at this level of specificity. The cohort model, in contrast, provides a theoretical basis for predicting the *recognition-point* for any given word. This is the point at which, starting from word-onset, a word can be discriminated from the other members of its word-initial cohort, taking into account both contextual and sensory constraints. For many words—especially monosyllables—this point may only be reached when all of the word has being heard. But for longer words—and for words of any length heard in constraining contexts—the recognition-point can occur well before the end of the word.[7]

---

[7]In a recent paper, Luce (1986) argues against the notion of recognition-point on the grounds that most common words are monosyllables and that most monosyllables (as he establishes by searching a lexical database) do not become unique until the end of the word or after. There are a number of problems with his argument.

The first is that he does not take into account the role of prosodic structure and of various types of anticipatory coarticulation in the recognition process. These will not only position the recognition-point earlier than a purely phonemic analysis would indicate, but will also reduce the potential problem created by short words that are also the first syllables of longer words. The second is that the claims of the cohort model derive, in the first instance, from observations of word-recognition in context, where even monosyllables are normally recognised before all of them have been heard (see Section 2 above). Thirdly, the important claim of the cohort →

Take, for example, the word "trespass". If this word is heard in isolation, then its recognition-point—the point at which it can be securely identified—is at the /p/, since it is here that it separates from words like "tress" and "trestle". The recognition-point for the same word in context might be at the first /s/, however, if these competitors were syntactically or semantically excluded. Similar predictions can be derived for any word in any context, given a specification of the word-initial cohort for that word, and of the constraints derivable from the context in which it is uttered.

The crucial hypothesis underlying the notion of recognition-point is a claim about the *contingency* of the recognition process. The identification of a word does not depend simply on the information that a given word is present. It also depends on the information that other words are *not* present. The word "trespass", heard in isolation, is only identifiable at the /p/ if the decision process can take into account, in real-time, the status of other potential word-candidates. The calculation of recognition-points directly reflects this. If these predicted recognition-points are experimentally validated, then this rules out all models of spoken word-recognition that do not allow for these dependencies.

4.1.1. Evidence for recognition-points

Paralleling the various types of evidence for early selection summarised in Section 2, the evidence for the psychological validity of recognition-points derives from a mixture of reaction-time and gating tasks. In a first experiment (Marslen-Wilson, 1978; Marslen-Wilson, 1984) response-latencies in a phoneme-monitoring task were found to be closely correlated with recognition-points, both as calculated a priori on the basis of cohort analysis, and as operationally defined in a separate gating task.

In phoneme-monitoring, the subject is asked to monitor spoken materials for a phoneme target defined in advance. There are two major strategies listeners can use to do this (cf. Cutler & Norris, 1979). I exploited here the lexical strategy, where the listener determines that a given phoneme is present by reference to his stored phonological knowledge of the word involved. When this strategy is used, response-latency is related to the timing of word identification, since the phonological representation of the word in memory cannot be consulted until it is known which word is being heard. If cohort theory correctly specifies the timing of word-identification, then there should

---

model is, in any case, not whether the recognition-point falls early or late relative to the word-boundary, but rather that the word is uniquely discriminated as soon as the available constraints (sensory, contextual) make it possible for the system to do so. Wherever the recognition-point falls, that is where the listener should identify the word in question. And for content words heard in utterance context, this will be, more often than not, before all of the word has been heard.

be a close dependency between the monitoring response and the distance between the phoneme-target and the recognition-point for that word. In particular, response-latency should decrease the later the target occurs relative to the recognition-point, since there will be less of a delay before the subject can identify the word and access its phonological representation.

I evaluated this question for a set of 60 three-syllable words, which contained phoneme targets varying in position from the end of the first syllable until the end of the third syllable. I had already confirmed that a lexical strategy was being used for these stimuli, since overall response-latencies dropped sharply over serial-positions, compared to a control set of nonsense words where there was no change in latency as a function of position (for further details, see Marslen-Wilson, 1984). The cohort structure of the materials was analysed to determine the recognition-point for each word, and the distances measured between the recognition-points and the monitoring targets. These recognition-points could occur as much as two or three hundred ms before or after the target-phoneme.

A linear regression analysis showed that there was a close relationship between these distances and the monitoring response $(r = +.89)$.[8] The variations in distance accounted for over 80% of the variance in the mean latencies for the 60 individual words containing targets. This strong correlation with phoneme-monitoring latency shows that recognition-points derived from cohort analysis have a real status in the immediate, on-line processing of the word. The subjects in this experiment were using a lexical strategy, so that their response-latencies reflected the timing of word-recognition processes, and the cohort model correctly specified the timing of these processes for the words involved.

These results were checked in a follow-up study, which used the gating task to operationally define the recognition-points for the same set of materials. Gating offers a variety of methods for calculating recognition-points, depending on whether or not confidence ratings are taken into account. The most satisfactory results are obtained when confidence ratings are included, since this reduces the distorting effects of various response biases. Gating recognition-points were therefore defined as the point in a word at which 85% of the subjects had correctly identified the word, and where these subjects were at least 85% confident.[9] These operationally derived recognition-

---

[8]The correlation is positive because the earlier the recognition-point occurs, relative to the position of the target phoneme (which is also the point from which response-time is measured), the longer the subjects have to wait until they can identify the word, access its phonological representation, and then make their response.

[9]The exact percentage chosen as criterial is not critical. Setting the level at 80 or 90%, for example, gives equivalent results.

points correlated very highly both with the previous set of recognition-points (calculated on an a priori basis) and with the phoneme-monitoring response latencies ($r = +.92$).

The comparison between gating recognition-points and a priori recognition-points is further evidence that the cohort model does provide a basis for correctly determining when a word can be recognised. The point at which a word becomes uniquely identifiable, as established through an analysis of that word's initial cohort, corresponds very well to the point at which listeners will confidently identify a word in the gating task. This has been confirmed for a new set of materials, and, in particular, extended to words heard in utterance contexts, in a recent study by Tyler and Wessels (1983). The gating recognition-points calculated in this study are indeed the points at which a single candidate is left, and this point is not only quite independent of the total length of the word, but also varies in the manner predicted by the theory as a function of the availability of contextual constraints.

4.1.2. Implications of on-line recognition-points

The evidence for the psychological reality of the recognition-points specified by cohort analysis poses severe problems for certain classes of word-recognition model. The recognition-points were calculated on the basis not only of the positive information accumulating over time that a given word was present, but also, and equally important, the information that certain other words were *not* present. There is nothing, for example, about *trespass* by itself that predicts a recognition-point at the /p/—or indeed, anywhere else in the word. It is only in terms of the relationship of *trespass* to its initial cohort that the recognition-point can be computed. This contingency of the recognition response on the state of the ensemble of alternatives is in conflict with the basic decision mechanisms employed both by logogen-based theories and by serial search theories.

The results exclude, first, those recognition-models that depend on a self-terminating serial search, in the manner of Forster's models of access and selection (Forster, 1976, 1979, 1981). In this type of model, word-forms are stored in peripheral access files. These access files are organised into "bins", with the words within any one bin arranged in sequential order according to frequency. Once a bin has been accessed, there follows a serial search through the contents of the bin, terminating as soon as a word-form is encountered which matches the search parameters. The search must be self-terminating, since it is this that gives the model its ability to deal with frequency effects— frequent words are recognised more quickly because they are encountered earlier in the search process. Such a procedure could only take into account the status of competing word-candidates if they were higher in frequency than the actual best match. This would not predict the correct recognition-points.

It is in general a problem for sequential search models if the outcome of the recognition process needs to reflect the state of the entire ensemble of possibilities, since this makes the process extremely sensitive to the size of this ensemble. In fact, evidence I will cite later shows that the timing of word-recognition processes is not affected by the number of alternatives that need to be considered. Parallel access and selection processes are far better suited to the task of providing information about the status of several word-candidates simultaneously. But this by no means guarantees the suitability of all parallel models.

One type of parallel model that is excluded by the present results (as well as by the data reported in the next section) are the logogen-based models. These models depend on the accumulation of positive evidence within a single recognition device as the basis for recognition. Each device has a decision threshold, and the word that is recognised is the one whose corresponding recognition device (or logogen) crosses the threshold first, without reference to the state of any other recognition devices. The model has no mechanism for allowing the behaviour of one unit to take into account the behaviour of other units in the ensemble. This means that it has no basis for computing the recognition-point for a given word as a function of the timing with which that word emerges from the ensemble of its competitors, and, therefore, cannot explain the effectiveness of cohort-based recognition-points in accounting for response variation in the phoneme-monitoring task.

4.2. Optimal real-time analysis

The evidence for the psychological reality of recognition-points is also evidence for a more general claim about the properties of the word-recognition system. In a distributed model of access and selection, information coming into the system is made simultaneously available to all of the processing entities to which it might be relevant. This makes the system capable, in principle, of extracting the maximum *information-value* from the speech signal, in real-time as it is heard.

The information-value of the signal is defined with respect to the information that it provides, over time, for the discrimination of the correct word-candidate from among the total set of possible words that might be uttered. To use this information in an optimally efficient manner requires an access and selection process that can continuously assess the sensory input against all possible word-candidates. It is only by considering all possible lexical interpretations of the accumulating sensory input that the system can be sure, on the one hand, of not selecting an incorrect candidate, and, on the other, of being able to select the single correct candidate as soon as it becomes uniquely discriminable—that is, at the point where all other candidates become excluded by the sensory input. A series of experiments, using an auditory lexical decision task, show that listeners do have access, in real time, to information about the sensory input that could only have derived from an analysis process with these properties (Marslen-Wilson, 1980, 1984).

These experiments focused on the discrimination of nonwords, rather than on the timing of real-word recognition, because this made it possible to ask a wider range of questions about the processes of access and selection. The nonword stimuli—which the subjects heard mixed in with an equal number of real words—were constructed by analysing the cohort structure of sets of English words. The sequence "trenker", for example, becomes a nonword at the /k/, since there are no words in English beginning with /tren/ which have /k/ as a continuation. The use of this type of material allowed us to ask the following questions.

First, can listeners detect that a sound sequence is a nonword at precisely the point where the sequence diverges from the existing possibilities in English—that is, from the offset of the last phoneme in the nonword sequence that could be part of the beginning of a real word in English? If the selection process does continuously assess the incoming speech against possible word-candidates, then decision-time should be constant relative to critical phoneme offset. It should be independent both of the position of the critical phoneme in the sequence, and of the length of the sequence as a whole.

The results were unambiguous. Decision-time, measured from the offset of the last real word phoneme, was remarkably constant, at around 450 ms.[10] It was unaffected either by variations in the position of the nonword point (from the second to the fifth phoneme in the sequence), or by variations in the length of the nonword sequences (from one to three syllables). It appears that not only is there a continuous lexical assessment of the speech input, but also that this input itself is not organised into processing units any larger than a phoneme.

This latter point was investigated in a subsequent experiment (Marslen-Wilson, 1984), which looked specifically at the role of a larger unit—the syllable—in access and selection. If the speech input is fed to the mental

---

[10]We can also look at the results in terms of the relationship between overall reaction-time (measured from sequence onset) and the delay from sequence onset until the offset of the critical phoneme. In an optimal system, the slope of this relationship should approach 1.0, since reaction-time from sequence onset should increase as a linear function of the delay until the sequence becomes a nonword. The outcome is very close to this, with an observed slope of +.90, and with a correlation coefficient of +.97.

lexicon in syllable-sized chunks, then nonword decision-time, which depends on access to the lexicon, should increase the further the critical phoneme is from the end of the syllable. To test this, I used nonword sequences where the critical phoneme was either at the beginning, in the middle, or at the end of a syllable. This variation in position had no effect on decision-time, which remained constant at around 450 ms. The absence of any delay for syllable-internal targets shows that subjects do not need to wait until the end of a syllable to make contact with the lexicon. This is consistent with recent evidence (Cutler, Mehler, Norris, & Segui, 1983) that the syllable does not function as a processing unit in English.

The absence of length effects in these experiments appears to be fatal for standard logogen models. A weak point in this type of model, as I have noted elsewhere (Marslen-Wilson & Welsh, 1978), is its treatment of nonwords. A logogen-based recognition system cannot directly identify a nonword, since recognition depends on the triggering of a logogen, and there can be no logogen for a nonword. The system can only determine that a nonword has occurred if no logogen fires in response to some sensory input. But to know that no logogen will fire, it must wait until all of the relevant input has been heard. In the present experiment, therefore, nonword decision-times should have been closely related to item length. In fact, there was no relationship at all between these two variables.

The predicted effect of length derives directly from the fundamental decision mechanism around which logogen-based recognition models are constructed. The failure of this prediction means that we must reject such mechanisms as the building blocks for models of spoken word-recognition.

The second main question I was able to ask, using nonword stimuli, addressed more directly the claim for a parallel access and selection process. A major diagnostic of a parallel, as opposed to serial system, is its relative insensitivity to set size effects. For a distributed system like the cohort model, it need make no difference to the timing of the word-recognition decision whether two candidates have to be considered or two hundred. In either case, the timing of the selection process reflects the point at which a unique solution emerges. This is purely a matter of cohort structure, and has nothing to do with the number of alternatives per se. For a serial process, however, which moves through the alternatives in the decision space one item at a time, an increase in the number of alternatives must mean an increase in decision-time.

I investigated this in two experiments, in which I varied the size of the "terminal cohort" of sets of nonword sequences. This refers to the number of real words that are compatible with the nonword sequences at the point where they start to become nonwords—that is, at the offset of the last real-word phoneme. To make the nonword decision, all of these words presumably need to be analysed, to determine whether the subsequent speech input is a possible continuation of any of them. In the first experiment, the size of these terminal sets varied from one to 30. In the second, replicating the first, the range was from one to over 70. In neither case did I find an effect of set-size. Decision-time was constant, as predicted by the model, from the offset of the last real-word phoneme in the sequence, irrespective of whether only one real word remained consistent with the input up to this decision point, or of whether more than 70 still remained. This is evidence against any sequential search model of spoken word-recognition, whether self-terminating or not.

4.3. The early activation of multiple semantic codes

The two preceding sections focused on the way the cohort model leads one to think about the relationship between the sensory input and the mechanisms of access and selection. Here I consider the role of contextual constraints in the operation of these mechanisms.

The cohort model places severe restrictions on the ways in which contextual variables can affect the access and selection process. In particular, it prohibits the top-down pre-selection of potential word-candidates. It is the sensory input that activates the initial set of candidates, which can then be assessed against context. There is no top-down flow of activation (or inhibition) from higher centers, but, rather, the bottom-up activation of the syntactic and semantic information associated with each of the word-forms that has been accessed.

This has two major consequences. It means, first, that contextual constraints cannot prevent the initial accessing (i.e., the entry into the word-initial cohort) of words that do not fit the context. There is already indirect evidence for this from earlier work on lexical ambiguity (e.g., Seidenberg, Tanenhaus, Leiman, & Bienkowski, 1982; Swinney, 1979). More recently, research by Tyler (1984) and Tyler and Wessels (1983) shows that subjects in the gating task produce a substantial proportion of contextually inappropriate responses at the earlier gates–that is, when they have heard between 50 and 200 ms of the word. These are responses that are compatible with the available sensory input, but which do not fit the semantic and syntactic context in which these fragments occur. The existence of these responses at the early gates is evidence for the priority given by the system to the bottom-up input, and for the inability of context to suppress the initial activation of inappropriate candidates.

The second major consequence is that early in the recognition process there will be the activation of multiple semantic and syntactic codes.[11] If contextual constraints are to affect the selection process, they can only do so, within this framework, if they have access to the syntactic and semantic properties of the potential word-candidates. This information must be made available not only about the word that is actually being heard, but also about the other words that are compatible with the sensory input—that is, the other members of the current cohort.

We have evaluated these two claims by using cross-modal priming tasks to tap the activation of different semantic codes early in the recognition process. In these experiments (Marslen-Wilson, Brown, & Zwitserlood, in preparation; Zwitserlood, 1985), the subjects heard spoken words, and made lexical decision judgements to visual probes that were presented concurrently with these words. Previous research by Swinney and his colleagues (e.g., Onifer & Swinney, 1981; Swinney, 1979) had shown that lexical decisions to visually presented stimuli are facilitated when these words are associatively related to spoken words that are being presented at the same time.

The spoken words in our experiments were drawn from pairs of words such as CAPTAIN and CAPTIVE, which only diverge from each other relatively late in the word—in this case at the onset of the vowel following the /t/-burst. The visual probes, to which the subjects made their lexical decisions, were semantically associated with one or the other member of the pair of spoken words—in this case, for example, the probes might be the words SHIP and GUARD, where SHIP is frequently produced as an associate to CAPTAIN but never to CAPTIVE, and vice versa for GUARD. The critical variable, however, was the timing with which the visual probes were presented, relative to the separation-point in the spoken words. We contrasted two probe positions in particular: an Early position, where the probe appeared just before the separation-point, and a Late position, where it occurred at the end of the word, well after the separation-point.

The cohort model claims that both CAPTAIN and CAPTIVE will be accessed early in the selection process, and that this will make available the semantic codes linked to both of them. If this is correct, then there should be facilitation of the lexical decision for both visual probes when they occur

---

[11]It is important not to equate the kind of activation being postulated here with the activation effects detected by Swinney (1979) and Seidenberg et al. (1982) in experiments using homophones. In these experiments, subjects hear a complete word-form—like "bug" or "rose"—that has two or more different meanings. Under these conditions, there is a strong activation of both meanings, which appears to persist for as much as a second after word offset. This is not the same as the phenomena predicted here, where the transient match, early in the word, of the incoming signal with a number of different word-forms leads to the transient activation of the semantic and syntactic codes associated with these forms. These effects are only the faint precursors of the activation effects to be expected when there is a full match of the input to a given word-form, as in the homophone experiments.

in the Early position. Decision-time for SHIP and GUARD should, therefore, be affected equally when these probes are presented on or before the /t/ in either CAPTIVE or CAPTAIN. In contrast, when the probes are presented in the Late position, then only the probe related to the actual word should be facilitated. If the word is CAPTAIN, for example, there should be facilitation of SHIP at the end of the word but not of GUARD.

This pattern should hold both for isolated words and for the same words in context. If the initial access, first of word-forms, and then of the syntactic and semantic information associated with these word-forms, is triggered from the bottom-up, and if contextual effects can only operate on this information after it has been accessed in this way, then the presence or absence of contextual constraints should not affect the pattern of activation of semantic codes at the early positions.

In a series of experiments this was exactly what we found. For words in isolation we see facilitation of both probes for the Early locations, but only facilitation of one probe at the Late positions (Marslen-Wilson et al., in preparation; Zwitserlood, 1985). The same pattern holds for words in context (Zwitserlood, 1985). The differential facilitation of probes associated with contextually appropriate as opposed to contextually less appropriate words only begins to appear after about 200 ms. At earlier probe positions, there is evidence for the activation of semantic codes linked to contextually inappropriate words, just as we find for words in isolation.

These results support the fundamental claim of the cohort model that the recognition process is based not only on multiple bottom-up access, but also on multiple contextual assessment (as discussed in Section 3). They also demonstrate that the involvement of contextual variables early in the selection process takes place under highly constrained conditions. No contextual preselection is permitted, and context cannot prevent the accessing and activation of contextually inappropriate word-candidates.

These conclusions distinguish the first version of the cohort model both from standard autonomy models and from standard interactive models. The cohort model differs from autonomous models, because it allows contextual variables to affect the selection process. But it shares with autonomy theories the assumption that initial access is autonomous, in the sense that top-down inputs cannot activate perceptual structures in the recognition lexicon.

This partial "autonomy" distinguishes the cohort model from theories which do permit top-down influences on initial access. One example is the logogen model, where logogens can be activated by inputs from the cognitive system as well as by bottom-up inputs. Another, more topical example, is the interactive activation model put forward by Rumelhart and McClelland

(1981), and recently applied to spoken word-recognition in the form of the TRACE model (Elman & McClelland, 1984). This is an approach that can accommodate many of the phenomena driving the cohort model—and, indeed, this was what it was initially designed to do.

It is not clear, however, whether TRACE (or its predecessor COHORT), with its mixture of excitatory connections between levels and inhibitory connections within levels, can accommodate the pattern of semantic activation described here for members of the same cohort heard in context and isolation. It should, first, predict differential patterns early in recognition for the contextually appropriate word, because of feed-forward from excitatory top-down connections. Secondly, because of the inhibitory connections between units within a level, there should be very little early activation of competing words like CAPTAIN and CAPTIVE. They should mutually inhibit each other until after their separation-point. Neither prediction is consistent with our results.

Finally, it is worth remembering that any evidence which reinforces the claims for multiple contextual assessment also serves to underline the fundamental inability of sequential search models to explain the observed properties of the on-line transfer-function of the recognition system—namely, the convergence of two sets of criteria, sensory and contextual, onto a unique solution within 200 ms of word-onset.

5. Information and decision in the cohort model: Some revisions and extensions

The results summarised in the preceding sections illustrate the value of the cohort approach as a basis for research into spoken word-recognition, and they support the accuracy of the claims it embodies about the functional characteristics of the recognition process. Nonetheless, it is also clear that the internal structure of the model, as originally stated, is over-simplified and inadequate on several counts.

In this final section of the paper I want to discuss some problems with the handling of information and decision in the cohort theory. These problems concern the nature of the information coming into the system, the way that information is represented within the system, and the way in which decisions are taken to exclude or include candidates for selection and recognition.

I will argue, in particular, that the cohort model has to move away from its binary concept of information and decision, where candidates are either in the cohort or out of it, towards a more fluid form of organisation, incorporating the concept of activation. The rationale for this derives, first of all, from some recent evidence for the role of word-frequency in the early stages of access and selection.

5.1. Activation and word-frequency

As originally stated, the cohort model made no mention at all of word-frequency. The main reason for this was the absence of compelling evidence that word-frequency was an effective variable in the kinds of on-line analysis processes with which the model is concerned. The older research in this area (e.g., Broadbent, 1967; Howes, 1957; Morton, 1969; Pollack, Rubinstein, & Decker, 1960) showed that word-frequency affects the intelligibility of spoken words heard in noise. But it was never clear whether these were immediate perceptual effects or due to post-perceptual response biases.

More recent research, using reaction-time techniques, was flawed by its failure to take into account the distribution of information over time in spoken words. Unless the high and low frequency words in an experiment are matched for recognition-point, and unless reaction-time is measured with respect to this point, then any measures of response-time to the two different classes of stimuli are difficult to interpret. This is the problem, for example, with the auditory lexical decision data reported by McCusker, Holley-Wilcox, and Hillinger (1979) and by Blosfeld and Bradley (1981). Both studies show faster response times to high frequency as opposed to low frequency monosyllables. But in each case reaction-time was measured from word-onset, with no correction for possible variations in recognition-point.

Two new studies provide better evidence for the role of word-frequency. In a preliminary study I looked at lexical decision latencies for matched pairs such as STREET and STREAK, where the recognition-point for each word is in the word-final stop-consonant.[12] This means that reaction-time can be measured from comparable points in each member of the pair—in this case, from the release of the final stop. For a set of 35 matched pairs, with mean frequencies, respectively, of 130 per million and 3 per million, there was a considerable advantage for the high-frequency words (387 vs. 474 ms).

Evidence of a different sort shows that these frequency effects can be detected early in the selection process. This evidence comes from the research on the early activation of semantic codes (see Section 4.3), where we found that the frequency of the spoken words being heard indirectly affected the amount of priming of the concurrent visual probe.

The effective variable was the *difference* in frequency between the word

---

[12]This was research carried out under my supervision by R. Sanders and E. Eden in 1983, as part of an undergraduate research project in the Cambridge Department of Experimental Psychology.

being heard and its closest competitor—in this experiment usually the other member of the stimulus pair. For the Early probes, presented before the spoken words had separated from each other, we regularly found more facilitation for the probe related to the more frequent member of the pair, with the size of this effect varying according to the size of the frequency difference between the two words.

The word CAPTAIN, for example, is more frequent than its close competitor CAPTIVE. For visual probes presented in the Early position, just before the /t/, there would be more facilitation of SHIP (the probe related to CAPTAIN) than of GUARD (the probe related to CAPTIVE), irrespective of whether the word actually being heard was CAPTAIN or CAPTIVE (Marslen-Wilson et al., in preparation). But for Late probes, presented at the end of the spoken word, these effects of relative frequency had disappeared, so that only the probe associated with the actual word being heard would be facilitated. Comparable effects were found by Zwitserlood (1985), in a study where the relative frequency of the members of such pairs was systematically varied.

These appear to be genuine perceptual effects, reflecting competition between different candidates early in the selection process. Alternative explanations, in terms of post-perceptual response-bias, can be excluded. If there are any bias effects in the data, they will reflect the properties of the visual probes rather than the spoken words, since it was the visual probes the subjects were actually responding to. They were not being asked to make any judgements about the identity or lexical status of the spoken words, nor, in general, did they seem to be aware that there was a relationship between these words and the visual probes. Furthermore, since the effects hold only for the Early probes, they reflect the state of the system *during* the selection phase, and not after it is completed.

Finally, and most significantly for the activation argument, these effects are transient. The effects of relative difference in frequency have dissipated by the time the Late probes are presented (between 200 to 300 ms later). What we appear to be picking up earlier in the word is a temporary advantage accorded to frequent word-forms, where the size of this advantage reflects the degree of differential activation of word-forms and their closest competitors.

Related transient effects can be seen in some other studies. For example, Blosfeld and Bradley (1981) only found significant frequency effects for monosyllables. In disyllabic words, lexical decision time did not vary according to frequency. This is because lexical decision is a task where the listener needs to wait until the end of the word before making a positive response, to make sure that he is not hearing a nonword. If the end of the word comes significantly later than the recognition-point, as will usually be the case for disyllables, then the effects of word-frequency at the recognition-point will have dissipated when the time comes for the subject to respond.[13] Finally, in the gating task the effects of frequency appear systematically only at the earliest gates (Tyler, 1984).

On the basis of this, I conclude the following. We can still assume that all word-forms which match a given input will be accessed by that input, and will remain active candidates as long as there is a satisfactory match with the sensory input. However, the response of higher-frequency word-forms appears to be enhanced in some way, such that the level of activation of these elements can rise more rapidly, per unit information, than the activation of less frequent elements (cf. Grosjean & Itzler, 1984).

This means that, early in the word, high-frequency words will be stronger candidates than lower-frequency words, just because their relative level of activation will be higher. This transient advantage is what the priming data reflect. And since the selection process is dependent on the emergence of one candidate from among a range of competitors, this should lead to faster recognition-times for high-frequency words than for low-frequency words, especially for low-frequency words with high-frequency competitors. This is because the activation of high-frequency competitors will take longer to drop below the level of the low-frequency candidate, once the critical sensory information has become available which excludes this high-frequency competitor.

To adopt this kind of account means that the behaviour of the cohort system can no longer be characterised in terms of the simple presence or absence of positive or negative information. Elements are not simply switched on or off as the sensory and contextual information accumulates, until a single candidate is left standing. Instead, the outcome and the timing of the recognition process will reflect the differential levels of activation of successful and unsuccessful candidates, and the rate at which their respective activation levels are rising and falling.

Some recent attempts to model a cohort-like analysis process have, in fact, represented the behaviour of the system in these or very similar terms (e.g., Elman & McClelland, 1984; Marcus, 1981, 1984; McClelland & Elman, 1986; Nusbaum & Slowiaczek, 1983). The results of these simulations show that an activation-based system is capable of exhibiting the main characteristics of a cohort selection process, with the correct candidate emerging from among its

---

[13] I should note, however, that recent research by Frauenfelder (personal communication) has failed to find this fall-off of frequency effects for disyllables.

competitors as the discriminating acoustic-phonetic information starts to accumulate.

But apart from being strongly suggested by the word-frequency data, the activation concept has advantages in other respects. In particular, it enables us to deal in a more satisfactory manner with a second set of issues raised by the cohort model's treatment of information and decision. These concern the nature of the sensory and contextual input to the decision process, and the way that the matching of these inputs to lexical representations affects this process.

5.2. Matching processes in access and selection

In the initial formulation of the cohort model it was assumed that the matching process was conducted on an all-or-none basis. The sensory and the contextual input either did or did not match the specifications for a given candidate. If it did not, then the candidate would be dropped from the cohort.

The trouble with this account is that it makes the successful outcome of the recognition process dependent on an unrealistically perfect match between the specifications of the correct candidate and the properties of the sensory input and the context. I will begin with the problems raised by variability in the bottom-up input.

5.2.1. Matching the sensory input

The cohort model emphasises the role of sensory information in determining the scope and characteristics of the access and selection process. It is this that determines the membership of the word-initial cohort, and that has the priority in determining which candidates remain in the cohort and which are dropped. The available evidence suggests that this is the correct view to take (see Section 4.3).

To take this view, however, is to run the risk of making the recognition process too sensitive to noise and variation in the sensory input. If sensory information is the primary determinant of cohort membership, and if the matching process operates on an all-or-none basis, then even a small amount of variability in the sensory signal could lead to problems in recognition, with the correct word-candidate either never making it into the word-initial cohort, or being dropped from it for spurious reasons.

In fact, the human spoken word-recognition system seems to be remarkably indifferent to noise in the signal, so long as the disrupted input occurs in an utterance context. Even when deviations are deliberately introduced into words—as in the mispronunciation detection task (Cole, 1973; Marslen-Wilson & Welsh, 1978)—listeners often fail to notice them. Over 70% of small changes (i.e., changes by a single distinctive feature) are not detected when they occur in words in utterance contexts, even though the same changes are readily detectable in isolated syllables (Cole, 1973).

To accommodate this type of result, the model must find some way of permitting deviant words to enter the cohort. The model can only allow context to compensate for deficiencies in the bottom-up specification of the correct candidate if this candidate nonetheless manages to find its way into the cohort.

There are two aspects to the solution of this problem. The first follows from the activation-based selection process sketched out in the previous section. This is not a decision process that requires all-or-none matching, since to discriminate the correct candidate it is not necessary to systematically reduce the cohort to a single member. Selection does not depend on simple presence or absence in the cohort, but on relative goodness of fit to the sensory input. This makes it in principle possible for candidates that do not fully match the sensory input to participate nonetheless in the recognition process.

The second aspect of the solution involves the model's assumptions about the nature of the input. The system will respond quite differently to deviant or noisy input, depending on the description under which this input is fed into the decision process. The more highly categorised the output of acoustic-phonetic analysis, the greater the problems that will be caused by variability and error (cf., Klatt, 1980). In fact, if the cohort model is going to be able to allow contextual constraint to compensate for bottom-up variability, then the input to the lexicon cannot be anything as abstract as a string of phonemes. Instead, a representation is required which preserves more information about the acoustic-phonetic properties of the input—for example, a representation in terms of a feature matrix.

To see this, consider the consequences of minor disruptions of the signal when we adopt different assumptions about the input. Suppose that the disturbance is such that a word-initial voiced stop—for example, /be/—is misidentified as a voiceless stop (/pe/). If the input to the word-recognition system takes the form of a string of phonemic labels, then this error will have drastic consequences for the membership of the cohort. A match will be established for all words beginning with /pe/, and these will be strongly activated. But the word intended by the speaker, beginning with a /b/, will receive no activation at all.

In contrast, if the input is specified in terms of a set of feature values, then such an error will have much less drastic consequences. A minimal pair like /b/ and /p/ only differ in their specifications along one feature parameter—in this case voicing. Even if a wrong assignment is made on this parameter, the input will still match the specifications for /b/ words along all of the other parameters. This means much less differentiation in the degree of match and mismatch between the /be/ and the /pe/ sets, so that the word-form intended by the speaker has a much better chance of receiving sufficient activation to be treated as a candidate for selection and recognition. In other words, the system will become more tolerant of minor deviations in the sensory input.

To assume a less highly categorised input to the lexicon does not sacrifice the ability of the system to discriminate among different alternatives. There is no inherent advantage to making phonemic distinctions at a pre-lexical decision stage, and the choice between two phonemes can be made just as well at the lexical level, as part of the choice between two words. In each case, the decision takes into account the same bottom-up information. The advantage of making the decision at the lexical level is that it enables the system to delay committing itself to final decisions about the properties of the sensory input until the other information relevant to this decision—including the lexical status of different alternatives and their contextual roles—can be taken into account (Klatt, 1980).

5.2.2. Matching the context

The evidence that selection is intimately bound up with integration lies at the heart of the argument for a distributed model of spoken word-recognition. But despite this, the way that the first version of the cohort model handles the relationship between selection and contextual constraints is seriously flawed.

Early statements of the model (e.g., Marslen-Wilson & Welsh, 1978) assert that candidates drop out of the pool of word-candidates when they do not fit the specifications of context, in the same way as when they do not fit the accumulating sensory input. This runs into similar problems to the all-or-none assumptions about sensory matching that I have just discussed. For the sensory input, the problem was to explain how mispronounced, or otherwise deviant words could nonetheless still be correctly identified. For context, the problem is to explain how contextually anomalous words can be identified (e.g., Norris, 1981).

Commonsense experience, as well as experimental evidence, tells us that contextually inappropriate words can, in fact, be readily perceived and identified, so long as they are unambiguously specified in the signal. In a recent experiment, for example, we compared monitoring latencies to the same target under conditions where it was either normal with respect to its context, or was anomalous in varying degrees of severity (Brown et al., unpublished). Consistent with earlier results, there was a clear effect of anomaly. Response latency to the word GUITAR increased by 27 ms over normal when it occurred in an implausible context ("John buried the guitar"), and by a further 22 ms when it occurred in a semantically anomalous context ("John drank the guitar"). But equally clearly, these anomalies are not causing a major break-down of the recognition process. In the semantically anomalous condition, for example, response-latencies remain well below 300 ms, and the error rate is essentially zero. Even for grossly anomalous targets ("John slept the guitar"), where verb sub-categorisation constraints are also violated, re-sponse-time is still a relatively rapid 320 ms, and the error-rate remains low.

The relative speed and accuracy of correct selection for contextually inap-propriate candidates is a reflection of the principle of bottom-up priority (Marslen-Wilson, & Tyler, 1980, 1983). The system is organised so that it cannot override unambiguous bottom-up information. This means that there is a considerable asymmetry in the degree to which context can override bottom-up mismatch as opposed to the ability of bottom-up information to override contextual mismatch. If the sensory input clearly differentiates one candidate from all others, then that is the candidate that will emerge from the perceptual process, irrespective of the degree of contextual anomaly. If contextual variables clearly indicate a given candidate, it will nonetheless not emerge as the choice of the system unless it also fits the bottom-up input (within the limits of variation indicated earlier).

The clear implication of this is that context does not function to exclude candidates from the cohort. There is no all-or-none matching with context, and no all-or-none inclusion or exclusion of candidates on this basis. This parallels the points made earlier (Section 4.3), prohibiting top-down influ-ences upon initial access. It looks as if contextual factors can neither deter-mine which candidates can enter the cohort, nor which candidates must leave it.

If we accept this conclusion, then there are two lines we can follow. One is to maintain an interactive model, but to restrict the kinds of top-down effects that are permitted. Since inhibitory effects are now excluded, context will only have facilitatory effects, perhaps by increasing the level of activation of candidates that fit the current context. Alternatively, we can turn towards a different type of model, where no top-down interactions of any sort are permitted. Different types of information are integrated together on-line to produce the perceptual output of the system, but they do not interact in the conventional sense. I will explore here the possibilities for this second kind of account.

The effects of context, within the general framework I have adopted in this paper, reflect the processing relationship between selection and integra-tion. This is the relationship between, on the one hand, the set of potential word-candidates, triggered from the bottom-up, and, on the other, the higher-level representation of the current utterance and discourse. This contextual representation provides a structured interpretative framework against which the senses associated with different word-forms can be assessed. In a non-interactive model, this framework does not, itself, operate directly on the activation levels of different candidates. These activation levels are a measure of the relative goodness of fit of the candidates to the bottom-up input, and context does not tamper with this measure.

We can capture, instead, the phenomena of early selection, and of contextual compensation for bottom-up deficiency, by exploiting the capacity of a parallel system for multiple access and multiple assessment. These will lead to a form of on-line competition between the most salient candidates (those most strongly activated by the sensory input) to occupy the available sites in the higher-level representation. Once the appropriate senses associated with a given word-form have been bound to these locations in the representation, then we can say that recognition has taken place.[14]

The speed with which this is accomplished will be the joint function of two variables: the extent to which the bottom-up fit for a given candidate differentiates it from its competitors, and the extent to which the contextual match similarly differentiates it. The facilitatory and compensatory effects of context reflect the tendency of the system to commit itself to a particular structural interpretation even though the sensory input may not have fully differentiated the word-form associated with this interpretation. The reason for this lack of full bottom-up differentiation may be either temporal—not all of the sensory input relevant to the decision has been heard yet, or it may be substantive— the sensory input is simply inadequate by itself to indicate a unique candidate.

On this account, both access and certain aspects of selection are autonomous processes, in the sense that they are driven strictly from the bottom-up. Whether the speech signal is heard in context or in isolation, the basic pattern-matching routines of the system will operate in the same way, providing information about the goodness of fit of the sensory signal to the array of lexical representations of word-forms.

This means that when the signal is heard in isolation, we will get something approximating the commonsense concept of word-recognition—that is, a process of form-based selection culminating in the explicit decision that a given word-form is present. But when the signal is heard in context—and note that normal context is fluent conversational speech—there need be no explicit form-based recognition decision. Selection—viewed as the decision that one particular word-form rather than another has been heard—becomes a by-

---

[14]It is at this point (Marslen-Wilson & Welsh, 1978) that the output of the system becomes perceptually available.

product of the primary process of mapping word-senses into higher-level representations. The bottom-up access and selection processes provide the essential basis for rapid on-line comprehension processes, but they provide no more than a partial input to an integrative system that is only peripherally concerned with identifying word-forms, and whose primary function is to uncover the meanings that the speaker is trying to communicate.

5.2.3. The new cohort

In the preceding section of this paper I have suggested a number of modifications in the way that the cohort concept should be realised as a processing model. These include the use of the activation concept, the introduction of frequency effects into the early stages of the recognition process, the specification of the bottom-up input in terms of some form of sub-phonemic representation, and the exclusion of top-down contextual influences on the state of the actual lexical recognition units. What do these changes mean for the central concepts of the approach, with its emphasis on the contingency of perceptual choice, and on the processing concept of the word-initial cohort?

By moving away from the concept of all-or-none matching against sensory and contextual criteria, and by adopting an activation metaphor to represent the goodness of fit of a given candidate to the bottom-up input, the model abandons the convenient fiction that the cohort is a discrete, well-demarcated entity in the mental life of the listener. The selection process does not depend on the membership of the cohort reducing to a single candidate. It depends instead on the process of mutual differentiation of levels of activation of different candidates. The operation of the system still reflects the state of the entire ensemble of possibilities, but the state of this ensemble is no longer represented simply in terms of the all-or-none presence or absence of different candidates.

Functionally, however, the cohort still exists. The effective core of salient candidates will be much the same as it would have been under an all-or-none regime. Although very many candidates will be momentarily activated as aspects of their phonological representations transiently match the accumulating input, the preceding and subsequent input will not match, and they will fall back into semi-quiescence. It takes some amount of time and input for candidates to start to participate fully in the selection and integration process. The effect of this is that the set of candidates which must be discriminated among will look very similar to the membership of the word-initial cohort as defined on an all-or-none basis. But by not defining it on this all-or-none basis, the system becomes far better equipped to deal with the intrinsic and constant variability of the speech signal.

Overall, none of the modifications I have suggested change the fundamental functional characteristics of the cohort-based word-recognition process. It still embodies the concepts of multiple access and multiple assessment, allowing a maximally efficient recognition process, based on the principle of the contingency of real-time perceptual choice.

References

Blosfeld, M.E., & Bradley, D.C. (1981). Visual and auditory word recognition: Effects of frequency and syllabicity. Paper presented at the Third Australian Language and Speech Conference, Melbourne.

Broadbent, D.E. (1967). Word-frequency effect and response-bias. *Psychological Review, 74,* 504–506.

Brown, C.M., Marslen-Wilson, W.D., & Tyler, L.K. (no date). Sensory and contextual factors in spoken word-recognition. Unpublished manuscript, Max-Planck Institute, Nijmegen.

Cole, R.A. (1973). Listening for mispronunciations: A measure of what we hear during speech. *Perception & Psychophysics, 13,* 153–156.

Cotton, S., & Grosjean, F. (1984). The gating paradigm: A comparison of successive and individual presentation formats. *Perception & Psychophysics, 35,* 41–48.

Cutler, A., Mehler, J., Norris, D., & Segui, J. (1983). A language-specific comprehension strategy. *Nature, 304,* 159–160.

Cutler, A., & Norris, D. (1979). Monitoring sentence comprehension. In W.E. Cooper & E. Walker (Eds.), *Sentence processing: Psycholinguistic studies presented to Merrill Garrett.* Hillsdale, NJ: Erlbaum.

Elman, J.L., & McClelland, J.L. (1984). Speech perception as a cognitive process: The interactive activation model. In N. Lass (Ed.), *Speech and Language, Vol. 10.* New York: Academic Press.

Fahlman, S.E. (1979). *NETL: A system for representing and using real-world knowledge.* Cambridge, MA: MIT Press.

Forster, K.I. (1976). Accessing the mental lexicon. In R.J. Wales & E. Walker (Eds.) *New approaches to language mechanisms.* Amsterdam: North-Holland.

Forster, K.I. (1979). Levels of processing and the structure of the language processor. In W.E. Cooper & E. Walker (Eds.) *Sentence processing: Psycholinguistic studies presented to Merrill Garrett.* Hillsdale, NJ: Erlbaum.

Forster, K.I. (1981). Priming and the effects of sentence and lexical contexts on naming time: Evidence for autonomous lexical processing. *Quarterly Journal of Experimental Psychology, 33A,* 465–495.

Grosjean, F. (1980). Spoken word recognition processes and the gating paradigm. *Perception & Psychophysics, 28,* 267–283.

Grosjean, F. (1985). The recognition of words after their acoustic offset: Evidence and implications. *Perception & Psychophysics, 28,* 299–310.

Grosjean, F., & Gee, J.P. (1987). Another view of spoken word recognition. *Cognition, 25,* this issue.

Grosjean, F., & Itzler, J. (1984). Can semantic constraint reduce the role of word frequency during spoken-word recognition? *Bulletin of the Psychonomic Society, 22,* 180–182.

Hinton, G.E., & Anderson, J.A. (Eds.) (1981). *Parallel models of associative memory.* Hillsdale, NJ: Erlbaum.

Howes, D. (1957). On the relationship between the intelligibility and the frequency of occurrence of English words. *Journal of the Acoustical Society of America, 29,* 296–305.

Klatt, D.H. (1980). Speech perception: A model of acoustic-phonetic analysis and lexical access. In R.A. Cole (Ed.) *Perception and production of fluent speech.* Hillsdale, NJ: Erlbaum.

Luce, P.A. (1986). A computational analysis of uniqueness points in auditory word recognition. *Perception & Psychophysics, 39,* 155–159.

Marcel, A.J. (1983). Conscious and unconscious perception: An approach to the relations between phenomenal experience and perceptual processes. *Cognitive Psychology, 15,* 238–300.

Marcus, S.M, (1981). ERIS—context-sensitive coding in speech perception. *Journal of Phonetics, 9,* 197–220.

Marcus, S.M. (1984). Recognizing speech: On the mapping from sound to word. In H. Bouma & D.G. Bouwhuis (Eds.) *Attention and Performance X: Control of language processes.* Hillsdale, NJ: Erlbaum.

Marslen-Wilson, W.D. (1973). Linguistic structure and speech shadowing at very short latencies. *Nature, 244,* 522–523.

Marslen-Wilson, W.D. (1978). Sequential decision processes during spoken word recognition. Paper presented to the Psychonomic Society, San Antonio, Texas.

Marslen-Wilson, W.D. (1980). Speech understanding as a psychological process. In J.C. Simon (Ed.) *Spoken language understanding and generation.* Dordrecht: Reidel.

Marslen-Wilson, W.D. (1984). Function and process in spoken word-recognition. In H. Bouma and D.G. Bouwhuis (Eds.) *Attention and Performance X: Control of language processes.* Hillsdale, NJ: Erlbaum.

Marslen-Wilson, W.D. (1985). Speech shadowing and speech comprehension. *Speech Communication, 4,* 55–73.

Marslen-Wilson, W., Brown, C.M. & Zwitserlood, P. (in preparation). Spoken word-recognition: early activation of multiple semantic codes. Manuscript in preparation. Max-Planck Institute, Nijmegen.

Marslen-Wilson, W.D., & Tyler, L.K. (1975). Processing structure of sentence perception. *Nature, 257,* 784–786.

Marslen-Wilson, W.D., & Tyler, L.K. (1980). The temporal structure of spoken language understanding. *Cognition, 8,* 1–71.

Marslen-Wilson, W.D., & Tyler, L.K. (1981). Central processes in speech understanding. *Philosophical Transactions of the Royal Society, Series B, 295,* 317–332.

Marslen-Wilson, W.D., & Welsh, A. (1978). Processing interactions during word-recognition in continuous speech. *Cognitive Psychology, 10,* 29–63.

McClelland, J.L., & Elman, J.L. (1986). The TRACE model of speech perception. In McClelland, J.L., & Rumelhart, D.E. (Eds.) *Parallel distributed processing: Explorations in the microstructure of cognition.* Cambridge, Mass. Bradford Books.

McCusker, L.X., Holley-Wilcox, P., & Hillinger, M.L. (1979). Frequency effects in auditory and visual word recognition. Paper presented to the Southwestern Psychological Association, San Antonio, Texas.

Morton, J. (1969). Interaction of information in word recognition. *Psychological Review, 76,* 165–178.

Morton, J., & Long, J. (1976). Effect of word transitional probability on phoneme identification. *Journal of Verbal Learning and Verbal Behavior, 15,* 43–52.

Norris, D. (1981). Autonomous processes in comprehension. *Cognition, 11,* 97–101.

Nusbaum, H.C., & Slowiaczek, L.M. (1983). An activation model of the cohort theory of auditory word recognition. Paper presented at the Society for Mathematical Psychology, Boulder, Colorado.

Onifer, W., & Swinney, D.A. (1981). Accessing lexical ambiguities during sentence comprehension: Effects of frequency of meaning and contextual bias. *Memory & Cognition, 9,* 225–236.

Pollack, I., Rubinstein, H., & Decker, L. (1960). Analysis of correct responses to an unknown message set. *Journal of the Acoustical Society of America, 32,* 454–457.

Rumelhart, D.E., & McClelland, J.L. (1981). An interactive activation model of context effects in letter perception, Part II: The contextual enhancement effect and some tests and extensions of the model. *Psychological Review, 89,* 60–94.

Salasoo, A., & Pisoni, D. (1985). Interaction of knowledge sources in spoken word identification. *Journal of Verbal Learning and Verbal Behavior, 24,* 210–231.

Seidenberg, M.S., & Tanenhaus, M.K. (1979). Orthographic effects on rhyme monitoring. *Journal of Experimental Psychology: Human Learning and Memory, 5,* 546–554.

Seidenberg, M.S., Tanenhaus, M.K., Leiman, J.M., & Bienkowski, M. (1982). Automatic access of the meanings of ambiguous words in context: Some limitations of knowledge-based processing. *Cognitive Psychology, 14*, 489–537.

Swinney, D. (1979). Lexical access during sentence comprehension: (Re)consideration of context effects. *Journal of Verbal Learning and Verbal Behavior, 14*, 645–660.

Tyler, L.K. (1984). The structure of the initial cohort: evidence from gating. *Perception & Psychophysics, 36*, 217–222.

Tyler, L.K., & Wessels, J. (1983). Quantifying contextual contributions to word-recognition processes. *Perception & Psychophysics, 34*, 409–420.

Tyler, L.K., & Wessels, J. (1985). Is gating an on-line task? Evidence from naming latency data. *Perception & Psychophysics, 38*, 217–222.

Zwitserlood, P. (1985). Activation of word candidates during spoken word-recognition. Paper presented to Psychonomic Society Meetings, Boston, Mass.

Résumé

La reconnaissance de mots (dans la chaîne parlée) englobe trois fonctions fondamentales: l'accès, la sélection et l'intégration. L'*accès* se réfère à l'appareillement de l'onde sonore avec les représentations de formes lexicales; la *sélection*, désigne la discrimination du meilleur "pareil" (match) lexical avec le stimulus, et l'*intégration* recouvre l'appareillement de l'information syntaxique et sémantique avec les niveaux de traitement supérieures.

Cet article décrit comment deux versions d'un modèle (de type "cohorte") rendent compte de ces processus, en traçant son évolution à partir d'une première version comportant un principe d'interaction partielle où l'accès est strictement autonome mais où la sélection est soumise à des contrôles "de haut en bas" vers une deuxième version (à fonctionnement entièrement "de bas en haut") où le contexte n'intervient plus dans les processus d'accès et de sélection.

Par conséquent, le contexte n'intervient qu'à l'interface entre les représentations supérieures et l'information générée en temps réel sur les propriétés syntaxiques et sémantiques des membres du cohorte. Ce nouveau modèle garde intactes les caractéristiques essentielles d'un processus de reconnaissance de type cohorte. Il intègre les notions d'accès et d'évaluation multiples permettant ainsi un processus de reconnaissance optimal fondé sur le principe de contingence de choix perceptif.

5

A reader's view of listening

DIANNE C. BRADLEY*
KENNETH I. FORSTER
Monash University

Abstract

There is a view that the fundamental processes involved in word recognition might somehow be different for speech and print. We argue that this view is unjustified, and that the models of lexical access developed for the written form are also appropriate for speech, provided that we allow for obvious differences due to the physical characteristics of speech signals. Particular emphasis is given to the role of word frequency in the recognition process, since this places restrictions on the types of models that can be considered (e.g., the cohort model). We reject the view that there are no frequency effects in spoken word recognition, and we also reject the view that frequency effects in printed word recognition can be relegated to the minor status of a post-access decision effect.

1. Introduction

Most research into language processing has been based on reading, despite the fact that most use of language (and clearly, over the population, truly skilled use) involves the spoken form. The reason for this is straightforward: the visual stimulus is relatively easy to manipulate, so that the circumstances of presentation are readily controlled or subjected to systematic alteration. Making an implicit assumption that the important characteristics of word and sentence recognition are shared by visual and auditory modes, researchers have tended to concentrate their efforts on the experimentally expedient case. That is, when psycholinguists investigate the performance of skilled adult readers, the research is more often than not taken to be about *language* processes, rather than *reading* processes per se. Levelt and Flores D'Arcais' (1978) book of reviews and original studies illustrates this point rather nicely:

*Reprint requests should be sent to Dianne Bradley, Department of Psychology, Monash University, Clayton, Victoria 3168, Australia.

much of the research considered relevant to the "perception of language" in fact uses written presentations of word and sentence materials.

From another point of view, the concentration on visual recognition might be surprising. Among the language behaviours, writing and reading are relative latecomers, and presumably are not those for which human language processing systems are evolved. It might be that the processes underlying comprehension in the skilled reader are quite parallel to those employed in auditory recognition; on the other hand, it might not. The differences between auditory and visual inputs are so striking, and so often the object of comment, that there is little need for an enumeration. We might, however, point to the areas of contrast which have most exercised those interested in spoken word recognition, and that is, that the acoustic signal is both evanescent and continuous, with no discrete physical representation of elements of the language at the level of phones or even words. Properties like these would seem to confront recognition processes with a problem.

That problem may become acute, given the following observation: phenomenally, at least, the comprehension of spoken language seems very much to be a real-time process (Chodorow, 1979), with understanding following closely on the input as it is deployed over time (Marslen-Wilson, 1973). It has been suggested that the very character of auditory inputs, taken together with an intuition of the immediacy of comprehension, require processing which is "optimally efficient" moment-to-moment (Cole & Jakimik, 1980; Grosjean, 1980; Grosjean & Gee, 1987, this issue; Marslen-Wilson, 1984; Marslen-Wilson & Welsh, 1978; Tyler & Marslen-Wilson, 1981). An essential aspect of the strongest version of these claims is that the speed and ease of normal speech understanding point to the exploitation of all and any information which might constrain the interpretation of an inherently difficult signal. That is, while in principle (or, indeed, in a grammar) we might distinguish among the informational types which contribute in the end to sentence meaning—for example, information about the physical and phonetic form of the elements of the sentence, about the non-redundant properties of contributing lexical items, about their assembly into phrasal units, and about the meaning of those phrases—the language processor needs to be organised for auditory recognition so that these informational types flow together, in a "parallel and highly interactive" system (Tyler & Marslen-Wilson, 1981).

The processes underlying listening and reading necessarily differ at some level, simply in virtue of decoding from inputs in separate modalities. And they must also converge at some level, for the common goal of these behaviors is the comprehension of language inputs. In the mental operations intervening between the initial analysis of a physical signal and the recovery of an intended interpretation, where do the differences between reading and listening disappear? The question here need not be one of the point at which inputs are handled in a code which is strictly neutral as to stimulus modality—though this is not an independent problem. The issue can be cast in terms of the extent to which the operations allowing comprehension of spoken and written messages are equivalent, whether or not representational codes respect input modality. The recognition problem created by the properties peculiar to the speech signal must have its solution; insofar as that solution closely determines a style of processing, comprehension processes in listening may differ radically from those supporting performance in reading. Commonality may well be limited to the endpoint, that is, to the analysis into meaning.

Framed this way, a mild-mannered question of the convergence or otherwise of reading and listening, having some bearing on a working assumption of the field, might assume an unmanageably broad shape. Here, as elsewhere, some progress can be achieved by concentrating on the problem of lexical identification. The immediate advantages of this move are self-evident: we know something of (or can propose investigations about) the processes leading up to the identification of words, with due attention to relevant stimulus attributes. A restriction to the lexical level is not unduly limiting: notice that it would be possible to examine questions of processor organization, though that will not be our focus here; if interaction among informational types is pervasive, it ought to be evident at the lexical level. Further, there seems available a non-controversial construal of the job of lexical identification devices: they perform a type-token assignment, that is, the pairing of an input with a stored mental representation.

Finally, a concentration on issues in lexical processing provides some kind of framework for the discussion which follows, since in our view models of lexical access must specify three things, in the end: the *input descriptions* under which the mental inventory is to be addressed; the way in which representations which are candidates for a pairing are to be discovered or encountered, which we will call, neutrally, the *mechanism of association*; and the *metric* under which the "fit" of a candidate is to be evaluated, fixing the degree to which variation can be tolerated, without blocking the assignment of an input to the type of which it is truly an instance. We note that specifications here may not be independent of each other.

These remarks are intended to set the background to the exercise that follows, in which we examine the possible commonalities of reading and listening, in ways which are suggested by our carving up of the lexical access problem. We first consider briefly (and negatively) a proposal that convergence is to be found at a very early stage, in the sharing of input descriptions. In pursuit of commonality of process, we then examine the fit of a model of lexical access, whose empirical support rests by and large on data derived from performances with written forms, to the case of spoken stimuli: in short, a reader's view of the solution to the listener's problem. Our attention here is focused on the mechanism by which input tokens are to be associated with mental types, reflecting a conviction that it is this area of specification which is central to model construction. (The issue of the evaluation metric is not given separate consideration, since we find that some choices on the earlier points deny options that are available, for others.) Beyond general considerations of the theoretical and empirical commitments which different mechanisms of association bring, we consider in detail the treatment that they afford to the frequency sensitivity of recognition performance, and end by evaluating the recent evidence which has cast earlier interpretations of frequency effects in doubt.

2. Input descriptions: Common access codes?

Convergence for listening and reading at an early stage of lexical processing would have its simplest expression if there were a common pre-lexical code for speech and print, despite signals with different properties. Differences in physical description do not dictate that the relevant description from the point of view of lexical access differs, since it may be that the input descriptions for access are only abstractly related to the physical input. The phonological recoding hypothesis (see McCusker, Hillinger, & Bias, 1981, for a review) is to be taken as an example: it asserts that visual representations must be converted into phonological representations before access can occur. This input description, which we will call the *access code*, might well be invariant across modalities.

The strongest argument one could make for commonality at the level of input descriptions would be to claim that the lexicon is so structured that it can *only* be accessed via one type of code. Since speech recognition is universal but reading is not, this code would be speech-related (and hence learning to read would involve learning how to convert print into a code designed in the first instance for spoken forms).

For languages with shallow orthographies, a rule system can provide this conversion, but for languages with non-shallow orthographies (in particular, ideographic scripts), the correspondence between the orthographic and speech-related form would have to be specified separately for each word. But this makes the conversion rather pointless—once the orthographic representation has been located, then all the information necessary to recover the full lexical properties of the word is available. That is, the orthographic entry for each word in this table of code-correspondences might just as well be associated with the full lexical entry as with the appropriate speech-related code.

Thus, considerations of computational efficiency suggest that an *obligatory* conversion to a speech-related code is unlikely. This is not to deny that there might nevertheless be some circumstances in which an optional conversion is carried out. For example, if the orthographic representation cannot be located, then a rule-system of some sort might be used to construct the speech-related code, even though (in the case of a language such as English) it may not always give a correct rendition. Such a mechanism might explain why the "regularity" of the spelling-sound relationship influences measures of access-time only for low-frequency words (Seidenberg, Waters, Barnes, & Tannenhaus, 1984).

In a two-stage access system (e.g., Forster, 1976), a coded version of the input signal first contacts an entry in an file, which then cross-references the entry to its full representation in the lexicon proper. With different input descriptions for speech and print, the first point of contact between a stimulus and the lexicon is necessarily modality-specific (in access files which take either letter, or acoustic-phonetic descriptions), but the second is not. Modality differences in the initial point of contact between inputs and the lexicon do not, of course, close off the possibilities for commonality at this level. As our introductory remarks pointed out, there is a construal of the speech/print convergence question which talks in terms of equivalence rather than identity. Consideration might now turn to the construction of the access code: we might ask, for example, whether input descriptions for spoken stimuli are couched in terms of phonetic categories (analogous to the assumed letter-based code for written stimuli), or in terms of acoustic cues. This is set aside here, as an avenue of inquiry which is likely to be unprofitable: though traditional acoustic-phonetics, with its focus on the "lack of invariance" problem, seems implicitly to assume that lexical addressing is cast in phonetic rather than acoustic terms, there are counter-proposals (e.g., Klatt, 1979; Marcus, 1984) which rely on spectral features, recovering phonetic or phonological descriptions post-lexically. The terms of input codes for speech are thus still in play, to a great extent. The issues, moreover, are outside our competence (though see Pisoni & Luce, 1987, this issue).

Continuing on, we might examine issues arising in the mapping between these input descriptions (whether equivalently couched or not), and the mental representations of lexical items—that is, in what we have called the mechanism of association. The remainder of the paper is devoted to this examination, which is organized around the claims of a particular model of lexical access. The model stands in contrast to the general flavour of those developed in the first instance for spoken recognition, since it proposes, as an essential feature, that form-based access proceeds via a *search* over lexical subsets, which is *frequency-ordered*, moreover. Our concerns are twofold: on the one hand, to spell out the considerations which motivate such a model, exploring their relevance to the case of spoken language; and on the other, to suggest where possible the options which are open where the empirical evidence is slim or apparently counter to the proposal. As a preliminary to this discussion, we begin with a setting out of the details of the model, establishing some terminology, along the way.

3. The model

In the model, lexical retrieval, the entire operation of finding a particular mental representation (or lexical entry) for a word within the lexical inventory, is taken to consist of several subprocesses, as follows (see Forster, 1976, 1979, for greater detail, and supporting argument).

(a) *Form-recognition.* The treatment of a written stimulus begins with the recognition of its orthographic properties (a letter-access procedure).

(b) *Access-code construction.* On the basis of this abstract representation of the input, an access code is constructed. This is the description under which the inventory of forms is to be first addressed, but may reflect something less than the full input; stripping operations (of prefixes, and of all but the first syllable, as per Taft & Forster, 1976; Taft, 1979) limit its scope, since the access code need correspond only to the headings under which words are mentally represented.

(c) *Bin selection.* The access code has its first use in the selection of an appropriate subset of the lexicon, over which a detailed search is to be made. Lexical subsets have predetermined boundaries (that is, they are fixed bins), and bin selection is given by a hashing operation on the access code.

(d) *Search.* Within the selected bin, entries are searched serially, under an order of encounter which depends on relative frequency, until a match with the access code is found; this is the second use of that code. The criterion for a match is the same for all entries, but may be uniformly raised or lowered (as required to recover from misspellings, O'Connor & Forster, 1981). The search is normally thought of as self-terminating, but it is probably more accurate to say that it is an exhaustive search that outputs the addresses of all entries that meet the match criterion, as they are located. In lexical decision experiments, only the first of these is necessary to reach a decision, and hence for this situation, the search is effectively self-terminating (since further outputs will be ignored). But in a sentence-processing situation, where there is evidence that all meanings of an ambiguous word are considered (e.g., Swinney, 1979), we need to have the search continue automatically past the entry first encountered.

(e) *Post-search check*. The orthographic specification contained within an entry whose heading gives an access code match is then compared with the full orthographic properties of the stimulus. If a match is not obtained in this more detailed comparison, search resumes automatically.

(f) *Readout*. If a detailed match is obtained, the relevant contents of the entry are made available to the relevant processors (e.g., syntactic properties for the parser, semantic properties for the interpreter).

Within this system, *access* is taken to include steps (b) through (e), and thus covers the process of locating the correct entry. Whatever happens subsequently is a post-access process (the post-search check was termed a post-access check in some previous writings (e.g., O'Connor & Forster, 1981), but this is misleading and inconsistent with other usage). Post-access processes fall into two broad classes. These include decision processes (typically, the computation of the central cognitive system that selects a response in a classification experiment), and context-checking processes (in which the appropriateness of the input to the context is evaluated).

3.1. Lexical identification: Access and recognition

As a final preliminary to considering the proposal that treatments at the lexical level might differ for speech and print, it is perhaps worth emphasizing that, in our view, a theory of lexical access is not the same thing as a theory of word recognition. Of the areas requiring specification that we have outlined earlier, the first two (relating to input descriptions, and the mechanisms of association) are quite clearly linked to questions of access, for they are directed to the processes by which information is extracted from the stimulus to permit the isolation of the appropriate memory structures in the mental lexicon. It is in the final area of specification (concerned with the evaluation metric) that we see potential separation of access and recognition. Where the access system's form-based evaluations of the fit of an input to a type represented mentally are less than entirely secure, a theory of word recognition might deal with a broader problem, that of construal: it considers how the information yielded by the access system is used to drive inferences about the probable lexical stimulus.

To take an example, consider the case of a speech input which contains a speech error, for example, "tircus sent" instead of "circus tent". As anyone knows who has tried collecting speech errors, they are easily missed (but note, critically, not inevitably missed)—and hence it is likely that hearers will sometimes report that they heard the intended rather than the actual form. In such a case, is it appropriate to say that they *perceived* the intended form, or should we say that they perceived the actual form but *inferred* the intended form? Clearly, this question raises the vexed problem of mediate and immediate perception, and the problem of deciding where perception ends and inference begins. Since it is by no means clear what the term "perception" refers to, we pose a different question: was it the lexical access system that identified the intended form, or was it the recognition system? Obviously, recovery of the intended form requires fairly complicated reasoning (e.g., noticing that the sound exchange mechanism offers a better explanation of the data than does a less constraining double incidence of poor segment rendition). To build this kind of power into the lexical access system seems undesirable. It is hard to imagine that anyone would want to postulate a system of word-detectors that are capable of making such inferences by themselves.

If we feel that this ought to be resisted at all costs, then we need to make a distinction between lexical access and word recognition, and to treat the latter as a case of fixation of perceptual belief, to use Fodor's phrase (Fodor, 1983). That is, auditory/visual recognition of word X occurs when a hearer forms the belief that he heard/saw the word X. Such beliefs are based in part on the output of the access system, but also may be based on other considerations. For example, it is undoubtedly significant that the lexicon is a component of a device recovering intended linguistic messages, where a powerful bias to the construal of inputs as words is to be expected.

Much of the current discussion about "post-access processes", "post-lexical processes", "decision processes" and the like is based on a similar distinction. When we obtain measurements of word-naming time, or lexical decision time, or accuracy of identification, we are necessarily measuring properties of the recognition process. These are determined in part by the properties of the access system, but also by other (post-access) processes, which use the information provided by access to arrive at conclusions about the stimulus input. There is, of course, an inevitable danger that a distinction between access and recognition might totally protect any theory of lexical access from disconfirmation, since any unwelcome facts about language performance can be attributed to the recognition system. That danger does not argue against the stand adopted here, but against its inappropriate use: the distinction between access and recognition is vacuous, and should be discarded, only if it were to achieve nothing other than saving a theory.

4. Mechanisms of association: General considerations

We now turn to the question of the mechanism that associates the access code with the appropriate lexical entry, and consider the proposals of three models of recognition, which seem representative of the options that recur in the literature of this area. In the search model outlined above, the mapping begins with a simple table look-up procedure: an operation over input data is assumed, the output of which is used to pick out a set of broadly compatible lexical candidates (the bin elements) which are to be examined in detail for their congruence with another, more fully specified description of the token. In logogen models (Morton, 1969, 1979), it is assumed that for each word there is an evidence-collecting detector which is selectively tuned to an appropriate constellation of stimulus features. Where the features that any single word detector likes to see as part of an input array actually occur, the excitation level of that detector is increased, with recognition depending on excitation exceeding a pre-set threshold. In neither of these two models is there any suggestion that the associative mechanisms for speech and print are different. However, the cohort model (e.g., inter alia, Marslen-Wilson, 1984; Marslen-Wilson & Welsh, 1978; Tyler & Marslen-Wilson, 1981) proposes a special associative mechanism for speech, which is responsive to the deployment of the stimulus over time. In this system, successive elements of the input description are made available in turn to detectors representing the lexical pool (the cohort), to drive a progressive attrition in that set; cases of detector/input mis-match drop out, until there is either only one or no cohort member remaining. An "optimality" assumption proposes that lexical identification occurs at the earliest possible point. Thus, as soon as only one member remains in the cohort, that word can be recognized. If all members have been eliminated, then the input can immediately be classified as a nonword.

4.1. Content-addressing and search

The proposal that access for written stimuli uses an association mechanism incorporating a search, and that speech is served by a cohort system, gives no commonality of process across modalities at this level. Our exploration of the divergence begins, curiously enough, with a question about the relationship between the cohort system and the logogen model, the latter being one which we have explicitly rejected as a model of access for print stimuli (Forster, 1976). One feature these systems share is the notion of content-addressability. In both, it is claimed that physical features of the input are sufficient to determine a precise "location" of the appropriate lexical entry. It is in this respect that these models differ fundamentally from the search model, in which a description derived from the input determines only an approximate location, in the first instance.

However, cohort and logogen models acquire the property of content-addressability in quite different ways. The cohort procedure is essentially a tree-search algorithm. Each node in the tree corresponds to a state of the processor, and each branch is associated with an element of the input; interconnected nodes define "legal" transitions. In its initial state, the recognition process begins at the highest node, and descends via the branch that corresponds to the first element of the input; the path to be followed through the rest of the tree is controlled by succeeding elements. Thus, to recognize the word /trɛspəs/, the search begins at the highest node, and descends via the branch labelled /t/ (for ease of exposition, we take elements to be phones). The search then descends via the branches for /r/, /ɛ/, and so on, until a terminal node is reached. At this point, the location of the lexical entry for the word "trespass" is specified, and the word has been identified. At any given point in the recognition process, the cohort is simply defined as the set of terminal nodes in the subtree dominated by the current node. There are two important features to note: first, branches are provided for *existing* words but not for *potential* words, that is, the tree is pruned, so that only attested paths are legal paths; and second, a sequence of non-branching nodes dominating a single terminal node is telescoped. These capture the optimality assumption of the original.

We shall return to this model later, but for the moment consider how this differs from the logogen account. To make the contrast clear, we could try to implement the logogen system on a tree of precisely the same kind. Instead of tracing a path through the tree, we could imagine activation flowing down the branches, to accumulate at terminal nodes. Thus, for the "trespass" case, when initial /t/ occurs, activation flows down the initial /t/ branch, and continues to reticulate down through the tree, so that the terminal nodes for *all* words beginning with /t/ receive some activation. When the element /r/ is detected, activation flows down each of the /r/ branches at the second level (not the highest level, since that would only be activated for a word with an initial /r/). If this process continues, with activation injected at successively lower levels, then obviously the accumulated activation level for the terminal node corresponding to the word "trespass" will receive more activation than any other. If we incorporate the notion of a threshold, so that detectors located at the terminal nodes "fire" when their activation level reaches a pre-set level, then we appear to have duplicated all the essential properties of the logogen model.

However, the following consideration shows that this is not the case. Suppose that the initial phonetic element (or indeed, any subsequent one) has been incorrectly coded, for one reason or another. This is catastrophic for the cohort system, since it will descend on the wrong path, and can never recover (a familiar problem with hierarchically-ordered systems, of which we have more to say below). However, a logogen system would not necessarily be affected. All that would happen is that activation from the initial /t/ would be missing, but there would still be activation at the relevant terminal node from the remaining elements, sufficient perhaps to reach threshold.

A miscoded initial element produces such different effects, precisely because the cohort system uses a hierarchically-ordered testing procedure whereas the logogen system does not (despite the fact that our example makes it appear as if it does). Thus in the cohort system, the consequences for branch-choice at the second level depend crucially on the identification of the first element: an /r/ branch from a /t/ node bears no relation to one with superior node /p/. But in a logogen system, activation flows from all second-level /r/ nodes regardless of what has previously happened, and hence the absence of information about the first element is not necessarily critical.

Viewed in this way, the pattern of activation in a logogen system is context-free (the activation produced by a given phonetic element is independent of its immediate context), but in a cohort system it is context-sensitive. If we decided to make the logogen system sensitive to context as well, then any difference between the systems would disappear. Thus, for example, if the /r/ of "trespass" produced activation only from the second-level /r/ node dominated by a first-level /t/ node, and so on, then this would amount to a context-sensitive logogen system, differing in association mechanism from the cohort model only in its terminology. The remaining differences (the logogen models's pre-set threshold, and the cohort's optimality assumption) might prove difficult to resolve. We note, though, that suitably adjusted thresholds may well allow the former to mimic the latter, to achieve lexical identification as early as possible. That is, the optimality which is sought in the cohort system by a telescoping of non-branching nodes might have its expression in a logogen system in a manipulation of thresholds, so that stimulus information up to the point of non-branching, by itself, is sufficient to give appropriately high activation levels.

The most distinctive feature of the cohort model, then, is that it involves a hierarchically-ordered series of tests on the input sequence. This also may turn out to be its weakest point, since it predicts that miscoding of any of the elements of the input description will disrupt access. Very occasionally, the miscoding could give a path to a lexical "neighbour" (*single* miscoded as *shingle*); this could afford an account of the mishearings which listeners experience, very occasionally. But in the majority of cases, and those which are most telling, miscodings lead to recognition failure (*singlet* miscoded as *shinglet*): they give a descent on an incorrect path, to end at a point where a legal transition is simply not available for that stimulus—recall that the tree is "pruned". What is notable here is that the point at which the access attempt halts gives no information about the point where the problem began; in our example, the system runs out of legal options with the delivery of final /t/, itself not a miscoding of the input. Thus, the system can have no guidance, if it is to "back up", and re-analyse, to get the best-fitting lexical correspondence.

4.2. Content-addressability and access difficulty

This misdirection problem might be dealt with in a number of ways. It could be claimed, for example, that the access code is so constructed that no possibility of error exists, and hence no recovery procedure is necessary—a strong claim, indeed, given what we know of human performance systems. Alternatively, the cohort model might simply take the implicit prediction to be the right one to make, saying in fact, that the attested failures of recognition have precisely the distributional characteristics and rates of occurrence that one might expect. Whatever those might be, overall, they must include no privileged relation between a misanalysed form, and its closest lexical fit. However, there is experimental evidence (in addition to intuition) to suggest that either of these is the wrong stand to take firmly. Taft and Hambly (1985), for example, present evidence that response latencies for spoken nonwords in a lexical decision task are sensitive to their overall similarity to words, even when point of departure from word status is controlled in pairwise contrasts. (Note that when point of departure is fixed in this way, a cohort model predicts *no* response time difference.) So, for example, classification of the form *rhythlic* as a nonword takes longer than that of the form *rhythlan*. Now, nonwords are cases in which recognition "failure" is guaranteed, in the sense that they necessarily lead to a mismatch between input and branching options, at some point. What do these data tell us about the activities of the lexical access system, when it encounters such mismatch? First, that recovery procedures of some kind exist, since different kinds of nonwords produce different latencies. And second, that those recovery procedures manage to locate plausible lexical interpretations of the stimulus, since similarity to existing words is relevant.

Thus finally, and most plausibly, the cohort system might seek to *protect* itself, by incorporating additional devices. So, for example, we might start by supposing that misrecognition (*single/shingle*) can be covered by positing an obligatory post-access check of the type/=/token assignment, once a terminal node is reached: this check would compare a full specification of expected input with a description of the stimulus. The system could back up to the point of mismatch, which can now be identified (*s/sh*), to make a second pass, with an adjusted access code. An extension of the same device to cope with recognition failure (*singlet/shinglet*) introduces difficulties, but we might propose that points where the tree is pruned have an attached full specification, like those at terminal nodes—a kind of "you are here" device. Unfortunately, all nodes are pruned nodes, since only attested words are represented in the tree, and these clearly do not exhaust the space of legal forms (let alone illegal ones). The specifications which are the basis for a check have therefore to be proliferated throughout the entire tree. All in all, this seems an infelicitous move, on a number of grounds. It removes much of the force of the claim of content-addressability, that is, of an automatic location of lexical address. At the same time, it does damage to the notions of efficiency which motivated the cohort proposal in the first instance, and which prompted model features like the optimality assumption. Perhaps more critically, it acknowledges a difference in the security of the input descriptions which drive access, and those which support more straightforward pattern-matching procedures.

A more subtle consequence results from the situation which arises where the problem is not one of misrepresentation in the input description, but of uncertainty. We have in mind here, the cases where the input descriptions allow no secure assignment at some point in the access code (again, for whatever reason). Once uncertainty arises, the only option open for a system incorporating a hierarchical test sequence is to retreat to the last node reached before the uncertain element, and then to treat all terminal nodes in the subtree dominated by the last secure node as equally-likely candidates. It would then be necessary to evaluate each of these candidates to determine which fits the input best (that is, a search process). An access system which has reason to expect any such uncertainty, routinely, might well include the notion of search, as a design feature. Thus, it would standardly make location assignments which are only approximate, and select among the candidate entries at that approximate location with case by case evaluation.

Are there arguments which might distinguish between a system which resorts to search only when it encounters difficulties in making type-token assignments, and one which searches quite routinely? Certainly, arguments in principle are difficult here, but the following considerations may be suggestive. Full content-addressability is, we assume, burdensome, either in the computational costs that it entails, or in the capacity demands of its network representation. Thus, a system which is already expensive is to be backed up by an additional search machinery, and perhaps also a pattern-matching check, of the kind argued for earlier. To the extent that difficulty in type-token assignment is less than rare, it would seem preferable to design a system which is less ambitious in the first instance (in that it settles for approximate prediction of location), and makes constant use (because it must) of its search machinery. It's of interest here that a recent proposal for machine-recognition of speech captures just this spirit of the search models. Shipman and Zue (1982) suggest that the recognition problem for large lexicons may be substantially reduced by the use of an initially broad characterization of inputs (e.g., in terms of sequences captured only by broad manner categories), for which acoustic cues are particularly reliable.

Thus, our arguments for a search model amount in fact to arguments against the feasibility of a totally content-addressable lexicon, and they are not particular to any modality. In short, content-addressability (without additional support) seems neither sufficiently forgiving of errors in its input analyses, nor sufficiently responsive to the vagaries of inputs.

4.3. Input description reliability in different modalities

In pursuit of an argument of a different kind, let us suppose for the moment that the processes supporting speech recognition make use of content-addressing, while those for print stimuli employ a search process. Why should this be so? One would imagine that a fully content-addressable system maximises access efficiency, and if it can be implemented for speech, why not for print? We have noted that if corresponding lexical entries are only approximately located (in the first instance) from features of the physical form of inputs, then the need for a search procedure follows. Given the supposed contrast across modalities, on what basis might one argue that entry location would be only approximately predicted for written words, but given definitively for spoken stimuli? One line of argument might suggest that location is only approximately predicted, whenever it is only approximately predictable. That situation would apply, and in the right direction, if there were reason to believe that the mapping from orthographic properties onto lexical entries is somehow less secure or less selective than the mapping from acoustic or phonological properties.

It is not at all clear what kind of evidence would support a claim that absolute differences exist in the reliability or richness of the information contained in the two modalities. The problem is that one's view of what counts as signal or noise for a given process is subject to change, and the recent work of Church (1983) on allophonic variation is instructive here. Church argues that such variation is far from being a hindrance to speech processing, in its introduction of differences in the surface form of speech elements. Rather, the variation is to be exploited for positive benefit, since its presence can indicate the location of boundaries (word or phrase) whose identification is critical to the proper parsing of spoken utterances. So the grounds, here, are dangerous indeed.

An argument might possibly be constructed on the basis of performance data in tasks requiring monitoring for sub-lexical units; for example, phone and letter monitoring. We might say that a content-addressing system should be capable of secure identifications of the elements which will enter into its computation of addresses, while a system which relies on search to get precise entry location might take support, where it can. Marslen-Wilson's (1984) report of lexicality effects for phone/letter-monitoring with auditory and visual stimuli is very much to the point: for speech, there is evidence of lexical support in /t/ detection, in distinct functions of response time on target position, for words and nonwords carriers; for print, there is no evidence of lexical support, that is, the response time/target position function is indifferent to the lexical status of the target bearing item. The differences, then, run in the wrong direction, if we take the more secure sub-lexical identification to be the one which takes no higher-level support. Given this construal of the monitor data, content-addressability would seem to attach most plausibly to the print mode, and approximate lexical location to speech, rather than vice versa. Moreover, the following observation attests to the typicality of these data: while there has been a small industry in research with spoken materials, exploiting the sensitivity of the phone monitoring task to variables at the lexical level and above (see Cutler & Norris, 1979, for a review), there is a notable lack of equivalent research with written stimuli. This reflects more than simple oversight, if our experience is any guide: in our laboratory, we have *never* been successful in finding any useful sensitivity in letter-monitoring performance.

However, such an argument may not be sound. For one thing, it rests on the assumption that the monitor targets (phones or letters) are to be identified with the elements entering into the access codes. Thus, the phone-monitoring data might equally be taken as evidence against the use of phonetic descriptions as a basis for access. For another, we must note that monitoring decisions depend on the availability of subprocessor outputs to a central cognitive system; it remains possible that for speech but not print, there may be a privileged relation between a general decision-making system and the lexical processor, to give the observed data pattern. Why the "controlling level" for monitoring responses should differ in this way between modalities is not clear. We note only that if the argument is to be dismissed by appeal to this notion, there can be no mention of the security of sub-lexical identification, in the justification of a higher controlling level.

In sum, this argument for a difference in the inherent reliability of mappings from stimulus descriptions onto lexical entries produces, at best, the wrong result, for it suggests a pairing of content-addressing with print stimuli, and search with speech. At worst, it produces a null result, in that the patterns of the monitoring data are to be given an explanation in other terms. It was noted, earlier, that a system employing sequences of hierarchically-ordered tests runs at great risk: misdirected to an inappropriate path, it can never recover gracefully. We can think of no argument that gives the "right" result, that is, that the analysis of speech stimuli is markedly less prone to error than the analysis of print stimuli.

4.4. Lexical addressing with partial inputs

An alternative way to pursue the link between the initial treatment of inputs, and the precision of lexical addressing, is to suppose that entry-location might be predicted approximately, not because of any inherent upper limit on predictability in some stimulus type, but because of the way in which the access code is developed. Thus, our remarks here will be directed to an argument of a different kind for search processes in speech.

A search system makes available a theoretical device which may be denied to more powerful recognisers, or at best only awkwardly incorporated into them: it can permit the form-description allowing first contact with the lexical inventory to be specified independently of the one which allows the close evaluation of candidates. There are two basic requirements, only, which must be satisfied by a search code. First, and most importantly, it must define a search set which will contain the best input match, with some sufficiently high probability. Misdirections at the level of the search code, though less likely than misdirections for fully content-addressable systems (since the locations sought are approximate rather than absolute) guarantee failures of recognition of the same kind, and so reliability here is critical. The second requirement simply invests the "double-staging" of recognition operations inherent in these proposals with real force: the candidate pool which is picked out by the search code must reflect a significant decimation of the total lexical inventory, for the purpose of the exercise is to place limits on the number of match evaluations, which we might take to be computationally expensive. Neither of these demand that the search code be computed over the entire input, nor that all features be equally weighted, within any stretch of the input which is to be the basis of the code. What enters into the search code may differ from what must be taken into account in the final evaluation of the fit of any candidate to the input; for the initial step of defining a search set, what will count is reliability and expediency; but in the end, all features of form may matter, for the type assignment is a step to be taken with care.

The potential for separation of the descriptions used early and late in lexical access raises interesting possibilities: in particular, we have a natural place in the model for an exploitation of those portions of the input which are likely to have maximum signal clarity, and within those portions, for reliance on those features which are most cheaply computed, while giving the statistically greatest advantage in sub-dividing the lexicon. For the case of spoken words, there are suggestions from various sources and for various reasons (for a review, see Grosjean & Gee, 1987, this issue), that the main-stress syllable has a special role in access, since sublexical identifications are most reliably made here. There are, then, sufficient reasons for proposing different input codings for different access phases; in the search model, these can be characterized as an initial search code and a later detailed description. It's to be noted that some kind of weighting function over a single description may be a more arbitrary device whose effect is to give roughly the same end, that is, "processing prominence" to certain stimulus subparts. In consequence, these observations count as arguments for the operation of a search mechanism over spoken forms, only to the extent that naturalness in theory-construction is valued.

5. Mechanisms of association and the frequency effect

In the preceding section, we have concentrated on the general considerations raised by the contrast of models using content-addressing, and approximate addressing plus subsequent search, as the mechanisms by which input tokens are associated with lexically represented types. We now turn to a more specific issue: the treatment of performance sensitivity to word frequency. From the standpoint of a search model, a frequency effect is the single most important property associated with lexical access. The fact that high-frequency words are accessed faster than low-frequency words follows naturally from the model's assumptions: if retrieval of entries requires a search process because lexical location is only approximately predicted, then the most efficient procedure is to place entries which are to be accessed more often nearer to the beginning of the search path. In short, a frequency effect is to be predicted on grounds of efficiency in computation. Furthermore, the assumption of a frequency-ordered examination of candidate representations should be seen as the keystone of search theory; to abandon this assumption amounts to abandoning the whole notion of a search retrieval system. To put it another way, we see no point in trying to preserve a search model that has some factor other than relative frequency controlling search order, and which thus gives the frequency effect some other explanation (by, for example, relegating it to some post-access mechanism).

The relevance of the frequency issue to the contrast at hand is straightforward: there is simply no way to arrange a tree-search algorithm of the cohort variety so that words of high frequency are accessed before words of low frequency. This follows from the fact that each step in the computational path from initial state to terminal node is controlled solely by the nature of the successive sub-lexical units (e.g., phones). Hence *lexical* frequency cannot influence the computational path. This is not the case in a table look-up procedure, where each step in the computational path (i.e., selection of the next candidate entry to be evaluated) can be controlled by lexical frequency. The only avenue open to the cohort model is to suggest that the frequency effect occurs *after* the terminal node is reached, i.e., after the word has been recognized.

The general form of the argument which we will pursue in the remainder of this paper goes as follows: first, that there is frequency sensitivity in the recognition of spoken words, and that the patterns of that frequency sensitivity have a ready explanation with the assumption of a pre-access locus of effect; and second, that there is a theoretical usefulness and an empirical basis for according word frequency a pre-access role. On these grounds, we would suggest that the cohort model does not provide a compelling account of access, since it cannot by its nature incorporate frequency acting prior to access. Hence, the frequency issue adds another argument against the claim of divergence in the mechanism of association, in the recognition of speech and print.

The argument to be developed here obviously places great reliance on a particular interpretation of frequency effects. If there is any doubt about that interpretation, then much of what we will have said can be discounted. It is certainly true that the position we have adopted is not universally accepted. Morton (1979), for example, has recently argued that frequency does not affect the logogen system itself, but rather the cognitive system to which logogen outputs are referred, for the completion of recognition. In similar vein, Norris (1983) proposes that frequency does not influence the process which selects candidate entries, but instead affects a post-selection criterion for acceptance. That is, a candidate is more likely to be accepted as a correct analysis of the input signal if that candidate has a high occurrence frequency. These explanations of the frequency effect are post-access in the sense that the system which lists possible analyses of the input is presumed to ignore frequency. The system we propose does not. Thus, for example, if there are two competing interpretations of the input (each of them valid), then our system predicts that only the higher-frequency alternative will ever be considered, in cases where performance has an effectively self-terminating basis. We round out the whole argument, therefore, with an evaluation of the kind of evidence that has cast doubt on a pre-access interpretation.

5.1. Frequency effects in spoken word recognition

An empirical approach to the proposal of content-addressability in the recognition of spoken forms runs into immediate difficulty, for, curiously, there appears to be very little evidence which bears directly on the issue of frequency sensitivity, for stimuli presented in clear. We note, however, that early investigations (e.g., Savin, 1963) found evidence of greater recognition accuracy for words heard in a noise background, in accord with the findings for visual stimuli presented tachistoscopically (e.g., Howes & Solomon, 1951). The potential contribution of guessing strategies makes these less than ideal data on which to base our case, however.

More direct evidence would be provided by a simple lexical decision experiment, but we are unaware of any *published* results. In perhaps the clearest positive example which has come to our attention, Taft and Hambly (1985) report strong frequency effects for polysyllabic words; their cases are matched pairwise in terms of the point from word onset at which uniqueness of lexical construal occurs (e.g., *difficult/diffident*), and thus give data which is particularly relevant, in the light of the cohort model's optimality assumption. We could rest our case here, but there are details which might profitably be explored further.

Those details are concerned with circumstances in which frequency sensitivity for auditory stimuli seems to be diminished. McCusker, Hillinger and Bias (1981), for example, briefly discuss the lexical decision data of McCusker, Holley-Wilcox and Hillinger (1979), who found a significantly larger frequency effect for visual stimuli (86 ms) than for auditory stimuli (51 ms); no indication is given of the reliability of the latter effect. In an early experiment conducted in our laboratory by Elizabeth Bednall, lexical decision times for spoken words showed no correlation at all with frequency. However, there was an extremely high positive correlation between the acoustic duration of the stimulus and lexical decision time. What could explain this effect? It is compatible with an assumption (which we think has useful consequences, see below) that subjects were waiting for some time, perhaps as long as until stimulus offset, before they made their decision. If, as Marslen-Wilson argues, initial identification of a spoken word is completed before offset, and frequency only affects this initial identification process, then the frequency effect may be "absorbed" when the subject delays his match-evaluation or decision until the stimulus has been largely or even fully deployed. What's emerging here is a very nasty possibility: that the frequency sensitivity of a search mechanism for spoken words can be obscured, when access operates over stimuli with the durational properties peculiar to speech.

As an example of this type of process, consider the access model for printed polysyllabic words suggested by Taft and Forster (1976), which assumes that the initial access code is the stem-initial syllable. That is, for the target *postman*, the first syllable *post* is identified as the most likely description under which the access entry will be filed (if one exists). When the entry for *post* is located, the various possible endings (including those for *postbox*, *postoffice*, *postage*, and so on) have to be checked to see whether *man* is listed. (Note that our use of a compound example here is nothing more than an expository device.)[1]

Now, with visual presentations, the physical evidence concerning the input completion is available simultaneously with the evidence concerning the first syllable. As soon as the first syllable is accessed, the existing ending can be checked for compatibility with the stem, so that the sooner the entry for the first syllable is identified, the sooner the lexical status of the complete word can be decided. But with an acoustic presentation of *postman*, the system must wait until the complete word has been received. If this postponement is sufficiently long, then the speed with which the initial syllable was accessed becomes irrelevant. Hence it is entirely possible that first-syllable frequency effects might be quite undetectable with a spoken stimulus. According to this analysis, the strength of the frequency effect for spoken polysyllabic words will vary inversely with the wait-time. The wait-time, in turn, will vary with the acoustic duration of whatever segment of the second and subsequent syllables is considered, and possibly, with the strategy adopted by the subject, should this be a situation where strategies can be called into play. McCusker, Holley-Wilcox and Hillinger's (1979) comparison of frequency effects in auditory and visual lexical decision is at least compatible with the analysis being suggested here: to the extent that there is enforced delay in the exploitation of the outputs of initial-syllable access mechanisms, frequency-sensitivity in lexical decision performance will reduce, relative to normal visual presentation.

If this view is correct, frequency effects for spoken words should be stronger for monosyllabic than for polysyllabic words, and that seems to be the case. Blosfelds (1981), in our laboratory, found in one case that the

---

[1] The use of a compound example allows us to avoid the difficulties inherent in the definition of what is to count as "syllable" for access purposes (Sánchez-Casas, Bradley, & García-Albea, 1984; Taft, 1979), and of what surface forms have shared lexical representation (Bradley, 1981). A treatment of these is beyond the scope of this paper.

frequency effects evident for monosyllables (50 ms) were markedly reduced for disyllables (6 ms), though they were less robust than for the same items in a visual version; however, in another, where stimulus duration made the contrast of frequency classes problematic, frequency sensitivity was weak for both syllabic classes (18 ms for monosyllables, 25 ms for disyllables). More recent work confirms the original claim, with effects of 58 ms and 28 ms for monosyllabic and disyllabic stimuli, respectively (Savage, 1985).

Moreover, the proposal that evidence of the frequency sensitivity of initial access procedures can be lost in a postponement of full stimulus match-evaluation is not tied to spoken words per se, but only to their durational properties. It should thus be possible, for written words, to "simulate" the postponement effect by using a staggered presentation of the individual letters of the word, so that the visual display mimics, albeit crudely, the serial deployment of the auditory case. That is, instead of presenting *postman* as a complete unit, one could present the word one letter at a time, with each new letter being added to the existing display, for example, *p*, *po*, *pos*, *post*, *postm*, *postma*, *postman*. With each new letter being added 80 ms after the previous one, the display roughly matches the phone rate (and only that) of the normal speech signal. Certainly this is a peculiar mode of visual presentation, and we are sensitive to the possibility that it might totally distort normal recognition processes. Here, we take some comfort from the ease with which subjects adapt to it, in contrast to their rejection of a *non*-incremental version, in which there is a strictly letter-by-letter display, as if with a moving window.

For visually presented stimuli, access is assumed to be controlled by the initial syllable; thus for monosyllabic words, an input stretch required for access corresponds to what is required for full match evaluation. Hence, the frequency-sensitive processes of access should be minimally obscured. However, for polysyllabic words, the confirmation of lexical status must be delayed until the compatibility of the second syllable has been assessed. With normal visual presentation, this check can be carried out immediately, but with a slow incremental display, the second syllable is not complete until a further 160–240 ms has elapsed (depending on the number of letters); this forced wait-time should be enough to absorb much of the frequency effect. Using the materials of her earlier experiments in spoken word recognition, Blosfelds (1981) found in one version, a significant 46 ms effect of frequency for monosyllable word targets, but for disyllabic words, a nonsignificant frequency effect of only 18 ms; in a replication using a new set of materials, the same pattern was found, the frequency effects being 58 and 23 ms respectively.

For the moment, then, we are inclined to accept the proposition that spoken word recognition contains a subprocess which is frequency sensitive.

Additionally, the observed diminutions in the magnitude of frequency effects are quite compatible with the assumption of a pre-access siting, and are not necessarily peculiar to the auditory modality. This has the advantage of postulating that the same general principles of lexical retrieval are operative for both speech and print. Its disadvantage is that it postulates potentially undetectable frequency effects for spoken words which are other than monosyllabic, at least in standard whole-word recognition experiments; and that is certainly a disquietening position in which to find oneself.

5.2. Pre-access interpretation of the frequency effect

To attribute frequency $/=/$ sensitivity to post-access processes would, we believe, be an undesirable move on both theoretical and empirical grounds, although the latter are noticeably weaker than the former. Our firm adherence to the claim that the frequency-sensitivity of recognition performance is to be given an interpretation in terms of the ordering of elements in a search path has one strong motivation, and that is one which turns on the need for tools to theory construction. The break between pre- and post-access processes is a major one, and potentially highly identifiable: definitionally, the non-redundant properties of lexical items other than those built into the access path (e.g., their syntactic class, their semantics) cannot be known prior to access, but become available after it. In the stream of processing that takes input stimuli and delivers them as interpreted perceptual objects to higher level language processes and central cognitive systems, variously, there is as yet no other break which we can have marked out so definitively. Thus, if we are in the business of deciding what kinds of processes go where for a full theory of word recognition, with our decisions responsive to the available data, then locating one variable on one side of an identifiable breakpoint gives strong constraint to the interpretation of others.

In illustration of this, consider the following. The search model predicts that any variable which radically alters the search path should modulate the frequency effect. Thus the finding that the frequency effect is unaffected by sentential context (e.g., Schuberth, Spoehr & Lane, 1981) is a clear indication that the search path remains constant across different contexts, and hence that contextually generated candidates are not interpolated into the ordered set of form-based candidates. A much stronger prediction derived from the search model is that there should be no *other* word-property associated with access time, unless it is also correlated with relative frequency. If access time is a function of the rank-order of the lexical entry in the search path, and if entries are listed in order of their frequency of occurrence, then it follows that frequency will be the only variable to control access time. We can draw an interesting parallel: just as a full tree-search algorithm cannot countenance anything other than the form of temporally ordered elements as a determinant of the access path, the search mechanism cannot incorporate anything other than frequency to fix search-path order within lexical subsets.

So, for example, a finding that words which refer to concrete objects are recognized faster than words with more abstract reference (James, 1975) has no access interpretation in a search model, and some other explanation must be sought. For theory construction, then, a treatment of frequency of this kind places close constraints on the alternatives which are open. In this respect, the model differs from some early versions of the logogen model, where the chief explanatory mechanism is the threshold value associated with logogens. High frequency words are accessed faster because their thresholds are lower; if concrete words are accessed faster than abstract words, there is no reason at all to prevent this being similarly attributed to variations in thresholds. The dangers of such freedom are evident: theoretical interpretation can amount to nothing more than a re-description of findings. What's being advocated here is not the automatic acceptance of simply *any* device which limits the options available to models, but rather its reverse: we would like to avoid the loss of a constraint which has a more than plausible a priori motivation, especially if the grounds for its rejection are chiefly that it tends to create theoretical difficulties.

There are, at this time, no principled partitions of post-access processes, though these may well be forthcoming, to place their own constraints on model development. But currently, to treat frequency as a post-access effect means giving up a powerful constraint on models of access (and there are few enough of these), as well as giving up a method of investigating other properties of the access system, via a determination of the conditions (e.g., of stimulus quality, task, context, and so forth) under which the frequency effect is modulated. It might also mean that a theory of access becomes virtually content-free in the sense that there will be no lexical properties remaining to control access time (cf., Whaley, 1978). So, one ought to have good reason to make such a move; for example, there must either be solid evidence of the inappropriateness of the pre-access interpretation of frequency, or other phenomena which have no explanation at all if frequency is treated in this way.

So much for considerations of theory development. Are there any more or less direct empirical grounds for treating frequency as an access effect? We can think of three. First, the search model's assumption that frequency controls the search path provides a genuine explanation of the approximately logarithmic form of the function relating access time and frequency. The reason is that it is not frequency per se that controls access time, but relative frequency, that is, rank-order. For any particular search path (or bin, in the terms of the model), the difference in frequency between the first and second entries may be very large, whereas the difference in frequency between the next-to-last and last entries may be extremely small. But the access time differences between the members of these pairs will be the same, since what's relevant is the ordering that frequency gives, rather than frequency, absolutely. Since the function relating rank-order and access time is linear (by the assumptions of a search model, and empirically, Murray and Forster, 1979), and the function relating rank-order and frequency is approximately logarithmic (Zipf's law), it follows that frequency and access time should be related logarithmically. Post-access accounts are, of course, free to stipulate that same function, but this is arbitrary; they are free, also, to predict any function at all.

An alternative line of evidence is exemplified in Forster and Bednall's (1976) analysis of ambiguity judgments. To determine that a given letter sequence is associated with only one lexical entry, it is necessary to conduct an exhaustive search of the lexicon (or some form-delimited subset of it). Hence the frequency of the word should be irrelevant, as indeed it was. However, if frequency were associated with some post-access process (such as the time taken to extract the contents of the entry), then it should remain relevant. Similar arguments apply to classification by form-class. Forster and Bednall were able to show frequency effects for a set of unambiguous nouns in a noun/non-noun classification task, where search should be effecively self-terminating for noun inputs. However, in a verb/non-verb classification, search must continue past the first entry located for noun inputs and so be exhaustive (given the possibility of usage both as noun and unrelated verb): here, the same words showed no frequency effect.

Perhaps the clearest direct evidence for a system with pre-access expression of frequency has been reported by Taft and Forster (1975). They compared for frequency-matched words such as *vent* and *card*. Given prefix-stripping assumptions, *vent* could be taken as a stem, that is, *-vent* (as in *prevent, invent*) or as a word in its own right. Since *-vent* has a higher frequency than *vent*, this lexical interpretation is encountered first, to produce interference as the entry for *-vent* is checked to see whether the stem can occur as a free form. The input *card* has a similar ambiguity, except that the bound form *-card* (as in *discard*) has a lower frequency than the free form *card*. With the search model's assumption of a strict frequency ordering in the encounter of lexical entries, there should be no interference; the lower-frequency alternative is effectively never consulted in a task where one full lexical match is sufficient to support a response. This leads to the prediction that lexical decision times for items such as *vent* should be longer than for items such as *card*, which is exactly what Taft and Forster found.

5.3. Alternative interpretations of the frequency effect

There are two sources of evidence which are currently taken to provide empirical grounds for *not* treating frequency as an access effect in the way that the search model does. Interestingly, these arise in studies using *written* materials. The first is the so-called frequency-blocking effect observed in the lexical decision task. Since the effect is not predicted by the search model, it has been the basis for the development of alternative models (e.g., Glanzer & Ehrenreich, 1979; Gordon, 1983)—in which, we should note, frequency is still accorded a pre-access locus. The second source of evidence concerns the outcomes of frequency manipulations in experiments using tasks other than lexical decision: in semantic categorization, frequency effects are found which are much smaller than would be expected (Balota & Chumbley, 1984); but in delayed naming, a frequency effect is found when none is expected (Balota & Chumbley, 1985).

5.3.1. Frequency blocking effects

Normally, experimental evaluations of the frequency effect use a mixed-list design, in which words from various frequency ranges are randomly intermingled. However, a blocked design groups all words from a given range together. Briefly, the notion is that frequency-blocking alters *access* time, so that if a low-frequency word is presented in the context of other low-frequency words, it will be accessed faster than it would have been in a mixed list. This was the result claimed by Glanzer and Ehrenreich (1979). The explanation of a frequency-blocking advantage particular to low-frequency words might require an assumption that the set of lexical elements considered to be candidates for word recognition can be modified by context. This would be problematic for a search theory, since search sets are pre-determined and are, in any case, strictly *form*-delimited.

However, as noted by Gordon (1983), the low-frequency advantage is not in fact a reliable result; instead, what one finds is that low-frequency words are not affected by blocking, whereas *high*-frequency words are. Thus strictly, the frequency-blocking effect does not directly challenge the notion that frequency controls access time; critical findings would be that there is no effect of frequency at all in pure lists, or that there is no difference between medium- and low-frequency words in such designs. However, the fact is that Gordon finds a stronger frequency effect in pure lists than in mixed lists, and that in both cases, it is a graded effect.

Still, this is not the result one would predict from a frequency-ordered model (since search necessarily begins from the highest-frequency entry, to be already maximally efficient), and it therefore raises intriguing problems. We are inclined to think an account will rest in the mechanisms by which the outputs of lexical processes are made available to central decision-making systems.[2] In these terms, any frequency-blocking effect is not attributable to faster access, but to a faster use of the products of access. It is not an effect which is *predicted* by a search theory, but this is hardly a serious weakness, if the phenomenon in question has nothing more to do with lexical access than have, say, motivational effects. That is, as we suggested earlier, lexical search theory is a theory about lexical access, not about the whole person.

5.3.2. Task effects

The second half of the counter-frequency argument begins with the findings of Balota and Chumbley (1984). Briefly, they found that frequency had no significant impact on semantic categorization times, for example, on the time to decide that a robin is a bird. Since accessing the lexical entry for *robin* seems a necessary prerequisite to categorization, we should expect to find quite standard effects of frequency in the task, if frequency controls access time. The fact that this was not found prompts the following argument: frequency has no major role in the processes leading to access, and its strong influence on performance in the lexical decision task means only that *decision* processes are frequency-sensitive.

The normal counter to this argument appeals to the fact that frequency also has significant influence in a task where decision-making is kept to a minimum, that is, the naming task (Forster & Chambers, 1973; Frederiksen & Kroll, 1976). However, Balota and Chumbley (1985) suggest that the effect of frequency here is largely spurious, since it may affect response execution. Their suggestion comes from the finding that frequency effects still occur when the naming response is delayed. That is, subjects took longer to begin

---

[2]Gordon is sympathetic to the "list-difficulty" interpretation suggested by Kiger and Glass (1981), who showed that a given item in a sentence verification task produced faster response times when placed in a context of easy items compared with a context of difficult items; the precise nature of this effect is obscure, but presumably has something to do with the subject's confidence or expectations. Instead, his claim is that the search model cannot provide such an explanation without modification. We would not argue with this, but would add a rider: that to our way of thinking, explaining these effects will require a much richer theory of the transfer of information between input modules in Fodor's (1983) sense and the central cognitive system than is properly provided in the domain of theories of lexical *access*.

saying a low-frequency word, even when the stimulus had been freely available for 1400 ms.[3]

The first point to note is that nowhere do Balota and Chumbley claim that there is no residual frequency effect, or that frequency has *no* influence on access time. Their only claim is that the effects of frequency may be exaggerated in both lexical decision and naming tasks. We certainly would not wish to contest this general point. Perhaps the matter could simply be left there, with a conclusion that the only disagreement concerns the *size* of the exaggeration.

However, we are inclined to sketch an alternative, since there seems to be a curious variability in the size of residual frequency effects in the categorization task. For example, Bednall (1978) found secure frequency effects for both positive and negative responses using the category *parts of the body*; and Forster (1985) reported sizable but non-significant frequency effects in a membership task, using the category *objects bigger than a brick*. Finally, Thorp (1986), working in our laboratory, carried out an interesting post-hoc analysis of his categorization results: when the data were subcategorized according to item difficulty (by a median split on mean response time), he found a significant frequency effect for the easy items, but not for the difficult ones. (Note that if frequency effects are to be attached to decision processes, this latter finding is quite the wrong way about.)

We propose that the initial point of contact between an input and its mental representation is *always* made via a frequency-organized search,[4] so that categorization must involve a frequency-controlled component. Whether this component finally survives to be revealed in the categorization times

---

[3]Two points are to be made about the finding that a frequency effect doesn't go away when it should, in the delayed naming task (Balota & Chumbley, 1985). The first is one about method: to test whether there is a frequency effect for naming times, we need to ensure that the two samples of words do not differ systematically in the time to assemble the necessary motor commands and to begin executing them, or in the time required for the output signal to reach the energy level necessary to trigger a voice-operated switch. In fact, Seidenberg (1985) mentions a failure to replicate Balota and Chumbley's results using homophones (which are more than likely to be matched on the relevant variables).

The second point to be made is that the *delayed* naming task may induce a special strategy. After the target is accessed, and the appropriate motor commands have been assembled, the subject must inhibit his vocalization until an appropriate signal is received. Balota and Chumbley assume that once that signal is given, the vocalization response can be "released" in the normal way. But it is entirely possible that a long inhibitory interval totally disrupts the process of naming, so that the target entry must be re-accessed after the signal is presented. Since any re-access would still be frequency-controlled, we would expect a frequency effect to persist across a delay. Hence this finding needs further supporting evidence before it threatens the frequency-ordered search assumption.

[4]This means giving up the notion that semantic priming of the *doctor-nurse* variety can be explained by proposing that *nurse* is identified by a search of words related in meaning to *doctor*, as in Forster (1976).

themselves depends on other factors. As argued in Forster (1985), survival of any access effect depends on a strict sequentiality of processing stages. However, suppose there are two stages which are executed in parallel: one is the access process, and the other is some frequency-independent process that must be completed before the products of access can be acted upon. Once there is *any* stage which cannot proceed until two (or more) preceding stages have been completed, it is possible that the wait/=/time may absorb earlier effects; in particular, any advantage enjoyed by high-frequency words may disappear.

If a departure from strict sequentiality is to give an account of the case at hand, we need a plausible overlapping stage. We suggest that what produces the "wait" is the recovery of the category-rule. If this retrieval operation overlaps with access of the target entry but is not completed until after access has occured, then no frequency effect at all will survive, since the categorization task cannot proceed without the category-rule. To the extent that rule-retrieval takes less time than access of the lowest-frequency words, but more time than access of the highest-frequency words, the frequency effect will be attenuated rather than abolished. (The treatment here is in many ways parallel to the one given earlier for diminished frequency sensitivity in disyllables.)

Clearly, we need far more supporting evidence before this line of argument can be established—and we need to specify the conditions under which rule-retrieval would be slow enough to block the appearance of a frequency effect. But for present purposes, it is enough to point out that it is far too early to close the books on the issue of frequency effects in the categorization task. Balota and Chumbley's results raise interesting questions, but in the absence of a detailed theory of the categorization process, they do not have direct implications for a theory of lexical access.

6. Conclusion: Listening and reading

Our survey of arguments about the processes supporting lexical identification in speech and print leads, in the end, to a conclusion that may best be expressed negatively: and that is, that we find no grounds for supposing that the operations acting on spoken and written inputs differ fundamentally in character.

The very strongest claim—for shared access routines, following from common input descriptions—cannot be supported. But this does not deny the possibility of a commonality of another kind, that of an equivalence of representations and processes, across input modalities. In our assessment of this possibility, we have focused on the mechanism of association, since there is no real specification available of the content of input descriptions, or of the metric for evaluating the match of stimulus tokens to mentally represented types. Certainly there are marked differences, for speech and print, in the claims made about the ways in which candidate mental representations are discovered.

There is undoubtedly an appeal in a proposal that the evident speed and ease of spoken word recognition reflects an identification process being carried out, close to real-time, and we appreciate the concerns that motivate the cohort model of Marslen-Wilson and his colleagues. But, for us, the problems introduced by the model's content-addressability must outweigh the apparent immediacy it gives to the treatment of an on-going speech signal. In the end, arguments against content-addressing count as arguments for the kind of approximate-addressing-plus-search that has been proposed for written stimuli; and the grounds for such arguments are the recognition consequences of input uncertainty or miscoding, as telling in the speech domain as for print.

Finally, a search mechanism allows a placement of the frequency variable where it can act to increase computational efficiency, by putting more frequently accessed items earlier in the search path. We find no reason to suppose that the treatment of spoken words differs from that of written ones in this respect, but note only that the overlay of processes which make up recognition performance may be such as to sometimes obscure frequency-sensitivity.

The conclusion, then, is that the reader's solution suitably fits the listener's problem. However, to put it this way seems clearly to have the matter the wrong way about, given that any speaker's primary competence is in listening rather than reading. Our strong suspicion is that lexical processes for print are as they are, exactly because they have been straightforwardly inherited from the speech domain. Commonality has its basis in borrowing.

References

Balota, D.A., & Chumbley, J.I. (1984). Are lexical decisions a good measure of lexical access? The role of word frequency in the neglected decision stage. *Journal of Experimental Psychology: Human Perception and Performance, 10*, 340–357.

Balota, D.A., & Chumbley, J.I. (1985). The locus of word-frequency effects in the pronunciation task: Lexical access and/or production? *Journal of Memory and Language, 24*, 89–106.

Bednall, E.S. (1978). *Frequency, semantic priming, and ambiguity effects in word recognition.* Unpublished Ph.D. dissertation, Monash University.

Blosfelds, M. (1981). *Visual and auditory word recognition.* Unpublished honours thesis, Monash University.

Bradley, D.C. (1981). Lexical representation of derivational relation. In M. Aronoff & M.-L. Kean (Eds.) *Juncture.* Saratoga, Ca.: Anma Libri.

Chodorow, M.S. (1979). Time compressed speech and the study of lexical and syntactic processing. In W.E. Cooper & E.C.T. Walker (Eds.) *Sentence processing.* Hillsdale, NJ: Erlbaum.

Church, K.W. (1983). Phrase-structure parsing: a method for taking advantage of allophonic constraints. Bloomington, Indiana: Indiana University Linguistics Club.

Cole, R.A., & Jakimik, J. (1980). A model of speech perception. In R.A. Cole (Ed.) *Perception and production of fluent speech*. Hillsdale, NJ: Erlbaum.

Cutler, A., & Norris, D. (1979). Monitoring sentence comprehension. In W.E. Cooper & E.C.T. Walker (Eds.) *Sentence processing*. Hillsdale, NJ: Erlbaum.

Fodor, J.A. (1983). *The modularity of mind*. Cambridge, MA: The MIT Press.

Forster, K.I. (1976). Accessing the mental lexicon. In R.J. Wales & E.C.T. Walker (Eds.) *New approaches to language mechanisms*. Amsterdam: North-Holland.

Forster, K.I. (1979). Levels of processing and the structure of the language processor. In W.E. Cooper & E.C.T. Walker (Eds.) *Sentence processing*. Hillsdale, NJ: Erlbaum.

Forster, K.I. (1985). Lexical acquisition and the modular lexicon. *Language and Cognitive Processes, 1*, 87–108.

Forster, K.I., & Bednall, E.S. (1976). Terminating an exhaustive search in lexical access. *Memory & Cognition, 4*, 53–61.

Forster, K.I. & Chambers, S.M. (1973). Lexical access and naming time. *Journal of Verbal Learning and Verbal Behavior, 12*, 627–635.

Frederiksen, J.R. & Kroll, J.F. (1976). Spelling and sound: Approaches to the internal lexicon. *Journal of Experimental Psychology: Human Perception and Performance, 2*, 361–379.

Glanzer, M., & Ehrenreich, S.L. (1979). Structure and search of the mental lexicon. *Journal of Verbal Learning and Verbal Behaviour, 18*, 381–398.

Gordon, B. (1983). Lexical access and lexical decision: Mechanisms of frequency sensitivity. *Journal of Verbal Learning and Verbal Behavior, 22*, 24–44.

Grosjean, F. (1980). Spoken word recognition processes and the gating paradigm. *Perception and Psychophysics, 28*, 267–283.

Grosjean, F., & Gee, J.P. (1987). Another view of spoken word recognition. *Cognition, 25*, this issue.

Howes, D., & Solomon, R.I. (1951). Visual duration threshold as a function of word probability. *Journal of Experimental Psychology, 41*, 401–410.

James, C.T. (1975). The role of semantic information in lexical decisions. *Journal of Experimental Psychology: Human Perception and Performance, 104*, 130–136.

Kiger, J.I., & Glass, A.L. (1981). Context effects in sentence verification. *Journal of Experimental Psychology: Human Perception and Performance, 7*, 688–700.

Klatt, D.H. (1979). Speech perception: A model of acoustic-phonetic analysis and lexical access. *Journal of Phonetics, 7*, 279–312.

Levelt, W.J.M., & Flores D'Arcais, G.B. (1978). *Studies in the perception of language*. New York: Wiley.

Marcus, S.M. (1984). Recognizing speech: On the mapping from sound to word. In H. Bouma & D.G. Bouwhuis (Eds.) *Attention and performance X: Control of language processes*. Hillsdale, NJ: Erlbaum.

Marslen-Wilson, W.D. (1973). Linguistic structure and speech shadowing at very short latencies. *Nature, 244*, 522–523.

Marslen-Wilson, W.D. (1984). Function and process in spoken word recognition—a tutorial review. In H. Bouma & D.G. Bouwhuis (Eds.) *Attention and performance X: Control of language processes*. Hillsdale, NJ: Erlbaum.

Marslen-Wilson, W.D., & Welsh, A. (1978). Processing interactions and lexical access during word recognition in continuous speech. *Cognitive Psychology, 10*, 29–62.

McCusker, L.X., Hillinger, M.L., & Bias, R.G. (1981). Phonological recoding and reading. *Psychological Bulletin, 89*, 217–245.

McCusker, L.X., Holley-Wilcox, P., & Hillinger, M.L. (1977). Frequency effects in auditory and visual word recognition. Paper presented at the meeting of the Southwestern Psychological Association, Fort Worth, April.

Morton, J. (1969). Interaction of information in word recognition. *Psychological Review, 76*, 163–178.

Morton, J. (1979). Facilitation in word recognition: Experiments causing change in the logogen model. In

P.A. Kolers, M.E. Wrolstad, & M. Bouma (Eds.) *Processing of visible language*. New York: Plenum.

Murray, W.S., & Forster, K.I. (1979). Why the frequency effect is logarithmic. Paper presented at the Second Language & Speech Conference, University of Melbourne, November.

Norris, D. (1983). Word recognition: Context effects without priming. Unpublished paper, MRC Applied Psychology Unit, August.

O'Connor, R.E., & Forster, K.I. (1981). Criterion bias and search sequence bias in word recognition. *Memory & Cognition, 9*, 78–92.

Pisoni, D.B., & Luce, P.A. (1987). Acoustic-phonetic representations in word recognition. *Cognition, 25*, this issue.

Sánchez-Casas, R.M., Bradley, D.C., & García-Albea, J.E. (1984). Syllabification, stress and segmentation in lexical access. Paper presented to the Eleventh Experimental Psychology Conference, Deakin University, May.

Savage, G.R. (1985). Frequency effects in spoken word recognition. Paper presented to the Fifth Language and Speech Conference, University of Melbourne, November.

Savin, H.B. (1963). Word-frequency effect and errors in the perception of speech. *Journal of the Acoustical Society of America, 35*, 200–206.

Schuberth, R.W., Spoehr, K.T., & Lane, D.M. (1981). Effects of stimulus and contextual information on the lexical decision process. *Memory & Cognition, 9*, 68–77.

Seidenberg, M.S. (1985). Constraining models of word recognition. *Cognition, 20*, 169–190.

Seidenberg, M.S., Waters, G.S., Barnes, M.A., & Tanenhaus, M.K. (1984). When does irregular spelling or pronunciation influence word recognition? *Journal of Verbal Learning and Verbal Behavior, 23*, 383–404.

Shipman, D.W., & Zue, V.W. (1982). Properties of large lexicons: Implications for advanced isolated word systems. *Conference Record, IEEE*, 1982 International Conference on Acoustics, Speech and Signal Processing, 546–549.

Swinney, D.A. (1979). Lexical access during sentence comprehension: (Re)Consideration of context effects. *Journal of Verbal Learning and Verbal Behavior, 18*, 645–659.

Taft, M. (1979). Lexical access via an orthographic code: The basic orthographic syllabic structure (BOSS). *Journal of Verbal Learning and Verbal Behavior, 18*, 21–39.

Taft, M., & Forster, K.I. (1975). Lexical storage and retrieval of prefixed words. *Journal of Verbal Learning and Verbal Behavior, 14*, 638–647.

Taft, M., & Forster, K.I. (1976). Lexical storage and retrieval of polymorphic and polysyllabic words. *Journal of Verbal Learning and Verbal Behavior, 15*, 607–620.

Taft, M., & Hambly, G. (1985). Exploring the cohort model of spoken word recognition. Unpublished manuscript, University of New South Wales.

Thorp, G.R. (1986). *The categorization of natural and nominal kind terms*. Unpublished Ph. D. dissertation. Monash University.

Tyler, L., & Marslen-Wilson, M.W. (1981). Quick on the uptake. *New Scientist, 89*, 608–609.

Whaley, C.P. (1978). Word-nonword classification time. *Journal of Verbal Learning and Verbal Behavior, 17*, 143–154.

Résumé

Il existe un point de vue selon lequel des processus fondamentaux différents sont impliqués dans la reconnaissance des mots pour la parole et l'écriture. Nous soutenons que ce point de vue est infondé, et que les modèles de l'accès lexical mis au point pour l'écriture sont aussi appropriés pour la parole, compte tenu des différences évidentes dues aux propriétés physiques des signaux de la parole. Un accent particulier est mis sur le rôle de la fréquence des mots dans le processus de reconnaissance, car cela limite les types de modèles à prendre en considération (par exemple, le modèle de la cohorte). Nous rejetons le point de vue selon lequel il n'existe pas d'effets de fréquence dans la reconnaissance des mots parlés, et nous rejetons aussi le point de vue selon lequel les effets de fréquence dans la reconnaissance des mots écrits ne sont que le reflet de décisions post-accès lexical.

6

Prosodic structure and spoken word recognition

FRANÇOIS GROSJEAN*
Northeastern University

JAMES PAUL GEE
Boston University

Abstract

The aim of this paper is to call attention to the role played by prosodic structure in continuous word recognition. First we argue that the written language notion of the word has had too much impact on models of spoken word recognition. Next we discuss various characteristics of prosodic structure that bear on processing issues. Then we present a view of continuous word recognition which takes into account the alternating pattern of weak and strong syllables in the speech stream. A lexical search is conducted with the stressed syllables while the weak syllables are identified through a pattern-recognition-like analysis and the use of phonotactic and morphonemic rules. We end by discussing the content word vs. function word access controversy in the light of our view.

1. Introduction

The aim of this paper is to present a view of lexical access that takes into account the prosodic structure of spoken language. We first argue that current spoken word recognition models are overly influenced by the written language notion of the word. We then discuss aspects of prosodic structure, and stress the importance that should be given to them in models of language pro-

The authors are co-equal and only the laws of alternation are responsible for the order of the names. Much of the thinking behind this paper was done at the Max Planck Institute, Nijmegen, The Netherlands, while the authors were visiting research fellows there in July 1983. They are grateful to all those in the Institute who made their stay there so fruitful. This work was also supported in part by grants from the National Science Foundation (BNS-8404565), The National Institute of Health (RR 07143) and the Northeastern University RSDF funds. The authors are most grateful to Bill Cooper, Jean-Yves Dommergues, Uli Frauenfelder, Harlan Lane, Jacques Mehler, Joanne Miller and Lorraine Tyler for their helpful comments on a first draft of the paper. Very special thanks also go to three anonymous reviewers who, through their comments, have helped improve this paper. Requests for reprints should be sent to François Grosjean, Department of Psychology, Northeastern University, Boston, MA 02115, U.S.A.

cessing. Next we present a view of lexical access that parses the phonetic and syllabic representation of the speech stream into words. This is done through two types of analysis. On the one hand, the processing system searches for stressed syllables and uses these to initiate a lexical search. On the other hand, the system identifies the weak syllables on either side of the stressed syllable by subjecting them to a pattern-recognition-like analysis and by using the phonotactic and morphophonemic rules of the language. These two types of analysis interact with one another and with other sources of information to segment the speech stream into a string of words. We end by suggesting that the existing distinction between function words and content words in the domain of lexical access can be better understood in terms of the two types of analysis we propose.

2. The problem

Considerable advances have been made in the understanding of the processes that underlie spoken (as opposed to written) word recognition. We know, for example, that certain properties of words affect their recognition: their frequency of use (Howes, 1957; Rubenstein & Pollack, 1963); their length (Grosjean, 1980; Mehler, Segui & Carey, 1968); their phonotactic configuration (Jakimik, 1979) and their uniqueness point (Marslen-Wilson, 1984). We also know that when words are presented in context, their lexical properties interact with various sources of knowledge (linguistic rules, knowledge of the world, discourse, etc.) to speed up or slow down the recognition process (Cole & Jakimik, 1978; Grosjean, 1980; Marslen-Wilson & Welsh, 1978; Morton & Long, 1976; Tyler & Wessels, 1983). The exact nature of the "interaction" between the properties of the words and these sources of knowledge remains to be described adequately, and the controversy concerning the moment at which "top-down" information enters the lexical access process has yet to be resolved (Forster, 1976; Marslen-Wilson & Welsh, 1978; Morton, 1969; Swinney, 1982). One conclusion that emerges from this research is that recognizing a word may not be a simple mapping between its acoustic-phonetic properties and its entry in the mental lexicon (although, see Klatt, 1979). Instead, it may well be a rather complex process that involves various narrowing-in and monitoring stages, correcting strategies, post-access decision stages, and even look-ahead and look-back operations (Grosjean, 1980; Marslen-Wilson & Welsh, 1978; Nooteboom, 1981; Swinney, 1982).

Despite these advances in the field of word recognition, there is one problem that may be undermining current research—it is the over importance given to the written language notion of the word. Many researchers have assumed that the written word has an acoustic-phonetic correlate in the speech stream and that it is this "unit" that is involved in the recognition process. Whether there is direct access from the spectra (as in Klatt, 1979) or intermediary stages of representation that involve linguistic units such as the phoneme or the syllable (as in most other models), the assumption has been that the domain over which processing takes place is the spoken analog of the written dictionary word (the WD word). We agree that the final outcome of spoken word recognition is the stored lexical item in the internal lexicon (an item that shares many characteristics with the WD word)[1] but we question whether, in the earlier stages of lexical access, the WD word plays the important role many have assumed: either as a "unit of processing" or as the domain over which lexical access takes place.

Several reasons can explain the importance given to the WD word in the lexical access of spoken words. First, spoken word recognition research has always lagged behind the research on written word recognition and has therefore borrowed from it its unit of study—the WD word. Because written language is ever present in our everyday life, it is all too easy to think of spoken language as a concatenation of individual words, even though the actual acoustic-phonetic stream of spoken language does not reflect this. Second, research has usually investigated the recognition process of single words, presented in the speech stream or in their canonical form, and not the operations involved in continuous lexical access. The consequence of this has been to strengthen the importance given to the individual WD word during the recognition process. Third, the experimental tasks used in spoken word recognition are too often biased towards single WD-like words; thus, word monitoring and lexical decision, among other tasks, force the listener to focus on single words; this, in turn, encourages us to think that the human processing system may in fact use the WD word as a unit or domain of processing. Finally, many of the words that are used in experiments are content words (as opposed to function words) and have few, if any, inflections. One consequence of this is that they are often recognized before their acoustic-phonetic offset, and this result reinforces the view that the spoken word recognition

---

[1]Even this question is more complex than it might seem at first. In the case of words put together by productive morphology, the final outcome of spoken word recognition may not be the word itself but a set of morphemes. These morphemes have to be related to each other in some fashion—often hierarchically with one morpheme being taken as the "head" around which the rest of the word is organized—before the whole word is "recognized". Particularly interesting problems arise in the case of polysynthetic languages, where words are made up of large numbers of morphemes put together in quite productive ways and where sentences contain few words (Comrie, 1981). For the hierarchical structure of words in English, see Selkirk (1982) and Williams (1981).

system is WD word driven, from the segmentation of the speech stream to the final access of the lexicon.

The importance given to WD words in lexical access research has led to a number of critical assumptions about spoken word recognition. One that is assumed by many researchers is that words are recognized sequentially, left to right, one word at a time. Cole and Jakimik (1979, pp. 133–134) state this explicitly when they write:

> Speech is processed sequentially, word by word ... the words in an utterance are recognized one after another ... listeners know where words begin and end by recognizing them in order.

Likewise, Marslen-Wilson and Welsh (1978), Morton (1969) and Forster (1976), in their different models of word recognition, assume word by word processing. Thus, in the cohort model, the first segment of a WD word plays the critical role of activating a cohort of candidates; in the logogen model, each WD word has a logogen, and in the bin model, one accesses the master lexicon by first finding an entry for the WD word in question. There is ample evidence that many words are indeed recognized sequentially (Grosjean, 1980; Marslen-Wilson & Tyler, 1980; Tyler and Wessels, 1983), but as we will argue below, this may not be the case for ALL words, and word by word recognition models will have to account for this. (Note that more recent models, like that of McClelland & Elman, 1986, do not make the sequentiality assumption.)

Other assumptions fall out of this WD word by WD word approach. One is that the beginning of the word is critical in its recognition (but what happens if the system does not know it is dealing with the beginning of a word? See Marslen-Wilson & Welsh, 1978; Cole & Jakimik, 1979, for a discussion of this assumption), and another assumption is that words are recognized at that point in their acoustic-phonetic configuration where they distinguish themselves from every other word (again proposed by Marslen-Wilson & Welsh, and Cole & Jakimik). The above assumptions may be correct for many content words (especially if they occur in the appropriate context) but may not always apply to certain monosyllabic and low frequency words, unstressed function words, words stressed on the second syllable, and words with prefixes and suffixes.

One need only examine the spectrogram or waveform of an utterance to be reminded of the continuous nature of the speech stream and of the ever present segmentation problem faced by the speech perception and word recognition systems. There is, in fact, evidence in the literature which shows that WD words are not all recognized one at a time in a sequential manner. In a set of classic studies, Pollack and Pickett (1963, 1964) found, for example, that words extracted from the speech stream were not easily recognized by themselves. Only 55% of the words were identified correctly when presented in isolation, and this percentage only reached 70–80% accuracy when the words were presented in two or three word samples. Grosjean (1980) found similar results in a gating study when he extracted WD words from the speech stream and presented them to subjects from left to right in increments of increasing duration: only 50% of the one syllable low frequency words (and 75% of the high frequency words) were guessed correctly by 5 or more of the 8 subjects used. (See Cotton & Grosjean, 1984, and Tyler & Wessels, 1985, for evidence showing that the gating paradigm shares many of the characteristics of other on-line tasks.) These studies appear to show, therefore, that not all WD words are recognized before their acoustic offset, a claim that is made (explicitly or implicitly) by many current models of word recognition.

To show that these results were not due to the fact that the words were extracted from their natural context, Grosjean (1985) constructed sentences of the type:

(1)   I saw the bun in the store
(2)   I saw the plum on the tree

and gated from the beginning of the object noun ("bun", "plum") all the way to the end of the sentence. The subjects were asked to listen to "I saw the", guess the word being presented after it, indicate how confident they were of their guess, and finish off the sentence. Whereas all two- and three-syllable words were isolated (guessed correctly) before their acoustic offset, only 45% of the one-syllable words were identified correctly. The remainder were isolated during the following preposition or even during the article after that. An examination of the point at which subjects felt perfectly confident of their guess confirmed the isolation results. Whereas 80% of the two- and three-syllable words were given perfect confidence ratings before their acoustic offset, only 5% of the one-syllable words managed this; 50% were given perfect ratings during the next word, 20% had to wait for the following article, and 25% were only confirmed during the perception of the following noun—some 500 ms after the onset of the stimulus object noun! An examination of the erroneous guesses proposed by subjects before they isolated the appropriate word confirmed the isolation times and the confidence ratings. When presented with the acoustic information of the next WD word (the preposition), subjects often thought they were dealing with the second syllable of the stimulus word (e.g., "bunny", "bonnet" for "bun in"; "boring" for "boar in"; "plumber" for "plum on", etc.). These erroneous guesses remind one of the slips of the ear reported in the literature. For example, Bond and Garnes

(1980) state that some 70% of the multiple word slips they found concerned word boundary shifts (an ice bucket → a nice bucket), word boundary deletions (ten year party → tenure party), and word boundary additions (descriptive linguistics → the script of linguistics).

The WD word (as a linguistic unit in its own right, as an ensemble of smaller linguistic units, or as an acoustic-phonetic segment) may not after all be the ideal domain over which lexical processing takes place. WD words are rarely delineated clearly in the acoustic-phonetic stream and many may not always be processed by the listener before their acoustic offset. Some form of the WD word must be stored in the lexicon (but see footnote 1) and as such is the final product of the word recognition process (as listeners, we need to know which words have been said), but we question whether the early stages of lexical access involve strictly left to right, WD word by WD word processes. The problem is of course compounded when we reflect on how function words, which are often short, unstressed and reduced phonetically, are recognized on-line. It is doubtful whether strings of unstressed function words such as "could have been", "to the", "I'd have" are in fact recognized WD word by WD word, in a left to right sequential manner. Similar doubts can be expressed about content words that have undergone "deaccenting" in discourse context (Ladd, 1980).

Before presenting a view of word recognition that puts less stress on the left to right, WD word by WD word, process, it is important to discuss certain characteristics of the prosodic (phonological) structure of spoken language that may well play an important role in lexical access. This we do in the section below.

3. Prosodic structure and phonological words

Recent prosodic (phonological) theories of language propose that the utterance has a suprasegmental, hierarchical organization defined in terms of a metrical tree with binary branching and strong/weak prominence relations. These prominence relations are defined for all the elements that make up the units of the prosodic structure, from the syllable through the word and phrase to the utterance as a whole (Liberman, 1975; Liberman & Prince, 1977; Selkirk, 1978, 1980a,b).

According to one view of prosodic structure (Culicover & Rochemont, 1983; Gee & Grosjean, 1983; Nespor & Vogel, 1982, 1983; Selkirk, 1978, 1980a,b), at the lower level of the hierarchy, weak and strong syllables group together into feet. Feet in turn bundle into phonological words which may, or may not, correspond to traditional WD words. Thus, in the sentence:

(3)   John//has been avidly/ reading//the latest/news// from home

we note that some phonological words (marked off by one or two slashes) correspond to WD words (John, reading, news) but that others do not and instead are made up of two or three WD words (has been avidly, the latest, from home). In the latter case, unstressed function words have been appended to stressed content words.[2]

Phonological words, to which we will return below, bundle into phonological phrases which comprise all the material up to and including the head of a syntactic phrase. (Phonological phrases are marked off with two slashes in sentence 3.)[3] Of interest here is that phonological phrases are not always constituents in syntactic structure. Thus, in the above example, the phonological phrase boundaries after "reading" and "news" occur in the middle of syntactic phrases, and the phonological phrases "has been avidly reading" and "the latest news" are not syntactic constituents. Phonological phrases themselves bundle into intonational phrases. We should note that there is a great deal of freedom as to what can be an intonational phrase as this is contingent in part on the information that is put into focus in the discourse (Gee & Grosjean, 1983; Selkirk, 1984).

In a recent study, Gee and Grosjean (1983) showed that the segmentation that takes place during oral reading and that is reflected by silent pauses, can best be accounted for by prosodic structure: phonological words are separated from one another by few (if any) pauses which in turn are very short;

---

[2]The entity we are calling a "phonological word" is not given a uniform name, description, or treatment in the literature. In Selkirk (1978), a phonological rule, the "Monosyllable Rule", operating with the phonological phrase as its domain, causes monosyllabic words which are weak (unstressed) and which correspond to non-lexical items in the syntax (function words), to lose their word status at the prosodic level. In this case, they become attached to an adjacent strong syllable (the stressed syllable of some content word). They are thus turned into simple weak syllables, and undergo the phonological rules that other weak syllables undergo (e.g., the weak syllables of multisyllabic words). For a detailed characterization of phonological words, also see Kean (1979, 1980) and Garrett and Kean(1980).

[3]The principles determining the boundaries of phonological phrases are discussed in detail in Culicover and Rochemont (1983), Gee and Grosjean (1983), Nespor and Vogel (1979, 1983), and Selkirk (1979, 1980a,b). Phonological phrases represent phonological (in fact, prosodic) readjustments of syntactic structure. In syntactic theory, any phrase is defined in terms of its head (a noun phrase is headed by a noun, a verb phrase is headed by a verb, a prepositional phrase is headed by a preposition, and so forth). A phonological phrase is made up of all the material up to and including the head of a syntactic phrase. Material following the head normally constitutes a separate phonological phrase. There are several provisos however. First, at the level at which phonological phrases are assigned in the grammar, prepositions no longer count as heads of their phrases, since they are functors and have been destressed (or assigned no stress); thus the noun complement following the preposition serves as the final boundary of the phonological phrase. Second, given the way stressless items attach to stressed ones in English, unstressed object pronouns attach to the verb and become part of a phonological phrase with it (e.g., "him" is part of the second phrase in "The girl/ has hit him"). See Gee and Grosjean (1983) for suggestions about the role such details play in the production system.

phonological phrases are separated from one another by more and longer pauses, and intonational phrases are marked off by more numerous and longer pauses. Syntactic structure, with its traditional units (the WD word, the phrase, the clause) could not account for the pausing data as well. The hierarchical "performance" trees that were constructed from the pause data were often quite different from the syntactic trees but were practically identical to the prosodic trees.

Recent developments of prosodic theory have important implications for psycholinguistics, and models of language production, perception and comprehension will need to pay more attention to the prosodic structure of spoken language utterances. In the domain of lexical access, models will need to take into account prosodic units such as the syllable, the foot and the phonological word (Kean, 1979, 1980, for example). The unit that is of primary interest to us at this time is the phonological word. Although we will *not* argue that it is the unit of lexical access (we only have evidence for it as a unit of production), we will present certain of its characteristics that are important to understand our view of spoken word recognition. The phonological word is a tightly bound phonological unit that is made up of one stressed syllable and a number of weak (unstressed) syllables that are phonologically linked to it. The unit is the domain of various phonological rules, many of which tend to assimilate and blend sounds together (Zwicky, 1977, 1982). The weak syllables in the phonological word may be the unstressed syllables of a content word (e.g., "poral" in "temporal"), affixes attached to a stem ("un" and "ful" in "unhelpful"), clitics attached to a content word ("j' " in the French "j'peux"), reduced functors lexically attached to a content word ("have to" = "hafta", "out of" = "outta"), or function words phonologically linked to content words ("a" in "a dog", "him" in "hit him", etc).

What becomes clear from a study of phonological word is that speech is made up of alternations of weak and strong syllables where the weak syllables are always linked to strong syllables in rule governed ways. Thus certain syllables in the speech stream are more *salient* than others. In English, this saliency is marked by a complex interaction of pitch, duration, and amplitude, for which the term "stress" is often used (Bolinger, 1958a, 1965, 1981; Chomsky & Halle, 1968; Halle & Keyser, 1971). In other languages, saliency is physically realized in different ways (e.g., pitch accent, tone, characteristics of syllable structure, etc.). Salient syllables are realized in words that tend to carry the least redundant and most contentful meaning in a sentence (Bolinger, 1958b, 1961, 1965, 1972; Ladd, 1980). It is interesting to note that in historical change, words that carry less informational saliency tend to lose some of their phonological substance, eventually becoming function words or affixes to other words (Givon, 1975). Such historical changes give rise to a greater degree of alternation between more salient and less salient syllables, both in terms of information and in terms of physical realization. We note also that in early child language, and in the early stages of pidgin languages, nearly every word tends to carry stress. As these language forms develop, however, redundant or less salient information tends to get de-stressed; thus, for example, children in normal first language acquisition eventually add more function words, contract non-contracted forms, and de-stress redundant or "given" content words (Bickerton, 1981; Givon, 1979; Slobin, 1977, 1982). In every instance of developed language, then, we find alternations between elements that carry informational saliency and those that do not, and this alternation is often reflected in the speech stream by some form of prosodic marking of weak and strong syllables. It is our belief that these design features of human language should be integrated into models of language processing. In the next section, we propose a view of lexical access that attempts to do just that.[4]

4. A different view of continuous lexical access

A few points need to be made before presenting our view of lexical access. The first is that it is still very general and thus many aspects of it remain unspecified. The aim behind our presentation is not to argue for the replacement of better established models of word recognition with our own view, but rather to invite researchers to consider a proposal for lexical access that takes into account both the prosodic structure of language and the fact that word recognition may not be a strictly left to right, WD word by WD word process. The second point is that little direct and non-controversial evidence for our view is yet available. We will nevertheless present some indirect empirical data to support it. A third point is that several researchers, among them Cutler (1976) and Bradley (1980), have proposed very similar views of lexical access (see below); this makes our view much less "extreme" than some might think at first.

The approach we propose is basically one that parses the string of weak and strong syllables in the speech stream and that makes contact with the WD-like words in the lexicon. The analyses we will describe work on the output of the speech perception system which comes in the form of a phonetic

---

[4]The particular way in which we will relate lexical access to weak-strong prosodic relations does not give any grounds for choosing between metrical theory (Hayes, 1980, 1982; Kiparsky, 1979; Liberman & Prince, 1977; McCarthy, 1979; Safir, 1979; Selkirk, 1978, 1980b) and grid theory (Prince, 1983; Selkirk, 1984). For convenience we talk throughout in terms of metrical theory.

string marked in terms of weak and strong syllables. Thus unlike Klatt's (1979) model which does lexical access directly from the spectra, we propose an intermediary representation between the acoustic string and the stored lexical item: it is a string of phonetic segments grouped into syllables marked as weak or strong.[5] We have little to say at this time about the mapping that takes place between the acoustic stream and this intermediate level of representation. What we are concerned with here is the process that parses this representation in such a way as to ultimately make contact with the lexicon. Our view is as follows. On the one hand, stressed syllables (and only they) are used to initiate a lexical search. On the other hand, and concurrently, the weak syllables located on either side of the stressed syllable (functors, affixes, weak syllables of content words) are identified by means of a pattern-recognition-like analysis and with the help of the listener's knowledge of phonotactic and morphophonemic rules.

The actual work that is done with the stressed syllable during the lexical search is as yet unclear: there may be cohort activation, active search of a word, word detector triggering, etc. One possibility that comes to mind is that a series of cohorts are activated where the stressed syllable in question is the first syllable of a subset of candidates, the second syllable of another series of candidates, the third syllable of yet another subset, etc. The information that comes back from the lexical search will be used in two ways: it will help the system recognize the word which contains the stressed syllable and it will play a role in identifying the weak syllables (functors, affixes, etc.) on either side of the stressed syllable.

As a lexical search is taking place with the stressed syllable, the system is trying to identify the weak syllables around it. The identification process is done by bringing to bear the phonotactic and morphophonemic rules of the language as well as by doing a pattern-recognition-like analysis of weak (and weak-strong) syllable groups. We hypothesize here that the listener will be helped by his/her knowledge of well learned syllable patterns such as sequences of function words or beginnings of phonological words (for example, /ðə-----/, /ən----/, /təðə-----/, /aɪdəv------/). The system will also use all the information that comes back from the lexical search that is being conducted with the stressed syllable.

We should note at this point that the analysis of weak syllables may at

---

[5]We should point out that this intermediate representation need not always be as rich as this. In fact, a representation in terms of sonority of segments, syllable structure, and weak-strong relations would already be quite rich. We should further note that as our view becomes more refined, it may well use the hierarchical structure imposed on weak-strong relations by current metrical theories to much greater purpose than we do here.

times be able to identify certain functors[6] before getting feedback from the lexical search on the candidates containing the stressed syllable and thus indirectly on the unstressed syllables surrounding it. This is the case, for example, when the rules of the language mandate a particular function word or when the functors to the left and right of the stressed syllable cannot make up a possible WD word with it (note, for example, that /ð/ as in "the" or "this" only occurs in functors). This may also be the case with strings of functors that have rather precise and well-known phonetic patterns such as "could have been" (/kudəbɪn/), "I would have" (/aɪdəv/); these may be identified as they are heard. Thus, there is clearly a top-down aspect to this weak syllable analysis. Knowledge of the phonotactic rules of the language gives rise to decisions about which weak syllables may go with stressed syllables and which may not. Of course, this process can sometimes misinform the lexical search. For example, in the "bun in" → "bunny" example given above, the process sees /bʌnɪn/ as a possible phonotactic combination in English and tells the lexical search (working with /bʌn/) that it is a possible candidate (along with /bʌni/). It is only feedback from the lexical search that tells the system that there is no word that corresponds to /bʌnɪn/, and therefore that two words are involved: "bun" and "in".[7]

The constant interaction between these two types of analysis—the analysis conducted on the weak syllables and the lexical search taking place with the stressed syllable—and the ever present information of other sources of information (the listener's knowledge of the world and of the immediate situation,

---

[6]Fries (1952) contains one of the classic discussions of function words and content words. Fries points out that function words (he identifies 154 in English) must be recognized in a different way than content words, due to the role they play in the sentence. What at the level of syntax amounts to a difference of function translates at the level of prosodic structure into a difference of stress (or saliency). In both cases, we may have something more akin to a continuum than a categorical distinction. See the discussion in Section 5 below.

[7]It is important to realize that even with partial information about phonological segments, a system utilizing its linguistic knowledge of phonological structure (at the segment, syllable, foot, and phonological levels) can make good predictions about possible word boundaries. Lynn Frazier (1987, this issue), utilizing work by Taft (forthcoming) and Selkirk (1980a), demonstrates how information about the sonority of segments, syllable structure, and phonological word structure predicts, for example, that a string of syllables consisting of "strong-weak-strong-strong" will be initially parsed as two words, the first word having the structure "strong-weak-strong" and the second being a strong monosyllable. In addition, she points out that for such a system to work, it need only have partial information about segments: syllabic parsing (in the sense of parsing the string into syllables) "could proceed before the identity of the segment has been established assuming that the sonority relations between that segment and adjacent segments may be determined in the absence of a complete feature specification (e.g., if the place of articulation of a segment was still unspecified)." It is interesting to note also that sonority is just a weak-strong relation defined internal to a syllable, as stress is a weak-strong relation defined above the level of the syllable. Our hypothesis then is that the process analyzing weak syllables (or groups of weak and strong syllables) is computing phonological structure in order to gain information about boundaries and to aid the lexical search being conducted with the strong syllable.

the rules of the language, the discourse, etc.) will allow the appropriate segmentation of the speech stream into a string of WD-like words.

Two points need to be made at this time. First, whereas words which contain a stressed syllable are recognized as a consequence of a complex lexical search (involving the lexicon at all stages of the search), unstressed words (and especially unstressed functors) are identified in a more direct manner. It is only when these words have been (partly?) identified that direct contact is made with the lexicon in order to obtain the information needed about them (meaning, syntactic class, subcategorization information, etc.). Functors are probably listed in the lexicon by themselves as well as in the general lexicon (see Bradley, 1978); depending on their saliency, they will be "looked up" in the functor lexicon or go through the more complex lexical search (this point is discussed in Section 5).[8] Second, it is hypothesized that the processing that is done with the stressed syllable is, in a sense, "more demanding" than the analysis that is taking place concurrently on the weak syllables. This is because stressed syllable processing involves lexical search, with all the complexities that are linked to it (such as narrowing-in on the appropriate candidate), whereas weak syllable analysis does not.

To illustrate our proposal, we will consider the hypothetical processing of the sentence:

(4)   I put the bun in a bag

$$\text{w \quad s \quad w \quad s \quad w w \quad s}$$
/aɪ pʊt ðə bʌn ɪn ə bæg/

As soon as the listener perceives the first syllable /aɪ/, some analysis is done on it immediately. It may not be identified at this point as the various sources of information do not yet have much to offer. As this analysis is taking place, the system finds the first stressed syllable /pʊt/ and uses it to initiate a lexical search which activates all the words that have /pʊt/ as a stressed syllable. The search comes up with a number of candidates but none that begin with /aɪpʊt/

---

[8]If function words are listed separately in the lexicon, or in a functor lexicon, in addition to also being listed in the general lexicon, then they do not have to run against non-function word candidates in any search process. This is one of several ways to operationalize the notion of "directly recognizing" function words. It is interesting to add that researchers on discourse (Chafe, 1980, for example) have argued for some form of buffer that contains words (or concepts) that are in focus, that have recently been used, or that constitute common knowledge that is currently in the foreground of attention. When such items are mentioned, they usually pronominalize or delete altogether, but when they do not, they carry little or no stress and low pitch (as in Ladd's, 1980, examples of "destressing"); see for example, Clark and Haviland (1977), Chafe (1980, 1984), Heim (1982), and Kamp (1982). Thus, in addition or along with a function word lexicon, there may be a discourse buffer containing currently focused words. When such words are used, they do not have to compete with the whole lexicon for access, but only with the other words on the list.

and this information is used by the system along with its linguistic knowledge and pattern recognition information to segment /aɪ/ from /pʊt/ and to identify /aɪ/ as the pronoun "I". Information from the lexicon on words that begin with /pʊt/ interacts with the bottom-up, acoustic-phonetic, information as well as phonological, syntactic and semantic knowledge to segment /pʊt/ from /ðə/: no content word in English corresponds to /pʊtðə/, /pʊt/ is a perfectly good word in the growing context, /ðə/ is a very good continuation, etc. The system also knows that no polysyllabic word starts with /ðə/ and that it is therefore most probably the definite article "the". The system finds the next stressed syllable, /bʌn/, and initiates a second lexical search which will use all sources of information to isolate a word that corresponds to the appropriate form class and context. Because the syllable after /bʌn/ is /ɪn/, the system considers words like "bun", but also "bonnet" and "bunny" before appropriately segmenting "bun" and "in" when the nasal information in "in" reduces the possibilities. All this gives the system more syntactic, semantic, pragmatic and prosodic information to help predict and analyze the upcoming phonetic information. The /ə/ before /bæg/ is probably identified and segmented off before the stressed syllable is reached (based on phonotactic constraints, syntactic rules, etc.) but its status as an indefinite article is only confirmed when information comes back from the lexicon: /əbæg/ is not a content word and therefore the listener must be dealing with "a" and "bag".

As noted above, both Cutler (1976) and Bradley (1980) have made very similar proposals to ours. Cutler (1976) suggests that when a stressed syllable is identified, the sentence processor will locate in the lexicon the word of which it is a part, using information about the syllable itself but also about the unstressed syllables immediately before and after it. A number of possible matches may then be found and compared with the (incomplete) information about the unstressed syllables, and this before a choice is made. Once the match is decided upon, the word boundaries can be drawn and the preceding and succeeding words looked up. Cutler goes on to say that since some of the unstressed portions may themselves be words, it follows that words may not necessarily be processed in a left-to-right order. Bradley (1980) has made a very similar proposal. In it she claims that the stressed syllable is picked out of the speech stream and is used to search the lexicon. The candidates are selected on the basis of this syllable and are evaluated by how well they fit with the elements that appear to their left and right.

It is interesting to note that this view of word recognition makes certain predictions about the time it will take to monitor for words in various environments. For example, subjects should be very rapid at monitoring for functions words that do not make up a possible word with the preceding content word (e.g., "him" in "asked him"); they should be much slower when the two make up a possible word ("her" in "got her", in certain dialects, at least), and they should be slower still when the two words make up an actual word, but not the one being monitored for (e.g., "her" in "send her", which may be heard as "center" or "sender"). Some very preliminary data we have obtained would seem to show that such predictions may well be correct.

These first thoughts on a different view of lexical access are of course quite sketchy and general. We do not, for instance, detail how actual content word recognition takes place at the time the lexical search is initiated with the stressed syllable. This is because current models have emphasized this very point and much is known about content word narrowing-in (see Grosjean, 1980; Marslen-Wilson & Welsh, 1978; Nooteboom, 1981; Salasoo & Pisoni, 1985; Tyler & Wessels, 1983 for instance). Rather, we wish to emphasize those points that appear newer to us. First, lexical access is not a WD word by WD word, strictly left to right process (although it might appear to be under certain conditions). Rather, it is a process that uses the prosodic structure of the speech stream and puts particular emphasis on stressed syllables. (Note that this may be a useful approach both in analytic and polysynthetic languages.) Second, two types of analysis appear to take place—a lexical search using the stressed syllable, and a weak syllable analysis. These analyses interact constantly with one another and with the other sources of information (grammatical, situational, etc.) to help segment the speech stream. Third, the system is very much a feed-forward, feed-back system, where there are constant adjustments being made to early and/or partial analyses and constant prediction being made on what is to come.

Although we have little direct evidence for the view we propose, it is interesting to note that research both on speech production and speech perception has constantly emphasized the importance of the stressed syllable. This is precisely what we would expect if our view has any reality whatsoever. Phonetic analyses have shown the stressed syllable to be longer than unstressed syllables, and to have higher pitch and greater amplitude (Lehiste, 1970; Umeda, 1977). The perceptual consequence of this is that stressed syllables are more easily perceived in noise (Kozhevnikov & Chistovitch, 1965, for instance) and may override segmental cues in word identification. It has also been found that the reaction times to the first phoneme of stressed syllables are significantly faster than to phonemes similarly located in unstressed syllables (Cutler & Foss, 1977). Also, mispronunciations are detected more often when the altered segment occurs in stressed syllables than in unstressed syllables (Cole & Jakimik, 1978). And because the stressed syllables of a sentence are component parts of a hierarchical prosodic structure (Liberman & Prince, 1977), their temporal location can be predicted in advance, and this in turn is reflected in various monitoring tasks (Cutler, 1976; Shields, McHugh, &

Martin, 1974). We should note also that slips of the ear very rarely contain mistakes involving stressed syllables (in particular, the vowel of the syllable is seldom wrong) and this has led researchers (Bond & Garnes, 1980, for instance) to propose speech perception heuristics of the type: "Pay attention to stress"; "Pay attention to stressed vowels", etc.). Finally, Huttenlocher and Zue (1983) have found that when words are classified according to their stress pattern and to a broad phonetic transcription of their stressed syllable only, then 17% of these words are uniquely specified in the lexicon, 38% belong to a class of 5 or less and the average class size is 3.8. We can conclude from this that the stress pattern of a word, and the phonetics of its stressed syllable, are valuable information for the lexical access system; it would be surprising if it did not make use of it!

Thus, past and current research in the production and perception of language points to the stressed syllable as an important unit in processing. Given the evidence that stress is crucial to processing, it is interesting to conjecture why it has been ignored in almost all theories of lexical access. The reason, as we suggested above, is that psycholinguistic theories have almost always been constructed in terms of syntactic units—words and phrases. Once we think in terms of prosodic units, then our notion of the word and the phrase change, as does our view of processing.

5. The function word vs. content word issue

The distinction between function words and content words has played an important role in recent psycholinguistics (see, e.g., Bradley, 1978; Bradley, Garrett, & Zurif, 1979; Friederici & Schoenle, 1980; Garrett, 1975, 1976, 1978, 1980; Segui, Mehler, Frauenfelder, & Morton, 1982; Swinney, Zurif, & Cutler, 1980), and it is therefore important to examine it in light of our view of lexical access. We wish to argue that the distinction between the two types of words is not as relevant during lexical access as was once thought; rather a function word will be processed differently depending on its information load, its degree of stress, its length, and so on. The more salient a function word becomes (through slower and more careful pronunciation or through increased stress), the more it will be accessed like a content word. It is not that function words are processed one way and content words another, but rather that stressed and unstressed syllables are processed differently. In fact, Cutler and Foss (1977) have shown evidence for this in a phoneme monitoring task: they found no reaction time differences between function and content words when stress was held constant, showing thereby that form class itself is not the critical factor; it is the stress on the item that is. Note also that Kean (1979) makes precisely the same arguments in her work on aphasia.[9]

Some pilot data we have obtained appear to show that there is a strong negative correlation between the duration of a monosyllabic function word and its monitoring time: long functions words (such as "some") take less time to monitor than short function words (such as "a" and "of"). But duration is in part dependent on the information load carried by a word; the more important the content of the word and the less redundant its information in context, the more salient it will be at the prosodic level (in terms of pitch, amplitude and duration), and hence the more quickly it will be monitored. Thus, the information load of a word in various contexts will determine in large part its saliency. In turn this saliency will determine which of two sorts of analyses it falls under: whether it will be accessed in depth through the mental lexicon, or whether it will be subject to a weak syllable analysis. This implies that in a rich enough context, even content words might be redundant enough to lose saliency, and in other sorts of context, function words might become informationally important, bear stress, and be accessed through the main lexicon.

It is important to note, therefore, that there is no clear two-way distinction between function words and content words, but rather a continuum of cases ranging from forms with full contentful meaning that bear a lot of stress, to forms that carry less content but more grammatical meaning, and thus bear less stress. Forms towards the more contentful end of the continuum tend to retain more phonological identity in the speech stream, while forms towards the grammatical end tend to retain less phonological identity and to contract tighter bonds with the stressed forms they are phonologically linked to. Table 1 presents a continuum of forms that range from those that carry more information, more stress, and retain more phonological identity, to forms that carry less information, less stress and retain less phonological identity. The lower the form on the list, the more likely it is to "merge" with a form that carries stress. Although the table represents the unmarked cases, it is clear that particular contexts may render a more contentful form redundant, and a more grammatical form informationally important, thus changing their prosodic characteristics.

---

[9]It should also be noted that function words sometimes have different functions and meanings when they are stressed. For example, the differences between stressed and unstressed "some" and "many" (often represented as "sm" versus "some" by linguists) is well known. "Sm" is an indefinite plural article whereas "some" is usually a restricted existential quantifier (for differences in their behavior, and other such pairs, see Milsark, 1977).

There appears to be no principled way, therefore, to break the continuum into categories so as to obtain two classes of "words": function and content. It is our contention that a view of the lexical access process based on the prosodic structure of the speech stream can best account for the full range of cases in the table. They will fall under one or the other of our two types of analysis (and even under both at times) depending on the context they are in. The important distinction is not one between content and function words per se, but one between salient (strong) versus non-salient (weak) syllables and the two types of analysis they involve.

Table 1.   *A continuum of cases going from forms that typically carry more informa-tion, more stress, and retain more phonological identity to forms that carry less specific information, less stress, and retain less phonological identity. The lower a form on the list, the more likely it is to merge, in a more or less tight phonological bond, with a form that carries stress. However, in context, any form can be destressed or stressed*

1. Content words carrying new information in context
2. Content words carrying old information in context (destressed)
3. Numerals, quantifiers, adverbs
4. Stressed "some" and "many"
5. Unstressed "some" and "many"
6. Unreduced auxiliary verbs
7. Full pronouns
8. Reduced auxiliaries
9. Reduced pronouns
10. Bisyllabic prepositions
11. Content prepositions
12. Grammatical prepositions (case markers)
13. Demonstrative articles
14. The definite article "the"
15. The indefinite article "a(n)"
16. The infinitive marker "to"
17. The syntactically determined preposition "of"
18. Contracted forms, like "hadda" or "fronta"
19. Prefixes/suffixes
20. Inflectional morphemes
21. Secondary stressed syllables of polysyllabic words
22. Syllables with unreduced vowels in polysyllabic words
23. Unstressed syllables in polysyllabic words

6. Concluding remarks

The basic aim of our paper was to call attention to the important role that the prosodic structure of spoken language may play during the recognition of words in continuous speech. The strong influence of written language on current views of spoken language processing has led to the development of models of lexical access that are giving too much importance to the written notion of the word. Recent developments in prosodic theory encourage us to pay attention to prosodic units and to the alternation of weak and strong syllables in the speech stream. Our view of continuous spoken word recognition is an attempt to integrate the prosodic structure of language into a processing model. In addition, it helps explain why words are not all recognized sequentially, one after the other, and it has interesting implications for the controversy that surrounds the function versus content word issue. Our view may well be wrong, but it will have served its purpose if it forces us to take into account prosodic structure in our models of spoken language processing.

References

Bickerton, D. (1981). *Roots of language*. Ann Arbor: Karoma Publishers.

Bolinger, D. (1958a). A theory of pitch accent in English. *Word, 14*, 109–149.

Bolinger, D. (1958b). Stress and information. *American Speech, 33*, 5–20.

Bolinger, D. (1961). Contrastive accent and contrastive stress. *Language, 37*, 83–69.

Bolinger, D. (1965). *Forms of English: Accent, morpheme, order*. Cambridge, MA: Harvard University Press.

Bolinger, D. (1972). Accent is predictable (if you're a mind reader). *Language, 48*, 633–644.

Bolinger, D. (1981). Two kinds of vowels, two kinds of rhythm. Bloomington, Indiana: Indiana University Linguistics Club.

Bond, Z.S., & Garnes, S. (1980). Misperceptions of fluent speech. In R. Cole (Ed.) *Perception and production of fluent speech*. Hillsdale, NJ: Erlbaum.

Bradley, D. (1978). *Computational distinctions of vocabulary type*. Unpublished doctoral thesis, MIT.

Bradley, D. (1980). Lexical representation of derivational relation. In M. Aronoff & M.–L. Kean (Eds.) *Juncture*. Saratoga, CA: Anma Libri.

Bradley, D., Garrett, M.F., & Zurif, E.B. (1979). Syntactic deficits in Broca's aphasics. In D. Caplan (Ed.) *Biological studies of mental processes*. Cambridge, Mass.: MIT Press.

Chafe, W.L. (1980). The deployment of consciousness in the production of a narrative. In W.L. Chafe (Ed.) *The Pear Stories: Cognitive, cultural, and linguistic aspects of narrative production*. Norwood, NJ: Ablex.

Chafe, W. (1984). Cognitive constraints on information flow. *Berkeley Cognitive Science Report No. 26*. Berkeley Cognitive Science Program, Institute of Cognitive Studies, University of California at Berkeley.

Chomsky, N., & Halle, M. (1968). *The sound pattern of English*. New York: Harper and Row.

Clark, H.H., & Haviland, S.E. (1977). Comprehension and the given-new contract. In R.O. Freedle (Ed.) *Discourse production and comprehension*. Norwoord, NJ: Ablex.

Cole, R.A., & Jakimik, J. (1978). Understanding speech: How words are heard. In G. Underwood (Ed.) *Strategies of information processing*. New York: Academic Press.

Cole, R.A., & Jakimik, J. (1979). A model of speech perception. In R. Cole (Ed.) *Perception and production of fluent speech*. Hillsdale, NJ: Erlbaum.

Comrie, B. (1981). *Language universals and linguistic typology*. Chicago: University of Chicago Press.

Cotton, S., & Grosjean, F. (1984). The gating paradigm: A comparison of successive and individual presentation formats. *Perception and Psychophysics, 35*,41–48.

Culicover, P., & Rochemont, M. (1983). Stress and focus in English. *Language, 59*, 123–165.

Cutler, A. (1976). Phoneme monitoring reaction time as a function of preceding intonation contour. *Perception and Psychophysics, 20*, 55–60.

Cutler, A., & Foss, D.J. (1977). On the role of sentence stress in sentence processing. *Language and Speech, 20*, 1–10.

Forster, K. (1976). Accessing the mental lexicon. In R. Wales, & E. Walker (Eds.) *New approaches to language mechanisms*. Amsterdam: North-Holland.

Frazier, Lyn (1987). Structure in auditory word recognition. *Cognition, 25*, 157–187.

Friederici, A.D., & Schoenle, P.W. (1980). Computational dissociation of two vocabulary types: evidence from aphasia. *Neuropsychologia, 18*, 11–20.

Fries, C.C. (1952). *The structure of English: An introduction to the construction of English sentences*. New York: Harcourt, Brace.

Garrett, M.F. (1975). The analysis of sentence production. In G. Bower (Ed.) *Psychology of learning and motivation*. New York: Academic Press.

Garrett, M.F. (1976). Syntactic processes in sentence production. In R.J. Wales, & E. Walker (Eds.) *New approaches to language mechanisms*. Amsterdam: North-Holland.

Garrett, M.F. (1978). Word and sentence perception. In R. Held, H.W. Leibowitz, & H.L. Teuber (Eds.) *Handbook of sensory physiology, Vol. VIII: Perception*. Berlin: Springer-Verlag.

Garrett, M.F. (1980). Levels of processing in sentence production. In B. Butterworth (Ed.) *Sentence production*. London: Academic Press.

Garrett, M.F., & Kean, M.-L. (1980). Levels of representation and the analysis of speech errors. In M. Aronoff, & M.-L. Kean (Eds.) *Juncture*. Saratoga, Ca.: Anma Libri.

Gee, J.P., & Grosjean, F. (1983). Performance structures: A psycholinguistic and linguistic appraisal. *Cognitive Psychology, 15*, 411–458.

Givon, T. (1975). Serial verbs and syntactic change: Niger-Congo. In C.N. Li (Ed.) *Word order and word order change*. Austin/London: University of Texas Press.

Givon, T. (1979). *On understanding grammar*. New York: Academic Press.

Grosjean, F. (1980). Spoken word recognition processes and the gating paradigm. *Perception and Psychophysics, 28*(4), 267–283.

Grosjean, F. (1985). The recognition of words after their acoustic offset: Evidence and implications. *Perception and Psychophysics, 38*, 299–310.

Halle, M., & Keyser, S.J. (1971). *English stress: Its form, its growth, and its role in verse*. New York: Harper and Row.

Hayes, B. (1980). *A metrical theory of stress rules*. Unpublished Ph.D. Dissertation, MIT.

Hayes, B. (1982). Extrametricality and English stress. *Linguistic Inquiry, 13*, 227–276.

Heim, I. (1982). *The semantics of definite and indefinite noun phrases*. Doctoral dissertation, University of Massachusetts, Amherst.

Howes, D. (1957). On the relation between the intelligibility and frequency of occurrence of English words. *Journal of the Acoustical Society of America, 29*, 296–305.

Huttenlocher, D., & Zue, V. (1983). Phonotactic and lexical constraints in speech recognition. *Working Papers of the Speech Communication Group at MIT, 3*, 157–167.

Jakimik, J. (1979). Word recognition and the lexicon. In J. Wolf, & D. Klatt (Eds.) *Speech Communication Papers Presented at the 97th Meeting of the Acoustical Society of America*. New York: Acoustical Society of America.

Kamp, H. (1982). A theory of truth and semantic representation. In J. Groenendijk et al. (Eds.) *Formal methods in the study of language*. Amsterdam: North-Holland.

Kean, M.-L. (1979). Agrammatism: a phonological deficit? *Cognition, 7*, 69–83.

Kean, M.-L. (1980). Grammatical representations and the description of processing. In D. Caplan (Ed.) *Biological studies of mental processes*. Cambridge, Mass.: MIT Press.

Kiparsky, P. (1979). Metrical structure assignment is cyclic. *Linguistic Inquiry, 10*, 421–442.

Klatt, D. (1979). Speech perception: A model of acoustic-phonetic analysis and lexical access. *Journal of Phonetics, 7*, 279–312.

Kozhevnikov, V., & Chistovich, L. (1965). *Speech: Articulation and perception*. US Department of Commerce Translation, IPRS 30, 543, Washington, DC.

Ladd, D.R. (1980). *The structure of intonational meaning*. Bloomington: Indiana University Press.

Lehiste, I. (1970). *Suprasegmentals*. Cambridge, Mass.: MIT Press.

Liberman, M. (1975). *The intonational system of English*. Unpublished Ph.D. Dissertation, MIT.

Liberman, M., & Prince, A. (1977). On stress and linguistic rhythm. *Linguistic Inquiry, 8*, 249–336.

Marslen-Wilson, W. (1984). Function and process in spoken word recognition. In H. Bouma, & D. Bouwhuis (Eds.) *Attention and performance: Control of language processes*. Hillsdale, NJ: Erlbaum.

Marslen-Wilson, W., & Tyler, L.K. (1980). The temporal structure of spoken language understanding. *Cognition, 8*, 1–71.

Marslen-Wilson, W., & Welsh, A. (1978). Processing interactions and lexical access during word recognition in continuous speech. *Cognitive Psychology, 10*, 29–63.

McCarthy, J. (1979). On stress and syllabification. *Linguistic Inquiry, 10*, 443–466.

McClelland, J., & Elman, J. (1986). The Trace Model of Speech Perception. *Cognitive Psychology, 18*, 1–86.

Mehler, J., Segui, J., & Carey, P. (1968). Tails of words: Monitoring ambiguity. *Journal of Verbal Learning and Verbal Behavior, 17*, 29–35.

Milsark, G.L. (1977). Toward an explanation of certain peculiarities of the existential construction in English. *Linguistic Analysis, 3*, 1–29.

Morton, J. (1969). Interaction of information in word recognition. *Psychological Review, 76*, 165–178.

Morton, J., & Long, J. (1976). Effect of word transitional probability on phoneme identification. *Journal of Verbal Learning and Verbal Behavior, 15*, 43–51.

Nespor, M., & Vogel, I. (1979). Clash avoidance in Italian. *Linguistic Inquiry, 10*, 467–482.

Nespor, M., & Vogel, I. (1982). Prosodic domains of external sandhi rules. In H. van der Hulst, & N. Smith (Eds.) *The structure of phonological representations (Part 1)*. Dordrecht: Foris.

Nespor, M., & Vogel, I. (1983). Prosodic levels above the word and ambiguity. In A. Cutler, & D.R. Ladd (Eds.) *Prosody: Models and measurements*. Berlin/Heidelberg/New York: Springer-Verlag.

Nooteboom, S. (1981). Lexical retrieval from fragments of spoken words: Beginnings and endings. *Journal of Phonetics, 9*, 407–424.

Pollack, I., & Pickett, J.M. (1963). The intelligibility of excerpts from conversation. *Language and Speech, 6*, 165–171.

Pollack, I., & Pickett, J.M. (1964). Intelligibility of excerpts from fluent speech: Auditory vs. structural context. *Journal of Verbal Learning and Verbal Behavior, 3*, 79–84.

Prince, A. (1983). Relating to the grid. *Linguistic Inquiry, 14*, 19–100.

Rubenstein, H., & Pollack, I. (1963). Word predictability and intelligibility. *Journal of Verbal Learning and Verbal Behavior, 2*, 147–158.

Safir, K. (Ed.) (1979). Papers on syllable structure, metrical structure, and harmony processes. MIT Working Papers in Linguistics 1.

Salasoo, A., & Pisoni, D. (1985). Interaction of knowledge sources in spoken word identification. *Journal of Memory and Cognition, 2*, 210–231.

Segui. J., Mehler, J., Frauenfelder, U., & Morton, J. (1982). The word frequency effect and lexical access. *Neuropsychologia, 20*, 615–627.

Selkirk, E. (1978). On prosodic structure and its relation to syntactic structure. Paper presented at the Conference on the Mental Representation of Phonology, University of Massachusetts at Amherst, 1978. In T. Fretheim (Ed.) *Nordic Prosody II*. Trondheim: TAPIR.

Selkirk, E. (1980a). The role of prosodic categories in English word stress. *Linguistic Inquiry, 11*, 563–605.

Selkirk, E. (1980b). Prosodic domains in phonology: Sanskrit revisited. In M. Aronoff, & M.-L. Kean (Eds.) *Juncture*. Saratoga, Ca.: Anma Libri.

Selkirk, E.O. (1982). *The syntax of words. Linguistic Inquiry Monograph 7*. Cambridge, MA.: MIT Press.

Selkirk, E.O. (1984). *Phonology and syntax: The relation between sound and structure*. Cambridge, MA.: MIT Press.

Shields, J.L., McHugh, A., & Martin, J.G. (1974). Reaction time to phoneme targets as a function of rhythmic cues in continuous speech. *Journal of Experimental Psychology, 102*, 250–255.

Slobin, D.I. (1977). Language change in childhood and history. In J. Macnamara (Ed.) *Language learning and thought*. New York: Academic Press.

Slobin, D.I. (1982). Universal and particular in the acquisition of language. In E. Wanner, & L.R. Gleitman (Eds.) *Language acquisition: The state of the art*. Cambridge: Cambridge University Press.

Swinney, D. (1982). The structure and time-course of information interaction during speech comprehension: Lexical segmentation, access and interpretation. In J. Mehler, E. Walker, & M. Garrett (Eds.) *Perspectives on mental representation*. Hillsdale, NJ: Erlbaum.

Swinney, D., Zurif, E.B., & Cutler, A. (1980). Effects of sentential stress and word class upon comprehension in Broca's aphasics. *Brain and Language, 10*, 132–144.

Taft, L. (forthcoming). *Prosodic constraints and lexical parsing strategies*. Doctoral dissertation, University of Massachusetts, Amherst.

Tyler, L.K., & Wessels, J. (1983). Quantifying contextual contributions to word-recognition processes. *Perception and Psychophysics, 34*(5), 409–420.

Tyler, L.K., & Wessels, J. (1985). Is gating an on-line task? Evidence from naming latency data. *Perception and Psychophysics, 38*, 217–222.

Umeda, N. (1977). Consonant duration in American English. *Journal of the Acoustical Society of America, 61*, 846–858.

Williams, E. (1981). On the notions "lexically related" and "head of a word." *Linguistic Inquiry, 12*, 245–274.

Zwicky, A.M. (1977). On clitics. Paper presented at the 3rd International Phonologie-Tagung at the University of Vienna, 1976. Bloomington, Indiana: Indiana University Linguistics Club.

Zwicky, A.M. (1982). Stranded *to* and phonological phrasing in English. *Linguistics, 20*, 3–57.

Résumé

Le but de cet article est d'attirer l'attention sur le rôle que joue la structure prosodique dans la reconnaissance des mots. Nous commençons par soutenir que la notion de mot écrit a eu une influence bien trop grande sur les modèles de la reconnaissance des mots parlés. Nous discutons ensuite plusieurs propriétés de la structure prosodique qui sont importantes pour les questions de reconnaissance. Nous présentons ensuite une conception de la reconnaissance des mots "en continu" qui tient compte de l'alternance entre syllabes fortes et faibles dans le flux de la parole. L'Accès lexical est guidé par les syllabes fortes, tandis que les syllabes faibles sont identifiées par une analyse globale de leur distribution et par l'utilisation de règles phonotactiques et morphonémiques. Nous concluons par une discussion de la controverse sur les différences d'accès aux mots à contenu et aux mots à fonction à la lumière de notre conception.

7

Structure in auditory word recognition*

LYN FRAZIER

University of Massachusetts, Amherst

Abstract

Dominant models of auditory word recognition emphasize the lexical access component of the word identification problem. They thus cast the recognition process as a simple operation matching the input against stored lexical representations or direct activation of those representations. Given this characterization of the problem, it is entirely unclear how the perceiver's knowledge of language structure could facilitate the recognition of words. Yet it may be necessary to appeal to grammatical knowledge to solve many of the outstanding problems in theories of word recognition, e.g., segmentation, coping with variation in the acoustic instantiation of words, and recognizing novel words.

The current paper takes seriously the possibility that grammatical knowledge participates in word recognition. It investigates what kinds of information would be helpful for what purposes. It also attempts to sketch in the outlines of the general sort of recognition system which could take advantage of the kinds of regularities found in natural languages.

1. Introduction

Most everyone agrees that humans perceive an unfamiliar language with reference to the phonology of their native language. Ironically, they do not perceive their native language with reference to its phonology, at least according to dominant models of auditory word recognition. Though current models (e.g., Kempley & Morton, 1982; Marslen-Wilson & Tyler, 1980; Morton,

*This work was supported by grant NIH MH 35347. I am grateful to Janet Fodor, Yosef Grodzinsky, Jacques Mehler, Chuck Clifton, Emmon Bach, Lorraine Tyler, Uli Frauenfelder and several anonymous reviewers for comments on earlier drafts of this paper. Reprint requests should be sent to Lyn Frazier, Department of Linguistics, University of Massachusetts, Amherst, MA 01002, U.S.A.

1969)[1] do not explicitly deny the relevance of phonological structure in word recognition, they contain no principles or mechanisms which exploit phonological information. Indeed, acoustic or linguistic variation—even if it is rule-governed, for example, aspirating voiceless stops syllable-initially—is viewed as problematic noise in the signal, rather than as an important source of information about the linguistic analysis of the input.

There are three prevalent assumptions about word recognition which contribute to or make possible the view that the grammar plays at most a minor role in perceiving words. First, word recognition is often identified with lexical access, that is, with identifying in the perceiver's mental lexicon one or more already existing representations compatible with the input string. Of course, lexical access must be involved in word recognition. But, in the case of novel words derived by rule (e.g., recognizing 'glubbable' if I just told you "to glub" means to destroy with a feather), word recognition must involve something more than lexical access. In the case of familiar words, word recognition may or may not involve something more than lexical access, depending on what turns out to be the correct theory of the mental lexicon and the representations it contains. Thus, if we define word recognition as identifying the word or words that make up an input string, word recognition may well involve operations (e.g., selection of an appropriate lexical description from several locally possible alternatives, rule-governed computation of a representation, etc.) in addition to whatever operations are implicated in lexical access per se.[2]

The second assumption is that lexical access procedures themselves are extremely simple, consisting primarily of matching an input to prestored representations or direct sensory activation of those representations. Given this characterization of the recognition problem, any variation in the signal will obscure or complicate the relation between the input and prestored lexical representations.

---

[1]The LAFs model of Klatt (1979) does make use of some phonological information. Phonologically legal sequences of sounds are precompiled into a "spectral sequence decoding network"; and, some phonetic and phonological regularities participate in the evaluation of the signal, to determine how the recognition device can proceed through the network. However, this model has not really attracted the attention of psychologists investigating word recognition.

The role of morphological regularities in word recognition has also received some attention in the literature (see, for example, the references in Henderson, 1985). However, this work has been concerned almost exclusively with visual, not auditory, word recognition.

[2]Here and throughout the paper I will finesse important questions concerning the differences between phonological, morphological and syntactic definitions of "word". The general problem may be illustrated using the English possessive morpheme "'s", as in *the sad girl's hat* or *the girl who was on the corner's hat*. "Girl's" or "corner's" seem to act like words phonologically, but clearly they cannot be treated as syntactic words since the possessive behaves syntactically like a sister to the entire possessor noun phrase.

Finally, it is commonly assumed in psychological discussions that representational questions about the input and output of the lexical access mechanisms can (perhaps must) be finessed, for the simple reason that at present there is no clear psychological evidence about the nature of those representations. Thus, it is typically assumed that some sort of phonetic preprocessing precedes lexical access, but the nature of the output of the phonetic preprocessor is often not explicitly discussed. Similarly, the question of whether lexical representations are fully specified with respect to phonetic detail or are more abstract (systematic phonological representations) and the question of whether phonological or phonetic segments are hierarchically structured or merely linearly concatenated are recognized as being important, but they're not usually emphasized.

In short, by focusing on the lexical access problem (how do we contact prestored representations) without explicitly characterizing the nature of the input (the representation resulting from phonetic preprocessing), it is natural to cast word recognition in terms of pattern matching or sensory activation, apparently alleviating the need for the grammar to mediate in lexical processing. But, what if we take seriously the view that the grammar of one's native language participates in the perception of one's own language as well as in the perception of unfamiliar languages. This will lead to an alternative approach to the lexical access and word recognition problem. Let me briefly illustrate intuitively why it may ultimately lead to a superior approach, by drawing an analogy between lexical processing and syntactic processing.

Imagine a language in which all clauses are uniform in structure, for example, each clause contains an overt subject noun phrase which always precedes the verb phrase which itself exhibits some constant shape. Now, imagine we introduce some rule-governed variation into this language, say, permitting all and only relative clauses to begin with a word (relative pronoun) which precedes the subject noun phrase. According to a theory in which there are prestored syntactic frames, we have just complicated the syntactic processing problem by introducing variation, on the assumption that the processing system is concerned with clause recognition. However, viewed from the perspective of a processor which must determine the relation between clauses (i.e., the type of clause being processed), this variation may well facilitate syntactic processing, providing immediate disambiguating information about the type of clause being processed.

Now, let's return to the case of phonological variation, for example, aspirating syllable-initial voiceless stops. Given the traditional (above) characterization of the word recognition problem, permitting a segment to be instantiated in more than one way (aspirated or unaspirated) complicates word recognition. However, what if one aspect of word recognition involves

phonologically structuring the input string? In this case, rule-governed variation may facilitate word recognition, since it may provide disambiguating
information about the structural analysis of segments, that is, if a voiceless
stop is aspirated, it must be syllable-initial. Below I will suggest that there
may be several advantages to be gained from phonologically structuring an
input: (i) identifying likely hypotheses about lexical segmentation of a string;
(ii) facilitating classification of the string (i.e., determining the identity of
segments), (iii) increasing the informativeness of partial information about
segment identity, and (iv) helping to maintain the global consistency of locally
possible analyses.

Before turning to those arguments, however, I would like to lay to rest
certain apparently devastating objections to this approach to word recognition. The gross facts about word recognition are that it is immediate, seemingly effortless, unconscious and automatic or mandatory (Conrad, 1974, for
example). If, as suggested above, perceivers must perform the extensive computations required to phonologically structure or parse an input string, why
aren't perceivers aware of these computations, why are they so bad at making
certain conscious judgments about phonological structure, etc.? I am forced
to assume that humans are not aware of all the mental computations implicated in word recognition. But notice that this assumption is independently
required. It is simply not true in general that the above characteristics are
found only in cases where the underlying perceptual or cognitive mechanism
is known to consist merely of simple matching operations or sensory activation. For example, the above properties seem to characterize syntactic processing (e.g., Flores d'Arcais, 1982; Forster, 1979). Syntactic processing must
involve some active computations beyond accessing prestored representations, given that not all sentence structures can be precomputed (there being
indefinitely many of them). Hence, the fact that our intuitions about word
recognition seem to conflict with the view of word recognition advocated
here does not provide a compelling argument against this view or evidence
in favor of alternatives claiming that a more direct process is involved in
mapping an input onto lexical representations.

The rest of this paper attempts to flesh out the view that the grammar plays
an important role in auditory word recognition. It addresses two questions.
What grammatical information might be useful in lexical access? And, what
kind of system could exploit this information? Section 2 examines the possible
contribution of phonological information. Sections 3 and 4 take up the potential role of information about word-level syntax (morphology) and phrase/
sentence-level syntax, respectively. Section 5 takes a brief look at the problems involved in determining the particular wordform or lexical subentry that
is appropriate for an input sentence; this section raises questions about the

boundaries of the lexical access system by emphasizing that the information sources that would be useful for lexical-form selection are almost entirely distinct from those which could be helpful for purposes of lexical access.

2. Phonological structuring of an auditory input

Under what description is an input submitted to the mental lexicon? The fact that a word may be recognized regardless of whether it is spoken softly or loudly, by a speaker with a high or low fundamental frequency and often by a speaker of any of a number of dialects of a language is usually taken as evidence that an auditory input must be in terms of linguistic, not acoustic, features.[3] It seems implicit in models like the logogen and cohort models (Kempley & Morton, 1982; Marslen-Wilson & Tyler, 1980) that the output of the phonetic preprocessor corresponds to an unstructured concatenation of phonetic segments, or a corresponding matrix of distinctive features. As pointed out above, if further structure is assumed, it is not exploited by any explicit principles of the models.

Recent work in phonological theory, however, indicates clearly that explaining the phonological processes found in natural languages requires a much more elaborate view of phonological representations. In particular, it is necessary to pay attention to the relation between segments, for example, how they are combined into constituents that form syllables, feet, and words (cf. Kahn, 1976; Liberman & Prince, 1977; Selkirk, 1980). Of course, it is in principle possible that speakers utilize information about the organization of individual segments but that perceivers ignore this information altogether. But this seems unlikely given that perceivers are sensitive to the temporal patterning of speech which depends on the phonological organization of speech segments.

Psycholinguistic studies have certainly been concerned with the question of whether syllables play an important role in speech perception and word recognition. However, the question has usually been cast as follows: Is it the syllable *or* the phoneme which corresponds to the basic unit of speech perception? But, of course, this may not be the right question to ask. (See Norris & Cutler, in press, for review of this literature and discussion.) The answer may be that both play an important role and neither is primary. To draw a

---

[3]If we abandon the assumption that inputs are described in linguistic rather than acoustic features (as one reviewer suggests doing) we are simply left without any definition of the family of acoustic signals (tokens) which count as an instance of a single 'word' or lexical item (type).

syntactic analogy once again, this question may be on par with the question: Is it the syntactic phrase or the clause which is the basic unit of syntactic processing? If syntactic processing involves assigning a complete constituent structure representation to an input sentence, then both phrasal nodes and clausal nodes must be postulated and whether clausal nodes are postulated before or after the postulation of their constituent phrasal nodes may depend entirely on when the processor has sufficient information to warrant their postulation. There is no a priori reason to dismiss the possibility that the same is true of segments and syllables (or other higher-level phonological units): both may be important and whether syllabic structure is identified before or after the identity of the constituent segments may depend entirely on the information available to the processor.

For the sake of concreteness, I will now describe a system capable of assigning phonological structure to an input as an illustration of what such a system might look like. I will then take up possible advantages of this general approach, and mention some empirical evidence supporting the basic idea that phonological structuring is involved in auditory word recognition.

2.1. Phonological parsing

In what follows, I will assume the theory of syllable structure in Selkirk (1984a). Further, I will pretend that a phonological word of English may be characterized as in (1). Though this characterization is inadequate (see Selkirk, 1980), it will suffice for purposes of illustration.

(1) $W \rightarrow \Sigma(\Sigma)$

   $\Sigma \rightarrow \Sigma \left(\left\{ \begin{smallmatrix} \Sigma \\ \sigma_w \end{smallmatrix} \right\} \right)$

   $\Sigma \rightarrow (\sigma_w)\sigma_s(\sigma_w)$

Where W = word, Σ = foot, σ = syllable (σ_w = weak; σ_s = strong), and a syllable may be strong only if it is closed or contains a tense vowel.

(2a)

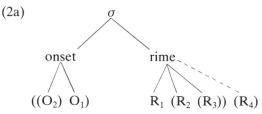

R$_4$ may consist of a coronal obstruent appendix and is permitted only in word-final syllables.

(2b) Sonority Sequencing Generalization: In any syllable, there is a segment constituting a sonority peak which is preceded and/or followed by a sequence of segments with progressively decreasing sonority values.

The rules in (1) claim that a word may contain one or more (stress) feet, where each stress foot must contain a strong syllable which may be preceded or followed by a weak syllable. A foot may also branch into two stress feet or correspond to a superfoot (i.e., a foot followed by a weak syllable). Selkirk's theory of syllable structure is summarized in (2). It claims that a syllable must contain a nucleus (R_1), which may be preceded and followed by one or two segments if they are of the appropriate sonority to satisfy (2b). (Selkirk gives more detailed restrictions on the sonority relations of the segments that may be inserted in the syllable template in (2a).) Treiman (1983) provides experimental evidence from novel word games that supports the view of syllable structure in (2a).

If we assume that phonological structuring of an acoustic input occurs in parallel with phonetic "preprocessing" of the input, then it is natural to assume that a distinctive feature representation of an input may be attached to a terminal position in the template in (2a) before a complete specification of its features is available. In other words, syllabic parsing of a segment could proceed before the identity of that segment has been established assuming that the sonority relations between that segment and adjacent segments may be determined in the absence of a complete feature specification (e.g., if the place of articulation of a segment was still unspecified). Thus in the string "*xyz*" if x has been analyzed as R_1 and y has been analyzed as R_2 and z is more sonorant than y, then z may (indeed, must) be analyzed as a constituent of a new syllable (regardless of whether it has been assigned any value for features which distinguish z from other members of its 'sonority class.')[4]

If we assume, say, that every segment of the input is minimally attached into the phonological word without postulating any potentially unnecessary nodes and that revisions of analysis are not made until or unless they become necessary, this sort of system will make several predictions about auditory word recognition. For example, it predicts that a string of syllables consisting of "strong-weak-strong-strong" will initially be analyzed as shown in (3).

---

[4]Presumably other principles will be needed as well. One likely candidate is a Maximal Onset Principle which preferentially assigns segments to an onset rather than a rime unless the segment is too sonorant to be analyzed as an onset, as in the case of a vowel, for example.

(3)

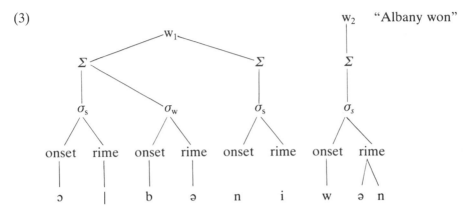

The analysis of the first three syllables follows directly from the minimal structure principle: attaching syllable one into a word requires postulating a foot node (given the rules in (1)), syllable two may be directly attached into this structure without postulating additional nodes, and (minimal) attachment of syllable three requires only a single foot node to be postulated. Syllable four could be attached into the first word but only by revising the attachment of the preceding syllable and this is excluded by the revisions as last resort principle.

Given the empirical results of Marslen-Wilson and his colleagues (e.g. Marslen-Wilson & Tyler, 1980; Marslen-Wilson & Welsh, 1978) we must assume that lexical analysis of an input is not delayed until after the phonological structuring of an entire word has been completed. Thus, if the only candidate in the cohort set established for syllable 1 in (3) was a one syllable lexical item (i.e., if the only English lexical item beginning with /ɔl/ was "all"), this would force syllable 2 to be taken as an onset and would force revision of the structure of word 1, that is, syllable 2 would have to be detached from word 1 as would the following syllable, resulting in (4).

(4)

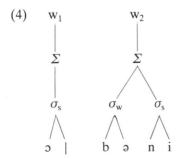

Of course, since "Albany" is a lexical item of English (and /bəni/ is not), the original phonological analysis of the string will be lexically confirmed in this particular example (but not, say, in "All replies ...").

We do not yet have a fully explicit model of phonological parsing. Important problems have been finessed, for example, are the salience relations between syllables to be captured by the branching pattern of their constituent structure or by principles stated over a metrical grid; what principles govern the revision of phonological structures, etc. However, notice that these problems and questions are also finessed in current models of auditory word recognition. What I have tried to show here is that a natural set of devices may be used to address those problems if we assume that perceivers do not ignore the grammar of their language during word recognition but rather exploit phonological constraints. We will now illustrate some potential advantages of assigning phonological structure.

2.2. Segmentation

Imagine, for a moment, that perceivers assign no phonological structure to an input beyond that implied by linear concatenation of segments. On this assumption, each segment might correspond to the initial segment of a lexical item. But clearly a lexical item is more likely to begin with a syllable-initial segment than a non-initial one. Perhaps perceivers make use of this information and initially ignore the possibility that syllable-internal or syllable-final segments correspond to the initial segment of a lexical item. In some cases, acoustic information per se may determine whether some segment is syllable-initial or not, for example, there are at times clear acoustic differences between syllable-initial and syllable-final stop consonants. However, in cases where no clear acoustic information is present, it may only be information about the possible syllable structures of the language which disambiguates the syllabic analysis of an item, thereby reducing the number of plausible lexical segmentation hypotheses.

For example, a perceiver of English could determine that (5) only has two possible lexical analyses, the two word analysis in (5a) and the three word analysis in (5b).

(5)   saemlarptstren

    a.   [saemlarpt] [stren]
    b.   [saem] [larpt] [stren]

(I'm ignoring the possibility of a compound.) In this case, the only information being exploited is information about the inventory of possible syllable structures in English, including the fact that *larpt* is a syllable with an "appendix", that is, an extra segment permitted only on word final syllables (see the definition of syllable structure in (2a)). Hence, a one-word noncompound analysis of the string is excluded by the fact that *larpt* is an impermissible syllable except in word-final position. Of course this type of argument cannot show that perceivers do use this sort of information during word recognition; it only shows that the information could be useful, drastically reducing the number of possible analyses of a string. The problem of segmenting an acoustic string is a notoriously difficult one. Perhaps the reason why so little progress has been made on the problem is because the representation provided by a simple linear concatenation of segments is too impoverished to permit useful generalizations about permissible segmentations to be exploited.

The prosodic information contained in phonological representations might also help to identify likely lexical-segmentation hypotheses. Lori Taft (1983) has recently presented evidence that the phonological structuring of segments into higher order constituents is responsible for the initial segmentation perceivers impose on a phonetically ambiguous string. She hypothesizes that in English every strong (stressed) syllable is taken as a potential onset of a (stress) foot, with following weak syllables associated as constituents of the foot (up to the limits imposed by the phonological constraints of the language). This initial hypothesis about the segmentation of an acoustic string thus determines the initial lexical analysis of the string in cases where other factors such as the relative frequency of occurrence of the words implicated by the alternative analyses are held constant. Hence the preferred segmentations of a two-syllable string with a strong-weak stress pattern (e.g., *lettuce*, *market*, *catcher*) will correspond to the one word analysis, whereas the preferred segmentation of a weak-strong string (e.g. *invests*, *attest*, *befriends*) will be more likely to give rise to a two word segmentation. Taft (1983) presents evidence that this effect holds for strings of nonsense syllables as well as word strings. (For further evidence, see results of the fast speech condition in Stinson & LaRiviere 1976.)

One important advantage of the view that higher level phonological structure is assigned to an acoustic signal is that this will drastically reduce the number of hypotheses about potential word onsets. As Taft points out this is particularly critical in the cohort model (see Marslen-Wilson, 1987, this issue), where initial segments must be identified to determine the cohort set of candidate items to be matched against the input. And, of course, it will be critical for establishing the identity of segments that have been affected by phonological rules whose application is contingent on the presence of a word boundary.

2.3. Classification

In addition to the problems posed by the "lack of invariance" in the speech signal, perceivers must cope with problems arising because speakers often mumble, make speech errors or persist in speaking despite the presence of considerable background noise. Hence, the classification problem (discovering the identity of the intended segments in a speech signal) is a nontrivial one, under any description. Fortunately, perceivers need not rely exclusively on the acoustic signal in solving this problem. Phonological constraints can disambiguate the identity of a segment, for example, a syllable-initial segment which might be acoustically ambiguous between "f" and "v" must be "f" if followed by "l", as well as the existence of a segment, for example, the existence of a reduced schwa in "ptato" (given that "pt" is not a possible syllable-initial cluster in English). Entirely parallel arguments exist showing that very partial information about a segment can be informative if constraints on phonological wellformedness are exploited by perceivers.

Massaro and Cohen (1983) show that perceivers do in fact rely on phonotactic constraints in identifying segments. Perceivers are more likely to report phonotactically legal sequences than illegal ones.

2.4. Maintaining global consistency

Studies of auditory word recognition have typically investigated the recognition or access of a single word. According to current models, the recognition system operates as follows: as an acoustic input is phonetically preprocessed, it is matched against stored lexical representations. This matching process changes the activation level of the representations in the lexicon (or their corresponding word detection devices). The activation level of a lexical representation increases if the input matches some aspect of its specification and possibly decreases (in the cohort model, not the logogen model) if there is a conflict or mismatch between the input signal and the lexical specification. Recognition occurs when some lexical representation (or its detection device) reaches its threshold level of activation (in the logogen model) or when it is the only active member of its cohort set of items sharing the same initial sounds (in the cohort model). Once the current item is recognized, presumably the process repeats itself, hopefully resulting in recognition of the following input item.

We might ask, however, how the recognition device is altered by the recognition of some input item. That is, having recognized item$_n$ and begun the analysis of item$_{n + 1}$, is the current state of the system precisely the same as it was before the recognition of the previous item(n)? The word recognition literature gives the impression that the only change is a possible change in the current activation level of lexical items. But clearly this can't be right. In any model, identifying the appropriate lexical representation for an input must somehow have the result of making information about that item available to the processing system, whether this is accomplished by placing the corresponding lexical entry in a special memory register, passing it to a syntactic processing system, or whatever. Further, presumably the lexical description of the input must be mapped onto whatever representation of the acoustic input is held in memory. If not, it is entirely unclear how the speech perception and word recognition systems can keep track of the consequences of the current analysis of the input for the lexical analysis of subsequent items, or recover from an inappropriate analysis of the signal. For example, if the recognition device succeeds in identifying "weather" in a simple phrase like "weather report", it cannot simply eliminate the corresponding portion of the acoustic signal from the representation available to the phonetic preprocessor and, say, store the lexical entry for "weather" in some memory register. The effect of this would be to leave the input signal too impoverished to permit recognition of the following word, since /iport/ does not correspond to any lexical item of English. In short, after recognition of "weather" the system must have available some representation that looks more like (6b) than (6a),

(6a)   σ σ

          # i p ɔ rt

(where "#" indicates the presence of a word boundary)

(6b)

permitting "r" to be treated as the offset of the final syllable of "weather" and as the onset of the initial syllable of "report".

If we examine a slightly more complicated example, the need to keep track of the analysis of the acoustic string may become clearer. At least, in fast speech, a phrase like "summer return" contains many local ambiguities. The initial syllable may constitute a word ("sum") or it may be the initial syllable of "summer" or of "summary"; and the final syllable of this phrase may constitute a word ("turn") or it may be the final syllable of "return". However the human word recognition system operates, it must have some way of avoiding the situation where it ends up accepting "sum" as the lexical analysis of the first syllable and "turn" as the lexical analysis of the final syllable, for the simple reason that this lexical analysis will not exhaust the input string (there being no English lexical item /əri/). In other words, the system must have some way to insure that locally possible analyses fit together into a globally coherent analysis that exhausts the input string.

One might consider any of several mechanisms for maintaining global consistency in the lexical analysis of the speech signal. There are two reasons for thinking it may be a phonologically structured representation of the acoustic signal which is used to perform this function, that is, that the results of the lexical access and recognition routines are used to confirm, disconfirm or supplement (further specify) the information in a phonological representation of the input. First, several studies of language processing indicate that perceivers must maintain a fairly global phonological representation to account for the effects of prosody (see e.g., Cutler & Foss, 1977; Liberman, 1975; Slowiacek, Carroll, & Speer, 1985). Second, if a phonological representation of the input is independently required for phonetic processing, for lexical access and to interpret prosodic information, then parsimony alone would argue that it is this same representation which is used to keep track of local phonological and lexical analyses and assess their global consistency and their consequences for the analysis of subsequent items.

2.5. Conclusions

Let me conclude this section by discussing apparent counterevidence to the present proposal and then drawing out what I take to be the general 'moral' of the above discussion. To my knowledge, there are only two sets of psycholinguistic studies whose standard interpretation runs counter to the approach advocated here. The first set involves syllable-monitoring studies (e.g., Cutler, Mehler, Norris, & Segui, 1983) showing that a mismatch between a target syllable (ba vs. bal) and the syllable structure of the word monitored (ba-lance vs. bal-con in the French materials) slows monitoring times for French subjects but not English subjects regardless of whether subjects are monitoring items in their native or non-native language. This result has been interpreted as showing that French perceivers rely more heavily on syllabic processing strategies than do English perceivers. However, an alternative interpretation of the result is that English and French perceivers are simply operating with different syllable structure rules. Since the rules of English (but not French) syllable structure permit the crucial medial consonant ("l" in the above example) to be ambisyllabic, English perceivers' representation of the target word will not be unambiguously inconsistent with either target. By contrast, in French, a CV target will be unambiguously inconsistent with the syllabic structure of an item like "balcon" and a CVC target will be inconsistent with the syllabic structure of "balance." Assuming that a perfect match between the structure of the target and the structure of the word being monitored leads to faster responses than does a partial match, differences in syllable structure, not differences in perceptual strategies, may account for these results. Of course, on this alternative interpretation, the results of the syllable monitoring study provide evidence that perceivers are assigning higher order phonological structure to segments, but do not indicate that syllabic structuring occurs only in some languages, for example, those lacking ambisyllabic segments.

The second study is one reported by Marslen-Wilson (1987, this issue). Briefly, what he finds is that word recognition times are unaffected by the position of a syllable-boundary with respect to the first distinguishing phoneme of a word (i.e., by whether the syllable boundary precedes or follows the first phoneme which differentiates a word from the others which begin with the same sounds). This finding does provide evidence against a system in which segments must be structured into a complete syllable before they are matched against the representations in the lexicon. However, notice that this finding is not problematic for the sort of system outlined here, where syllables are no more or less basic than segments and phonological structuring of an input is assumed to occur in tandem or concurrently with whatever lexical matching operations are implicated in lexical access.

Finally, I feel obliged to point out that there is an entire host of studies which might be taken as evidence about the precise nature of the higher-order phonological structure assigned to an acoustic input, as opposed to whether such structure is assigned. For example, while phonologists have at times postulated the existence of a more articulated syllable structure than is being assumed here (i.e., (2a))—specifically the division of the rime into nucleus and coda—the Treisman study cited above finds no evidence supporting this further articulation of rimes. Also, Norris and Cutler (in press) report evidence they interpret as arguing against the assignment of foot-level structure, raising the possibility that perceivers operate with a somewhat simpler definition of possible phonological word than that indicated in (1) or that foot-level structure is important for some purpose other than lexical identification (e.g., G. Bruce, personal communication, has made the intriguing suggestion that it may be at foot boundaries that perceivers align the F_o contour of a sentence with a segmental representation of the input).

Before leaving this section, I wish to emphasize again that my purpose here has not been to argue for the correctness of the details of the phonological parsing system outlined above. Rather, the purpose has been to indicate the advantages of assuming that the grammar participates in the mapping between an acoustic signal and lexical representations and to indicate what general type of lexical recognition device could exploit the phonological regularities of natural languages.

We might briefly compare this approach with the view that word recognition involves little or no structuring internal to words. In such models it is not clear what information other than isolated superficial cues to phonological or lexical structure could be useful during word recognition. Though some types of context independent cues clearly do exist (e.g., pauses, certain cues to juncture, cf. Nakatani & Dukes, 1977) the obvious fact about the phonological structure of languages is that they involve systems of relations, not isolated superficial 'markers.' In the cohort model, for example, it would be extremely useful for a language to simply select some distinguished segment from its inventory and reserve its use for marking the beginning of words. But this kind of superficial marking of word onsets is precisely what is not typically found in natural languages.

Instead one finds systems of rules or constraints that provide useful information about the segmentation of an acoustic input (e.g., in English a word typically begins with a syllable onset and there are limitations on what may constitute an onset). But these 'cues' in the surface string are informative primarily with respect to the structure assigned to surrounding material. There are exceptions to this generalization, of course. For example, the existence of a wider range of syllable types in word final position than in other positions (noted above) provides a superficial cue to word offsets. The existence of "appendices" permitting this situation is apparently not uncommon. However, notice that even in this case the restriction is not that a word must end with an identifiable word-final syllable; a syllable with an appendix is simply one of the possible syllables that may occur in word final position and thus provides a sufficient but not a necessary cue to word offsets. Similarly, in Korean *h* only occurs word-initially (E. Bach, personal communication) and thus it provides a sufficient but not a necessary cue to word onsets. In short, it appears that current models of auditory word recognition (e.g., the cohort and logogen models) could efficiently exploit grammatical constraints only if these constraints were of a quite different sort than the constraints typically found in the phonology of natural languages. Thus, turned around, the point is that if we are investigating processing systems that can efficiently and rapidly exploit the grammatical information about the sound patterns of languages, we must develop models that can utilize systems of rules and representational constraints, not just isolated superficial cues to phonological and lexical structures.

3. The role of word syntax

The structure of words can be viewed on par with the structure of phrases and sentences (e.g., Bach, 1983; Selkirk, 1982). For example, the co-occurrence possibilities of morphemes may be captured by strict subcategorization restrictions carried by derivational and inflectional morphemes, as illustrated in (7).

(7)

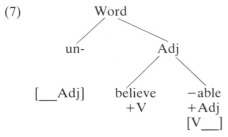

Here the strict subcategorization frame for the negative prefix *un-* indicates that this prefix may only attach to an adjective. This entails that the sister to this prefix ("believable") must be adjectival. If this adjectival element is morphologically simple, then the morpheme following the negative prefix must itself be an adjective (e.g., unhappy). However, if the sister to the prefix is itself morphologically complex (as in (7)) then it is the head of this constituent, not the immediately following morpheme, which must be adjectival. (See Williams, 1981, and discussion below in Section 4 for the notion "head of a word.")

Completely deactivating classes of lexical candidates on the basis of strict subcategorization restrictions would be risky. As the above example shows, the subcategorization restrictions of a prefix need not (directly) constrain the lexical category of the immediately following morpheme. And, of course, complete elimination of candidate lexical items not matching the subcategorization requirements of the prefix would also prove to be problematic in cases of ambiguity. For example, in (7) problems would arise due to the existence of a homophonous (reversative) prefix *un-* which strictly subcategorizes for verbs, as in "unzip."

However, we might consider alternative ways in which the strict subcategorization requirements of morphemes might be exploited. For example, they might prime or in some other manner lead the processor to give special consideration to lexical items of the appropriate category. Or, perhaps, the phonological structuring device has access to a list of closed class morphemes and their strict subcategorization frames, permitting this information to form part of the description of the input to the lexical access mechanisms (or, more likely, part of one such description, given the existence of pseudoprefixed items, e.g., realize).

This would permit rapid evaluation of lexical representations. Certainly both types of mechanisms seem worth considering, since either one could substantially reduce the ambiguity in the lexical analysis of a string. For example, *re-*, which subcategorizes for a verb, could immediately disambiguate the category of, say, the extensive noun-verb duals in English, as in *recycle, rexerox, recopy*, etc. Nevertheless, there is reason to favor the latter (closed class list) mechanism. This mechanism avoids the difficulties which arise for a priming model when a prefix is attached to a polymorphemic stem (where only the head of the stem—not its first constituent—need be of the predicted syntactic category). It would also permit productive closed class morphemes to be used generally and not just in cases where they happen to precede some open class lexical item. Thus, suffixes as well as prefixes could aid lexical analysis. In the case of inflectional suffixes this may be especially important since these items may provide particularly informative cues for segmentation, at least in a language like English where inflectional items typically do not occur word-internally.[5]

---

[5]Kempley and Morton (1982) demonstrate long-term (10-40 min) morphological priming effects on the recognition of spoken words presented in noise. Subjects first rated a list of words on their imagability. Prior exposure to a regularly inflected form of a test word facilitated later recognition of the word nearly as much as exposure to the identical form, although prior exposure to physically related words (e.g., *deflecting* vs. *reflecting*) had no effect on recognition. Because exposure to an irregularly related word (*man/men, held/holding*) did not facilitate later recognition, Kempley and Morton conclude that the effect is presemantic and that it argues morphemes are the units of analysis in auditory word recognition (e.g., that logogens correspond to morpheme-sized units). This evidence is reassuring for the sort of view explored here. However, several questions arise about the relation between this evidence and the hypothesis that morphemes are the units of analysis in auditory word recognition. Inflectional morphemes are a distinguished subclass of morphemes and thus their behavior may differ from other classes of morphemes. In particular, inflectional morphemes differ from one class of partially moribund derivational morphemes, known as "Nonneutral derivational morphemes" (cf., Allen, 1978; Chomsky & Halle, 1968; Selkirk, 1982). Unlike inflectional morphemes of English, these derivational morphemes may change the syntactic category and stress pattern of items they attach to, and frequently they are associated with idiosyncratic meanings that cannot be predicted by rule. Thus there is good reason to be cautious in generalizing these results. Further, if we assume that regularly inflected words are not stored in the mental lexicon but computed by rule, this assumption alone could explain the results (i.e., one would recover the same lexical representation for *reflect* and *reflecting* but not for *reflecting* and *deflecting* or for *man* or *men*, given that irregular forms must be stored, being unpredictable). Consequently, while this evidence is encouraging for the approach explored here, it certainly does not require this view, or the conclusion that lexical representations invariably correspond to individual morphemes.

4. The role of phrasal syntax

It has been argued in preceding sections that exploiting certain kinds of grammatical information (in particular, phonological regularities) could facilitate lexical recognition. But there is little reason to believe that every kind of grammatical information is exploited at this stage, that is, for purposes of lexical access. Despite the considerable interest in syntactic priming (see Tanenhaus & Lucas, 1987, this issue), it is argued below that there is reason to be skeptical that phrase-level syntactic information could facilitate lexical access.

4.1. Finding the head of the relevant word

Various observations about the syntax of words and phrases place limitations on the usefulness of exploiting expectations based on phrase-level syntax to either prime certain lexical items or remove certain lexical items from consideration.[6] Williams (1981) argues very convincingly that the head of a word determines the syntactic category of the word. He proposes that English words are "right-headed." Thus it is the rightmost daughter of a node that determines the categorial specification of that node (e.g., the agentive affix -er, is +N and thus send-er is +N; walk is +verb, so sleepwalk is +V). Williams' Righthand Head Rule explains why, for example, prefixes generally cannot change the category of the items they attach to in a language like English (with righthand heads). It immediately follows that any prediction derived from the phrasal syntax of English could at most constrain only the category of the head of some following word; it could not directly constrain the category of any other constituents of that word.

Now consider phrase-level syntactic predictions, for example, the expectation that a determiner will be followed by an adjective or noun. Presumably expectations derived from phrasal syntax will concern the expected con-

---

[6]How severe these limitations turn out to be will depend in a large part on precisely how much and what type of information can be extracted from the prosodic structure of speech. On the assumption that the boundaries of phonological phrases must coincide with word boundaries, several arguments given in the text below would not apply to words at the end of a phonological phrase if prosodic information can be used to predict the ends of phonological phrases, for example how many syllables will intervene between some word onset and the end of the phonological phrase. Using the gating paradigm, Grosjean (1984) has shown that half-way through a potentially (sentence) final word, subjects can accurately determine whether the sentence will end or whether it will continue. In this study, subjects knew the identity of the potentially final word in advance. Nevertheless, this finding raises the possibility that offsets of at least certain types of words (e.g., monosyllabic words and bisyllabic words with initial stress) can be predicted in advance when they occur at the end of prosodic units.

stituents of a phrase and the likely co-occurrence of phrases. A phrase may include items of several syntactic categories and, in English at least, many of these items are optional. Thus the most useful syntactic prediction is likely to be that concerning the head of the phrase, since it is the head of a phrase that is an obligatory member of the phrase and it is the head which must be of the same syntactic category as the phrase. The consequence of these observations is that syntactic expectations will not in general constrain the linear sequence of items in the input; instead, they concern the restrictions on the category of items (words and phrases) that are sisters in a constituent structure representation of a phrase or sentence.

Consider (8) for example. The real grammatical expectation in (8) is that the head of the word that serves as the head noun phrase introduced by the determiner *the* must be +N. Clearly this expectation does not concern some superficially identifiable item in the input string, for example, the lexical item adjacent to the word responsible for the prediction. But imagine that the

> *The* quickly deteriorating orange [[squeeze]er]

(9) The quickly deteriorating [[orange]$_N$ [[squeeze]$_V$er]$_N$]$_N$
(10) The quickly deteriorating [orange]$_A$ [[squeeze]$_V$er]$_N$

processor nevertheless uses the fact that a determiner introduces a noun phrase to predict that (an adjective may occur and) a noun must occur. In (8) several words intervene between the determiner and the noun which confirms the noun prediction (*orange-squeezer* in (9) or *squeezer* in (10)). Elimination of all lexical candidates other than adjectives and nouns would be disastrous. If derived words are stored as such, the adverb *quickly* would be deactivated and, if they're not, the verb *deteriorate* would be deactivated. Furthermore, taking the occurrence of *orange* (which in fact may be a noun in (8) if *orange-squeezer* is taken to be a compound) as confirmation of the predicted noun would be inappropriate since either *squeezer* or the compound *orange-squeezer* must be the head of the noun phrase.

4.2. Exploiting expectations about adjacent words

Rather than coping with predictions about words whose position in the input cannot be superficially determined, the processor might exploit predictions about adjacent words. It might adopt a strategy of assuming that each phrase will be expanded to include only its obligatory members. In this case, having processed a determiner, the processor would expect a noun to immediately follow. For example, in (11) this would lead to the hypothesis that *-er* is +N (the agentive affix) rather than +Adj (the comparative affix).

(11) The fast-er
    (a)   The faster car ...
    (b)   The faster starved.

This strategy would result in an initial correct analysis of (11b); however in (11a) the processor would be led astray.

Relying on a strategy which presupposes that phrases are minimally expanded to include only obligatory constituents would lead to the prediction that phrases are closed as early as possible. In an example like (12) this predicts a preference for the interpretation in (12a). Intuitions, at least, do not seem to confirm the predictions of the strategy in ambiguous phrases (e.g., (11) and (12)), with the possible exception of phrases

(12) All the runners over ...
    (a)   All the runners overate (and got sick).
    (b)   All the runners over eight (got sick).

in which the alternative analysis is a structurally complex compound (e.g., *squad helps dog bite victim.*).

4.3. Determining the correctness of a prediction

Notice that even a strategy which makes predictions about adjacent words in the input string will be helpful only once the input string has already been segmented into words. Otherwise substrings corresponding to potential words of the predicted category will incorrectly be given highest priority. For example, in (11), the prediction that a determiner will be followed by a noun would initially be confirmed by analyzing *fast* as a noun. Clearly, information about the expected category of adjacent words is not sufficient to predict the likely category of adjacent morphemes or lexical items. Thus, a strategy of exploiting syntactic information about the expected category of adjacent words either cannot apply until after (potential) words have already been identified or the strategy will not have the desired effect. It will give rise to spurious expectations about the segmentation of the input and about the category of the constituents of the following words. In terms of the schematic representation in (13), if x, y, or z could be labeled +N, the processor would incorrectly take the item to be the head of a word, leading to an incorrect segmentation of the string, and a bias in favor of a category that is in fact no more expected (as a *constituent* of a word following a determiner) than some other category. Further, this analysis in turn would set up false expectations about the category of the following word.

(13) [+Det]   [predict +N]

    the x y z head

    It should be noted that in English the heads of major phrases (NP, AP, VP, PP) all participate in compounds (e.g., *streetwalk, bluebird, undersell*) and adjectives, nouns and verbs at least participate in category changing derivations (e.g., *sulleness, girlish, selective*). It follows that syntactic predictions concerning the heads of major phrases other than noun phrases will also be useful only after the processor has identified the "domain" of the word that it takes to be the head of the phrase (i.e., once the relevant word has been segmented from the acoustic string and/or the head of the word has been identified).

    We might assume, for example, that when *to* occurs in circumstances where it is unambiguously an infinitival marker (rather than a preposition *to*, number *two* or adverbial *too*), it predicts that a verb will follow. This will lead to incorrect segmentations in verbal compounds like (14) and in adverbs containing either verbal constituents, for example (15a), or nominal constituents with verbal counterparts, for example (15b).

(14) a. to fire... ([[fire]$_N$ fight]$_V$ vs.   fire the employee)
     b. to bus... ([[bus]$_N$ drive]$_V$ vs.   bus the students)

(15) a. to willingly surrender ([[[will]$_V$ ing]$_A$ ly]$_{Adv}$ vs.   to will...)
     b. to hopelessly continue ([[[hope]$_V$ less]$_A$ ly]$_{Adv}$ vs.   to hope...

Nonsystematic segmentation errors will of course also result, for example segmenting *want* as a verb in "to wantonly destroy". Thus the problems noted above are quite general, and involve all the major phrases of English.

    To summarize, until words have been identified, the processor cannot know which item in the input a syntactic prediction is a prediction about. As a result it is essentially irrelevant to the validity of the prediction whether the immediately following lexical item does or does not confirm the prediction. The prediction that the word following the infinitival marker *to* will be a verb may be confirmed by the next item in the input as in (15a) and (15b), and still turn out to be false (i.e., an adverb, not a verb, follows *to*); or the prediction may be true even in cases where the item which immediately follows *to* disconfirms the prediction (as in (14), where the compound is in fact a verb, though its first element is not). Thus, using syntactic predictions in word recognition will often complicate processing even when the sentence (i.e., the ultimately correct analysis) conforms to the prediction.

Even in the case of using absolute categorial predictions about the word-level syntax (e.g., the strict subcategorization requirement of a prefix), the problem arises of not knowing whether the prediction concerns the immediately following lexical item or some other constituent. But, in the case of phrase level syntactic predictions, this problem is compounded in two ways. The presence of optional intervening words and phrases will further complicate the relation between the syntactic prediction and the determination of what particular element in the input string it is a prediction about. And, the presence of uncertainty concerning two distinct levels of structure (the structure internal to the word and the phrase level syntax) will often entail that there is no transparent relation between the presence of apparent confirming or apparent disconfirming evidence and the actual correctness of the analysis based on the prediction. It seems difficult to believe that probabilistic predictions are really useful guides to analysis under these conditions.

4.4. Supplementing syntactic predictions with prosodic information

In the existing literature on syntactic priming, one typically encounters hypotheses stated in roughly the following form: immediately following a determiner, a (monomorphemic) noun is predicted to be easier to recognize than a (monomorphemic) verb. As several reviewers pointed out to me, it may be that phrase level syntactic information can only be exploited beneficially by lexical access procedures if its use is coordinated with the use of prosodic information. Thus, while the arguments above may be relevant to simplistic syntactic priming hypotheses of the form tested to date, they may not be relevant to some more fully articulated hypothesis claiming lexical access is facilitated by syntactic contexts with certain specific prosodic properties.

Prosody seems to play a crucial role in language processing. Presumably it often disambiguates the speech signal and guides the processor's hypothesis about the analysis of the signal. Thus, it may well be true that phrase level syntactic expectations, together with prosodic information, facilitate lexical identification. The above arguments may need to be reconsidered in this light. Rather than showing inherent limitations on the usefulness of phrasal-level syntactic expectations in lexical access, they may only highlight the need for more explicit and refined hypotheses about syntactic priming.

It is clearly worthwhile to develop more precise hypotheses about what lexical and syntactic information is conveyed by prosody. Nevertheless, there are reasons for being skeptical that prosody will provide a general panacea for the difficulties involved in the lexical and syntactic analysis of speech. It appears that prosodic structure not only guides the analysis of speech, but is also *a product* of whatever analysis the perceiver assigns to the speech signal. For example, perceivers hear pauses between sentences, regardless of whether any pause actually occurs. It would, therefore, not be too surprising if local prosodic cues were interpreted not just with reference to the global prosodic structure of the sentence, but also with reference to the linguistic analysis assigned to the sentence. If so, then it may turn out that prosody is least informative in some of the cases when it is most needed by the processor, namely, in cases of lexical and syntactic ambiguity—at least for those ambiguities not involving the boundaries of lexical and syntactic constituents. Indeed, this would provide at least one account of the verbal transformation study of Lackner and Tuller (1976), where the perception of prosody and of syntactic structure 'flip' together (jointly undergo radical revision of analysis).

There is a second reason for being skeptical that a better understanding of prosody will entirely eliminate the restrictions on the usefulness of phrase level syntactic predictions in lexical access. It appears that constraints on the relation between prosodic structure and syntactic structure are sufficiently loose that they often permit more than one phonological phrasing of a sentence (see Selkirk, 1984b). The particular option chosen by speakers often depends on the details concerning the length of constituents (Gee & Grosjean, 1983). At least one natural way to break a sentence like (16) into phonological phrases is to divide it between the verb and its complement. The sentence may then be pronounced with a rising contour on "mumbled" and a slight pause preceding "that", with no phrasal accent on "girl" (i.e., with a prosody very similar to that in (17)).

(16) The pretty little girl múmbled / that her parents were in the store.
(17) The pretty little toy múppet / cost a fortune in our local store.

One potentially useful prosodic generalization is that lexical heads of phrases often receive some sort of phrasal accent. However, if the above impression about the phrasing of (16) is correct, this generalization will not be very helpful in solving or circumventing the problems associated with syntactic priming. Even though the presence of a phrasal accent might help to identify the presence of the head ("mumbled" in (16)) of some phrase, there is no guarantee that the accented item will be the head of the current phrase. This problem arises because the absence of a phrasal accent will not indicate the absence of some (intervening) head of a phrase.

4.5. Conclusions

In this section I have argued that a language like English is simply not set up to make phrase level syntactic predictions very useful in lexical access, at least not if they are used independently from prosodic information. It might turn out that for evolutionary reasons humans are endowed with a particular type of word recognition device that results in priming or deactivation of lexical candidates on the basis of phrase level syntactic expectations; and, this simply happens to be less than optimal for a language like English. Therefore, we might ask whether other languages seem better suited than English for a word recognition device with this feature.

The obvious way for grammars to accommodate a word recognition system that uses expectations about the permissible or expected category of adjacent words during lexical access is for the language to guarantee that words are (always or typically) monomorphemic. By prohibiting the grammar of a language from containing one set of morphological rules (i.e., a word syntax) distinct from the rules of phrasal syntax, the grammar could insure that syntactic predictions were relevant to adjacent items in the input. Thus we might expect a strong tendency, both within and across languages, for there to be a one-to-one correspondence between morphemes and words. Certain languages in Asia do seem to be of this type. For example, Chinese and Vietnamese (cf. Comrie, 1979) are often characterized in approximately this way (though Emmon Bach has informed me that lexicalized compounds still seem to be permitted in these languages). However, to my knowledge, nobody has claimed this is an unusually common language type. Further, if there were strong processing reasons to favor such languages, we would have expected to find this characteristic in languages in diverse geographical areas, since the processing pressure favoring the characteristic would presumably be universal.

Perhaps there is some independent reason why languages with processes permitting or creating polymorphemic words should be highly valued (e.g., for purposes of acquisition). In this case we would still expect a tendency for words to be left-headed, since this too would permit syntactically based predictions to be useful; it would guarantee that the head of a word would reliably follow the item responsible for a syntactic category prediction. But it is a well-known fact (cf. Greenberg, 1965) that languages tend to be suffixing rather than prefixing—exactly what we wouldn't expect if languages tended to have left-headed words. Thus, even a quick glance at the languages of the world suggests that if the human word recognition system is structured so that it is inevitably sensitive to syntactic expectations, then evolution has been less than kind.

Showing that some processing system is not optimal and that the grammars of natural languages do not show any clear signs of accommodating the system obviously cannot provide conclusive evidence for or against the system. The arguments presented here do, however, suggest that it is likely to be information about the phonological and morphological structure of a language, not phrase and sentence-level syntactic structures, that is important in early stages of word recognition. Empirical evidence on syntactic priming seems to at least be consistent with these conclusions (see Tanenhaus and Lucas, 1987, this issue).[7] The current findings may be interpreted as showing that syntactically integrating a word with its context is accomplished particularly fast when the word confirms a syntactic expectation, but lexical access per se is unaffected.

5. Selecting the particular lexical form appropriate to context

Obviously language processing involves more than the recognition of particular families of words defined by some shared phonological representation. Even if cases of accidental homophony (e.g., *bank*) are set aside, structuring and interpreting a sentence often requires choosing between alternative uses of a lexical item, for example, those corresponding to alternative syntactic categories, subcategories, predicate–argument structures and/or thematic structures. The selection of the appropriate form of a word interacts with several distinct types of information. Indeed, it seems that the information influencing the selection of a particular lexical form is almost entirely distinct from the information which could be helpful in lexical access.

Consider the sentences in (18) where the category of the word *swing* will determine which feature, if any, the word assigns to its mother (noun phrase or verb phrase) node.

(18a)   The swing sets evenly on the ground.
(18b)   The swing sets are placed evenly on the ground.
(18c)   They swing sets of five children at once.

In (18a) *swing* must be analyzed as the head noun of the subject and thus must assign the feature "singular" to the subject noun phrase node; in (18b) *swing* is not the head noun and thus assigns no feature to the noun phrase node; in (18c) *swing* must be analyzed as a verb that assigns the feature "plural" to its mother node.

Thus to disambiguate the category of *swing*, the processor must assess the

---

[7]Wright and Garrett (1984) found that lexical decisions about words were facilitated when the word corresponded to the head of a highly predictable syntactic phrase. This might be interpreted as an instance of syntactic priming during lexical access. If so, it would seem to imply that priming must be assumed for heads of predictable phrases (or perhaps all obligatory members of predictable phrases) *and* for all items intervening between the head and the first item responsible for th prediction. Alternatively, we might attribute the facilitation effect they observed to a postlexical decision process which is sensitive to the syntactic integration of words. It would certainly be natural to assume that syntactic analysis of an item is performed more rapidly when the item confirms an obligatory syntactic prediction than when it does not.

consequence of alternative categories and alternative word structures for the feature composition of the mother node and determine whether the resulting node would be consistent with surrounding syntactic context. The information disambiguating the word may be carried by items preceding the word (e.g., in (18c)) or following it (e.g. (18a) and (18b)), depending on the particular lexical items that occur in the sentence.

The information disambiguating the (subcategory) of a word may be of any of a large variety of types as illustrated in (19)–(21).

(19a)   The man rolled ... (down the hill vs. the ball down the hill)
(19b)   The ball rolled ...
(20a)   The dancers met ... (frequently vs. the choreographer)
(20b)   The dancer met ... (*frequently vs. the choreographer)
(21a)   Sam hit the girl with a wart.
(21b)   Sam hit the girl with a bat.

An "ergative" verb like *roll*, wich may take an "agent" subject and a "theme" object or just a "theme" expressed in subject position, may be disambiguated by the animacy of its subject (assuming it requires an animate agent). Thus (19a) with an animate subject is ambiguous between a transitive and intransitive form, whereas (19b) only permits the intransitive form. Inherently plural predicates like *meet* obligatorily require an object (or some other internal argument) when they occur with singular subjects, but may occur as intransitive (or monadic) predicates when they occur with plural subjects, as in (20a). And, of course, the semantic content of a sentence can influence the number and kinds of arguments and the intended form a word takes, as in (21), where *hit* takes a single "theme" argument in its complement in (21a) due to the implausibility of a wart being used as an instrument for hitting. By contrast, *hit* may take either a (complex) noun phrase or a noun phrase followed by an instrumental prepositional phrase in (21b).

Examples implicating other types of information in the selection of the appropriate form of a word could be enumerated easily. The above examples are offered only by way of illustration, to give a taste of the variety of computations and information sources that may be involved.[8] In the face of this

---

[8]Since I am not aware of any on-line investigations of these issues using speech, I will briefly review the results of relevant visual studies. Basically, there are two generalizations which have emerged: sentences are processed more quickly if they conform to the more frequent subcategorization frame of a verb than if they do not (cf., Clifton, Frazier, & Connine, 1984; Fodor, 1978; Tanenhaus, Stowe, & Carlson, in press); and, the ultimately preferred analysis of an ambiguous sentence can depend on the specific verb the sentence contains either because of the nature of its preferred "lexical form" (see Ford, Bresnan, & Caplan, 1983) or because of the semantic or pragmatic fit between particular verbs and one or another analysis of surrounding lexical items (Ford et al., 1983; Mitchell & Holmes, in press; Rayner, Carlson, & Frazier, 1983). However, all of these results are at least compatible with an interpretation attributing the effects to an interpretive stage of processing which follows lexical and syntactic analysis of an input.

variety, it seems unlikely that the process of identifying a particular lexical form falls under the domain of the lexical access system. To the extent that the selection process is not governed by lexicon-internal factors (e.g., frequency), any notion of a single monolithic word recognition system concerned with all aspects of lexical processing is suspect.

I take it that questions like this about the boundaries of the lexical recognition system are ultimately empirical in nature. Once we have a better understanding of the principles governing the lexical analysis of language, presumably it will be possible to determine whether all aspects of lexical processing are accomplished by a single system or whether several systems are implicated. One thing is clear. If it is a single system, it must be an extremely powerful one given the range and nature of the processing tasks involved.

6. Conclusions

I would like to conclude by raising the question of whether the current characterization of the auditory word recognition problem is a fruitful one. The divide-and-conquer approach to the study of complex systems has been productive in general, but it is unlikely to be revealing if the initial idealization of a problem is inappropriate, for example does not carve an area into natural domains. It seems implicit in most experimental investigations that a theory of word recognition will emerge if we develop a theory of speech perception, on the one hand, and a theory of lexical access, on the other. Taken jointly, the two theories will explain how lexical items are identified in speech.

The simplicity of the (matching or activation) operations involved in lexical access is central to the current view of auditory word recognition. Given the assumption of an independent phonetic preprocessor which identifies the segmental composition of an input string, it is indeed natural to think of lexical identification routines as operations which move through this representation from 'left-to-right' sequentially matching it with (or activating) the segments of stored representations in the mental lexicon. Once a string of segments has been matched successfully with a lexical representation, that string can effectively be removed from consideration (e.g., from a current input buffer) and the cycle may be repeated.

This view of word recognition rests crucially on the assumption that phonetic preprocessing may be accomplished locally in a left-to-right manner, independent of lexical information and the lexical access procedures. If we abandon the assumption that phonetic preprocessing is independent, the access procedures must take into account information about the acoustic shape of segments in various phonological environments. If we abandon the assumption that phonetic preprocessing is local and essentially left-to-right, then the mapping between the phonetic representation and lexical representations becomes complex (along with whatever segmentation and matching operations accomplish this mapping). It thus becomes important to ask whether these (implicit) assumptions about phonetic preprocessing are consistent with what is known about speech perception.

Several studies seem to indicate that 'phonetic preprocessing' is sensitive to the existence or nonexistence of particular lexical representations (e.g., Connine & Clifton, 1984; Ganong, 1980; Samuels, 1981). Thus the assumption of an independent phonetic preprocessor may not be correct. And, what we know from studies of timing and duration in speech perception indicates that 'phonetic preprocessing' cannot be local. The interpretation of durational cues is not isolated from global prosodic properties of at least the current phonological phrase (cf., Grosjean, 1984; Liberman, 1975; Luce & Luce, 1983; Martin, 1979; Scott, 1982, for example). Further, it has been shown that the nature of a following segment may affect the classification of preceding segments (cf., Massaro & Cohen, 1983) challenging the assumption of strictly left-to-right phonetic processing. In short, the crucial implicit assumptions about the nature of phonetic processing are highly questionable.

My worry here is not that these basic assumptions may lead us to idealize the actual facts of phonetic processing; the worry is a more serious one, namely, that these assumptions may have lead to an inappropriate characterization of the basic problem in auditory word recognition. Put crudely, the basic problem in accessing or 'looking up' lexical representations may have little to do with matching two representations that are already couched in the same vocabulary. Rather the basic problem of lexical access may be the problem of grammatically structuring an acoustic input to *develop* a representation capable (potentially) of matching a lexical representation, that is, developing a representation couched in the same vocabulary as the vocabulary of lexical representations.

It is rarely useful to suggest abandoning the current characterization of a problem if no alternative approach is available. Preceding sections of this paper have emphasized that an alternative approach to the problem of auditory word recognition may already be within reach, if we examine how systems of (relevant) constraints on wellformed grammatical representations are used to structure an input into a possible lexical item of the perceiver's language.

References

Allen, M. (1978). *Morphological investigations.* University of Connecticut doctoral dissertation.

Bach, E. (1983). On the relationship between word-grammar and phrase grammar. *Natural Language and Linguistic Theory, 1*, 65–90.

Chomsky, N., & Halle, M. (1968). *The sound pattern of English.* New York: Harper & Row.

Clifton, C., Frazier, L., & Connine, C. (1984). Lexical expectations in sentence comprehension. *Journal of Verbal Learning and Verbal Behavior, 23*, 696–708.

Comrie, B. (1979). *Language universals and language typology.* Chicago: University of Chicago Press.

Connine, C., & Clifton, C. (1984). Evidence for the interactive nature of Ganong's lexical effect. University of Massachusetts, manuscript.

Conrad, C. (1974). Context in language comprehension: a study of the subjective lexicon. *Memory & Cognition, 2*, 130–138.

Cutler, A., & Foss, D.J. (1977). On the role of sentence stress in sentence processing. *Language and Speech, 20*, 1–10.

Cutler, A., Mehler, J., Norris, D., & Segui, J. (1983). A language specific comprehension strategy. *Nature, 304*, 159–160.

Eimas, P., Miller, J.L., & Jusczyk, P. (in press). On infant speech and the acquisition of language. In S. Harnad (Ed.) *Categorical perception.* Cambridge: Cambridge University Press.

Flores d'Arcais, F.B. (1982). Automatic syntactic computation in sentence comprehension. *Psychological Research, 44*, 231–242.

Fodor, J.D. (1978). Parsing strategies and constraints on transformations. *Linguistic Inquiry, 9*, 427–474.

Ford, M., Bresnan, J., & Kaplan, R. (1983). A competence-based theory of syntactic closure. In J. Bresnan (Ed.) *The mental representation of grammatical relations* (pp. 727–796) Cambridge, Mass.: MIT Press.

Forster, K. (1979). Levels of processing and the structure of the language processor. In W.E. Cooper & E.C.T. Walker (Eds.) *Sentence Processing.* Hillsdale, N.J.: Erlbaum.

Frazier, L. (1983). Review of Bresnan's *The Mental Representation of Grammatical Relations. Natural Language and Linguistic Theory, 1*, 281–310.

Ganong, W.F. (1980). Phonetic categorization in auditory word perception. *Journal of Experimental Psychology: Human Perception and Performance, 6*, 11–125.

Gee, J.P., & Grosjean, F. (1983). Performance structures: A psycholinguistic and linguistics appraisal. *Cognitive Psychology, 15*, 411–458.

Greenberg, J.H. (1965). Some universals of grammar with particular reference to the order of meaningful elements. In J.H. Greenberg (Ed.), *Universals of language.* Cambridge, Mass.: MIT Press.

Grosjean, F. (1984). How long is the sentence? Prediction and prosody in the on-line processing of language. Northeastern University, manuscript.

Henderson, L. (1985). Toward a psychology of morphemes. In A.W. Ellis (Ed.) *Progress in the psychology of language,* Vol. 1. London: Erlbaum.

Jackendoff, R. (1975). Morphological and semantic regularities in the lexicon. *Language, 51*, 639–671.

Kahn, D. (1976). *Syllable based generalization in English phonology.* MIT doctoral dissertation.

Kempley, S.T., & Morton, J. (1982). The effects of priming with regularly and irregularly related words in auditory word recognition. *British Journal of Psychology, 73*, 441–454.

Klatt, D.H. (1979). Speech perception: A model of acoustic phonetic analysis and lexical access. *Journal of Phonetics, 7*, 279–312.

Lackner, J., & Tuller, B. (1976). The influence of syntactic segmentation on perceived stress. *Cognition, 4*, 303–308.

Lehiste, I. (1973). Phonetic disambiguation of syntactic ambiguity. *Glossa, 7*, 107–122.

Liberman, M. (1975). *The intonational system of English.* MIT doctoral dissertation.

Liberman, M., & Prince, A. (1977). On stress and linguistic rhythm. *Linguistic Inquiry, 8*, 249–336.

Luce, P., & Charles-Luce, J. (1983). The role of fundamental frequency and duration in the perception of clause boundaries. *Research on Speech Perception*, Progress Report No. 9, Indiana University.

Marslen-Wilson, W., & Tyler, L. (1980). The temporal structure of spoken language understanding. *Cognition, 8*, 1–71.

Marslen-Wilson, W. (1987). Functional parallelism in spoken word-recognition. *Cognition, 25*, this issue.

Marslen-Wilson, W., & Welsh, A. (1978). Processing interactions and lexical access during word-recognition in continuous speech. *Cognitive Psychology, 10*, 29–63.

Martin, J.G. (1979). Rhythmic and segmental perception are not independent. *Journal of the Acoustical Society of America, 65*, 1268–1297.

Massaro, D.W., & Cohen, M.M. (1983). Phonological context in speech perception. *Perception & Psychophysics, 34*, 338–348.

Miller, J.L., Green, K., & Schermer, T.M. (no date). Obligatory processing: A distinction between the effects of sentential speaking rate and semantic congruity on word identification. Submitted to *Journal of Experimental Psychology: Human Perception and Performance*.

Miller, J.L., & Grosjean, F. (1981). How components of speaking rate influence perception of phonetic segments. *Journal of Experimental Psychology: Human Perception and Performance, 7*, 208–215.

Mitchell, D.C., & Holmes, V.M. (in press) The role of specific information about the verb in parsing sentences with local structural ambiguity. *Journal of Memory and Language*.

Morton, J. (1969). Interaction of information in word recognition. *Psychological Review, 76*, 165–178.

Murrell, G.A., & Morton, J. (1974). Word recognition and morpheme structure. *Journal of Experimental Psychology, 102*, 963–68.

Nakatani, L., & Dukes, K. (1977). Locus of segmental cues for word juncture. *Journal of the Acoustical Society of America, 62*, 714–719.

Norris, D., & Cutler, A. (in press) Juncture detection as a processing universal. To appear in U. Frauenfelder (Ed.) *Cross-linguistic approaches to word recognition*.

Rayner, K., Carlson, M., & Frazier, L. (1983). The interaction of syntax and semantics during sentence processing: Eye movements in the analysis of semantically biased sentences. *Journal of Verbal Learning and Verbal Behavior, 22*, 358–374.

Samuels, A. (1981). Phoneme restoration: insights from a new methodology. *Journal of Experimental Psychology: General, 110*, 474–494.

Scott, D. (1982). Duration as a cue to the perception of a phrase boundary. *Journal of the Acoustical Society of America, 71*, 996–1007.

Scott, D., & Cutler, A. (1984). Segmental phonology and perception of syntax. *Journal of Verbal Learning and Verbal Behavior, 23*, 450–466.

Seidenberg, M.S., Tanenhaus, M.K., Leiman, J.M., & Bienkowski, M. (1982). Automatic access of the meanings of ambiguous words in context: Some limitations of knowledge-based processing. *Cognitive Psychology, 14*, 489–537.

Selkirk, E. (1980). The role of prosodic categories in English word stress. *Linguistic Inquiry, 11*, 563–606.

Selkirk, E. (1982). *The syntax of words*. Cambridge, Mass.: MIT Press.

Selkirk, E. (1984a). On the major class features and syllable theory. In M. Aronoff (Ed.), *Language sound structure*. Cambridge, Mass.: MIT Press.

Selkirk, E. (1984b). *Phonology and syntax: The relation between sound and structure*. Cambridge, MA.: MIT Press.

Shockey, L., & Reddy, D.R. (1975). Quantitative analysis of speech perception. In G. Fant (Ed.) *Proceedings of the Stockholm Speech Communications Seminar*. New York: Wiley.

Slowiacek, M., Carroll, P., & Speer, S. (1985). Temporal organization and working memory. Paper presented at the 57th Annual Meeting of the Midwestern Psychological Association.

Stinson, M., & LaRiviere, C. (1976). Effects of rate and word boundary ambiguity on recall by normal and impaired listeners. *Journal of Psycholinguistic Research, 5*, 185–194.

Taft, L. (1983). Prosodic constraints in lexical segmentation. Presented at the Annual Meeting of the Linguistic Society of America, Minneapolis, December 1983.

Taft, L. (1985). *Prosodic constraints and lexical parsing strategies.* University of Massachusetts doctoral dissertation.

Tanenhaus, M., & Lucas, M. (1987) Context effects in lexical processing. *Cognition, 25*, this issue.

Tanenhaus, M., Stowe, L., & Carlson, G. (in press) The interaction of lexical expectations and pragmatics in parsing filler-gap constructions. To appear in *Cognitive Science, 7.*

Treiman, R. (1983). Word games and syllable structure. *Cognition, 15*, 79–84.

Williams, E. (1981). On the notions "lexically related" and "head of a word". *Linguistics Inquiry, 12*, 245–274.

Wright, B., & Garrett, M. (1984). Lexical decision in sentences: Effects of syntactic structure. *Memory & Cognition, 12*, 31–45.

Résumé

Les modèles dominants de la reconnaissance des mots parlés font jouer un rôle essentiel au composant d'accès lexical dans l'identification des mots. Pour ces modèles, le processus de reconnaissance est une opération simple qui associe l'input à des représentations lexicales emmagasinéés en mémoire ou qui active directement ces représentations. Etant donnée cette caractérisation du problème, on voit mal comment la connaissance qu'a l'auditeur de la structure de sa langue pourrait faciliter la reconnaissance des mots. Et pourtant, il peut être nécessaire d'utiliser la connaissance grammaticale pour résoudre bien de problèmes considérés comme importants par les théories de la reconnaissance des mots: la segmentation, la variabilité de la réalisation acoustique des mots et la reconnaissance de mots nouveaux.

   Cet article prend au sérieux la possibilité que la connaissance grammaticale participe à la reconnaissance des mots. Il étudie quels types d'information pourraient servir à cette fin. Il essaye aussi d'esquisser quel type de système de reconnaissance des mots pourrait tirer profit des régularités que l'on rencontre dans les langues naturelles.

8

The mental representation of the meaning of words*

P.N. JOHNSON-LAIRD

*MRC Applied Psychology Unit,
Cambridge*

Abstract

Five phenomena concerning the meanings of words are outlined in this paper. They concern (1) our limited introspective access to the nature of lexical representations; (2) the existence of lexical entries that make accessible the sense of a word; (3) the effects of context on the interpretation of words; (4) the systematic gaps in the acquisition of lexical knowledge; and (5) the existence of different semantic types of open-class word. These phenomena are used as the basis for a psychological theory of meaning of words.

1. Introduction

Outside a psychological laboratory, the recognition of words is seldom an end in itself, because listeners want to understand what they hear. Comprehension requires them to know and to retrieve the meaning of the words they recognize. Lexical meanings are the ingredients from which the sense of an utterance is made up, and its syntactic structure is the recipe by which they are combined. Listeners must put together the meanings of the words they recognize according to the grammatical relations that they perceive between them. Comprehension, however, does not end there, since it transcends purely linguistic knowledge. For example, anyone who knows English can retrieve the ingredients and combine them appropriately for a sentence such as:

Do you know who those people are?

The ingredients are the sense of the word "you", the sense of the word "people", and the senses of the other words in the sentence. But, the sense of the expressions must be distinguished from their reference—the particular entities or indi-

*I am grateful to Lolly Tyler for forcing me to write this article and to Patrizia Tabossi and the referees for their cogent criticisms of it. Requests for reprints should be sent to P.N. Johnson-Laird, MRC Applied Psychology Unit, 15 Chaucer Road, Cambridge CB2 2EF. United Kingdom.

viduals that expressions pick out in the world. Reference from the standpoint of psychology is not merely a question of individuals in the real world: human beings invent imaginary and hypothetical worlds and regularly refer to individuals within them. Unlike certain logicians, ordinary people do not treat all expressions that refer to non-existent entities as equivalent.

To grasp the sense of a phrase such as "those people" is generally a precursor to determining its reference—the particular set of individuals to whom the speaker is referring in uttering the sentence. Grasping sense is a matter of knowing the language; determining reference is a matter of much more since it usually depends on knowledge of the situation, knowledge of the speaker, knowledge of the conventions governing discourse, and the ability to make inferences. In the absence of these components, no-one can go from the sense of a sentence to its real significance, which depends on who or what it is about and also on why the speaker uttered it. Listeners need to determine who is referred to by "you" and "those people" in the example above and whether the speaker is asking a simple question demanding only the answer "yes" or "no", or making an indirect request for identifying information. They grasp the significance of the question only when they establish these facts.

There is, of course, no end to the process of recovering a speaker's intentions. Listeners may infer that the speaker needs to identify the relevant people, they may infer why the speaker has that need, and so on. As the processing of speech proceeds from phonology through words to comprehension, it thus becomes increasingly dependent on inferences based on the social and physical circumstances of the utterance, on a knowledge of the situation to which it refers, and on general knowledge.

This article is about the mental representation of the meaning of words, but the inferential basis of the higher orders of comprehension must be borne in mind in trying to understand lexical semantics—if only because the major phenomena apply equally to the interpretation of both speech and writing.

The plan of the article is simple. It describes five phenomena that concern the mental representation of the meanings of words, that is, their senses, since their references depend on their contexts of use. These phenomena are important clues to how the mind represents meaning. After the description of these clues, they are used to motivate a theory of the mental representation of lexical meaning. Although the theory is driven by data—in much the same way that word recognition itself proceeds, the data were not collected as a result of theory-free observations. As many philosophers of science have emphasized, it is doubtful whether any observations can be made without at least the glimmerings of some theoretical motivation. In the present case, however, the observations were made over a number of years and there is no simple unitary theory that led to them.

2. Consciousness and lexical meaning

The single most obvious phenomenon about the meanings of words is the difficulty of focusing consciousness upon them. If I ask you what does the verb "sight" mean in the sentence:

He sighted a herd of elephants on the plain

then you are immediately aware that you know the meaning of the word, and that you understand the sentence with no difficulty. You should also be able to offer a paraphrase of the word, such as:

to see something at a distance.

But the formulation of this paraphrase is not an immediate and automatic process. You cannot turn to the appropriate definition in a mental dictionary and read out the contents that you find there. It may take a second or two to formulate a definition, and in some cases, as we shall see, you may be unable to give a helpful definition at all. In short, you have an immediate awareness of knowing the sense of a word, but you have no direct introspective access to the representation of its meaning.

The importance of this simple observation is twofold. First, it presents us with the problem that is the topic of this article, because if we had a ready access to lexical representations it would hardly be necessary to advance a theory about them. Second, the very distinction between what we can and cannot be conscious of constitutes an important clue to the architecture of the mind. A good theory of linguistic processing should explain why listeners can be aware of the words and intonation that speakers use, and aware of understanding (or not understanding) what the words mean. It should also explain why listeners lack immediate introspective access to the nature of the representations that underlie the meanings of words and sentences. An answer to this question will indeed be offered in the final section of the article.

3. The existence of lexical entries

Because theorists are in the same predicament as everyone else when it comes to introspection, they lack any immediate evidence for the existence of a mental representation of the senses of words. Indeed, a major psychological issue is whether there are lexical entries in the mind that give the meanings of words. Some theorists have assumed that the sense of a word consists of a structured set of semantic features into which its meaning is decomposed (e.g., Schaeffer & Wallace, 1970; Smith, Shoben, & Rips, 1974). Others assume that the mental lexicon takes the form of a semantic network (e.g., Anderson, 1976; Anderson & Bower, 1973; Collins & Quillian, 1969; Rumelhart, Lindsay, & Norman, 1972), or a combination of network and features (Glass & Holyoak, 1974/5). A third sort of theory, however, rejects the notion of semantic decomposition, and assumes that there are no semantic representations for words, only a vast set of rules of inference, or "meaning postulates" (see e.g., Fodor, Fodor, & Garrett, 1975; Fodor, 1977, Ch.5; Kintsch, 1974). Meaning postulates in such theories specify entailments that depend on words, for example

for any x, y, if x is on the right of y, then y is on the left of x.

It is difficult to obtain crucial psychological evidence to decide amongst these theories. But, on the one hand, comprehension does not appear to call for a process of decomposition (see Fodor et al., 1975; Johnson-Laird, 1983); and, on the other hand, there is evidence which, though it was designed with another issue in mind, casts doubt on the meaning postulate theories (see Johnson-Laird, Gibbs, & de Mowbray, 1978). If readers wish to participate in a single trial of the experiment, which takes only a few minutes, they should carry out each of the following instructions without looking ahead to the next instruction.

(1) Scan as quickly as possible the list of words in Table 1; ticking in pencil those that denote things that are both solid and ordinarily fit for human consumption, for example, tick "pear", but not "whisky" which is consumable but not solid, and not "ivory" which is solid but not consumable. This is a simple task that ordinarily takes only a few seconds.

Table 1.   *Search down these lists of words as quickly as possible for those that denote things that are normally solid (as opposed to liquid) and fit for human consumption*

sherry	knife	hammer	linoleum
ammonia	jug	ink	pippette
bucket	apple	cream	petrol
quartz	toaster	carafe	paraffin
skewer	syringe	needle	biscuit
broom	water	coal	plate
toffee	wood	veal	beer

(2) Cover up Table 1 so that it is no longer visible.

(3) Try to recall and to write down all the words in Table 1—every word, not just those that were ticked.

We carried out two experiments using a similar procedure, one in which the subjects listened to a brief auditory presentation of each word, and the other in which the subjects read through a list of words as quickly as possible. Both experiments showed that the more components that a word in the list had in common with the target category, the more likely it was to be remembered (see Table 2). Thus, a word such as "beer" which has one of the required components is more likely to be remembered than a word such as "petrol" which has neither of the key components. This result presumably reflects the amount of processing carried out on each word (Johnson-Laird et al., 1978; Ross, 1981), or the number of retrieval cues provided by the target components (McClelland, Rawles, & Sinclair, 1981), or both. It is neutral with respect to the existence of dictionary entries. However, Table 1 also includes words that denote, not substances, but utensils of various sorts. We found that such words in general were not so well recalled as the substance words, yet as Table 2 shows there was a significant trend within them. A word such as "plate" denotes a utensil that is used for consumable solids, whereas a word such as "vase" is used for non-consumable liquids. In general, the greater the match between the type of utensil and the target category the better the recall.

If there are no lexical entries but only a vast list of meaning postulates, subjects should reject all the utensils in the same way. Suppose the target category is "consumable solids", then they should search for postulates of the form:

$$\text{For any } x, \text{ if } x \text{ is a } \begin{Bmatrix} \text{plate} \\ \text{jug} \\ \text{hammer} \\ \text{vase} \end{Bmatrix} \text{ then } x \text{ is consumable,}$$

Table 2. *The percentages of words correctly recalled in the experiment carried out by Johnson-Laird, Gibbs, and de Mowbray (1978)*

| | Semantic components of the target category possessed by the words | | | |
	Both	One	Neither	Overall
Substance words	50.0	21.5	10.6	27.4
Utensil words	16.2	10.6	8.1	11.7

and fail to find them. Likewise, they would succeed in finding each of the postulates:

For any x, if x is a $\left\{ \begin{array}{c} \text{plate} \\ \text{jug} \\ \text{hammer} \\ \text{vase} \end{array} \right\}$ then x is solid.

Hence the postulate theory cannot explain the trend in the data. However, if there are lexical entries from which the semantic information about a word is readily accessible, then the entry for a word such as "plate" will make available the fact that plates are utensils used to serve *consumable solids*, whereas the entry for "vase" will not make available any information containing these target components. Subjects searching the list for consumable solids are therefore likely to carry out more processing in order to reject "plate" than to reject "vase", and this extra amount of processing accounts for the greater memorability of "plate". A similar explanation in terms of the cues to recall provided by "consumable" and "solid" again depends on the ease of recovering the target components from the lexical entry for "plate". The trend in the memorability for the utensil words can therefore be best explained on the assumption that there are comprehensive lexical entries containing specifications of the senses of words. The trend cannot readily be accounted for by inferences made after lexical access on the basis of independent meaning postulates.

4. Context and lexical meanings

Linguistic context has well-known effects on the recognition of spoken and written words (see e.g. Fischler & Bloom, 1979; Meyer & Schvaneveldt, 1971; Schuberth & Eimas, 1977; Swinney, Onifer, Prather, & Hirshkowitz, 1979; Tanenhaus, 1987, this issue; Tweedy, Lapinsky & Schvaneveldt, 1977). It also has effects on the interpretation of words. This phenomenon is hardly surprising because words are notoriously ambiguous. There is considerable evidence which suggests that all the different senses of an ambiguous word are initially activated (Cairns & Kamerman, 1975; Conrad, 1974; Holmes, Arwas, & Garrett, 1977; Swinney, 1979). Yet the evidence may not be decisive. Patrizia Tabossi (personal communication) has made an interesting observation using the "cross-modal lexical decision task" developed by Swinney in which subjects hear a sentence and then at some point within it have to decide whether or not a visually presented string of letters is a word in the language. Tabossi found that where the disambiguating sentential context brings to mind a salient aspect of the more frequent meaning of an ambiguous word within it, then the time to make the lexical decision is faster if the word relates to this salient feature than if it relates to the other meaning of the word. Thus, in Italian, the sentence:

> Because of the terrible climate the explorers almost died in an expedition to the pole, which was long and difficult.

contains the ambiguous word, "polo", which may refer either to one of the world's poles or to the game played on horseback. The sentence not only disambiguates the word, but brings to mind a salient aspect of the world's poles, namely, their coldness. The time to decide that the string, "cold", presented visually immediately after the spoken word "polo" in the sentence, is reliably faster than the decision for the string, "horse", which relates to the other meaning of "polo". Some further results of Tabossi suggest that the effect does not arise from associative cueing by other words in the sentence. Perhaps contexts that bring to mind salient features of the main meaning of an ambiguous word eliminate the need to retrieve all of its meanings.

Listeners are normally aware of an ambiguity only if it is unresolved by the rest of the sentence. Hence the mechanism for resolving lexical ambiguities operates rapidly, automatically, and outside awareness. The standard linguistic account is that the mechanism centres on "selectional restrictions", that is, specifications of the senses of other words occurring in construction with the ambiguous word. Thus, the ambiguity of "board" is resolved in the sentence, "He sued the board", because the verb "sue" takes as its object only people and institutions: one cannot sue a plank of wood. This standard piece of lexicography was elevated into linguistic theory by Katz and Fodor (1963). Unfortunately, however, it has become clear that the crucial disambiguating component is often, not the sense of a word, but its reference. Consider the following discourse, for example:

> The client received the cheque on Tuesday. He banked it.

The second sentence contains an ambiguous verb, which can be paraphrased as "to form a border or bank (out of some substance)", "to tilt (an aircraft) in flight", or "to deposit (money) in a bank". Yet, the sentence is unambiguous because the reference of "it" is plainly the cheque, and it is highly improbable that he formed a border or bank out of a cheque or was using it as an aircraft. For this and other reasons (Johnson-Laird, 1983, p. 233) it seems safer to assume that disambiguation generally depends on inferences based on a knowledge of the reference of expressions.

How many different meanings are there for a verb such as "eat"? Some linguists have argued that this verb, like many others, is highly polysemous.

Indeed, Weinreich (1966) claimed there are different senses of "eat" corresponding to eating soup with a spoon; eating a steak with a knife and fork; eating chop suey with chopsticks, and so on. Halff, Ortony, and Anderson (1976) have similarly claimed that words have many meanings and that a particular sense of a word is "instantiated" when it is used in context. Thus, in the sentence, "A fish attacked a swimmer," the sense of "fish" that is instantiated is likely to be equivalent to "shark". Anderson and his colleagues have reported a number of experiments in which a word corresponding to an instantiation, for example "shark", turns out to be a better recall cue to the sentence than the original word that occurred in it, e.g. "fish" (see Anderson & Ortony, 1975; Anderson, Pichert, Goetz, Schallert, Stevens, & Trollip, 1976). Garnham (1979) has obtained the same effect with verbs, for example "fried" is a better recall cue than the original verb for "The housewife cooked the chips", though not, as is to be expected, for "The housewife cooked the peas".

In fact, there has been too much emphasis on polysemy and in consequence a mistaken view about the mechanism of instantiation. Linguists have formulated more accurate linguistic criteria for ambiguity (Zwicky & Sadock, 1973), and the crucial psychological criterion is whether or not it is necessary to postulate more than one semantic representation for a word in order to account for the interpretations of the sentences in which it occurs. Instead of asking how many different meanings can be squeezed out of the word, psycholinguists need to ask what is the minimum number of different senses that are necessary to cope with all of its different uses. If "eat" were truly polysemous then the sentence:

He eats the food

should be highly ambiguous. It should have many wholly distinct senses. Yet it remains unequivocal. What is true, however, is that the sentence in common with others can be truthfully asserted of an infinite number of different situations: "he" can refer to any male individual, "food" can designate an indefinite number of different types of food served in an indefinite number of different conditions, and the manner by which the food is eaten can vary in an indefinite number of different ways from chewing it like cud to straining it through the teeth. This indeterminacy of reference is not sufficient to establish ambiguity because, if it were, all open-class words would be infinitely ambiguous and their meanings could not be contained by a finite brain. Hence the sentence above, which truly applies to a variety of situations, is referentially indeterminate, but not ambiguous. Its syntax is unambiguous, and its words are unambiguous: they each have in ordinary usage a single sense, but these senses suffice, as do the senses of all words, to embrace many different situations. The sentence requires only a single representation of its meaning.

A comparable mistake has been made in the standard interpretation of instantiation. Context can, of course, pick out the appropriate sense of a genuinely ambiguous word, for example "He banked the cheque." However, the instantiation of an unambiguous word such as "fish" by a sentential context does not depend on picking out one sense from a long list of possibilities. A simple thought experiment, which was proposed in Johnson-Laird (1981), suggests a more plausible interpretation. Consider the sentence:

> It frightened the swimmer.

It may well be that the word "shark" would make a better recall cue for this sentence than the original word, the pronoun "it", that functions as its subject. However, it is obvious that this pronoun does not have a vast set of different senses: it has a single sense that enables it to refer to any of a potentially infinite set of entities. Its reference can depend on its linguistic context if it is used to refer to something that is identified elsewhere in the discourse, or it can depend directly on the reference situation if it is used deictically. Instantiation is therefore a process, not of eliminating senses from a list in a lexical entry, but of imagining a more specific situation than is warranted solely by the meanings of words (see also Gumenik, 1979, for results that can be interpreted in the same way).

All open-class words, such as "fish" and "eat", are closer to being pronouns than is commonly recognized: they provide a relatively simple semantic framework that can be enriched by inferences based on knowledge. These inferences concern the situation designated by the sentence, and different linguistic contexts highlight different aspects of lexical meaning. Consider, for instance, the following sentences:

> The tomato rolled across the floor.
> The sun was a ripe tomato.
> He accidentally sat on a tomato.

The first sentence calls to mind the characteristic shape of a tomato, the second its characteristic colour, and the third its characteristic squashiness (see Johnson-Laird, 1975). Listeners know all these aspects of tomatoes, and many more, but when they initially interpret a sentence they are most unlikely to call to mind all of this information (*pace* Gibson, 1971) or none of it (*pace* Fodor, Fodor, & Garrett, 1975). Instead, they are likely to retrieve some information—the most relevant for imagining the state of affairs depicted by the sentence, and the rest of the sentence is one obvious cue to what is relevant.

This hypothesis has been corroborated in a number of experiments carried out by the author and his colleagues. Thus, the occurrence of a verb such as "pleased" suggests that the object of the sentence will be something that is animate, and subjects are indeed faster to detect the presence of an animate noun when it occurs in such a sentence than when it occurs in a sentence with a verb such as "soaked" (see Hodgkin, 1977). The facilitation occurs even when the target noun occurs prior to the verb. Similarly, if subjects are asked a specific question that hinges on the sense of a word, such as:

Is a diamond brilliant?

then, as Tabossi and Johnson-Laird (1980) have shown, their response is faster when the question follows a sentence such as:

The mirror dispersed the light from the diamond

than when it follows a sentence that does not call to mind the relevant aspect of diamonds:

The film showed the person with the diamond.

As we expected, subjects are slower to answer the question when the preceding sentence calls to mind some other but irrelevant aspect of diamonds, such as their hardness:

The goldsmith cut the glass with the diamond.

Table 3 presents the mean latencies to respond correctly to the questions and the mean numbers of errors. Subsequent experiments have shown that the phenomenon is equally apparent whether the priming is a result of selectional restrictions on the sense of a word or factual inferences about its likely referent (Tabossi, 1982).

For all of these experiments, independent panels of judges established that the priming sentences genuinely called to mind the relevant element of meaning, and the design made it very difficult for the subjects to guess which word in a sentence the subsequent question would be about or what the question

Table 3.   *The mean latencies (ms) and mean errors (max = 12) to respond to questions about nouns in the Tabossi and Johnson-Laird (1980) experiment*

	Responses after a relevant priming sentence	Responses after a non-priming sentence	Responses after an irrelevant priming sentence
Latencies	1016	1089	1142
Errors	0.54	0.88	1.33

would be. Tabossi (1983) has even shown that there is a more general form of priming in which the initial sentence need not contain any of the nouns in the question. Thus, for example, the sentence:

The fountain pen left a spot in the desk drawer

enables subjects to respond faster to the subsequent question:

Does ink leave a stain?

than when it occurs after a neutral sentence that does not call to mind the relevant property of ink.

Linguistic context evidently has at least three different effects on the interpretation of words. First, it can enable the listener to select the appropriate sense of a truly ambiguous word. Second, it can lead to a representation of more specific referents than is strictly warranted by the sense of an unambiguous word. For example, a listener imagines a shark as an instance of the generic term, "fish", since a shark is a plausible actor in the situation described by the sentence. Third, it can call to mind particular aspects of a word's interpretation—at the expense of other aspects. Thus, it plays a major part in the interpretation of compound nouns, such as "hot dog man" (see Clark, 1983). The context of a cooperative game can even lead people to a tacit negotiation of specific meanings for general nouns, such as "row" and "column" (Anderson, 1983). What has sometimes been underestimated in all of these cases is the importance of reference, or more properly, its psychological correlate: the representation of specific referents, real or imaginary, in particular situations. What the context refers to can disambiguate a word; it can instantiate a more specific referent; and it can suggest an aspect of a word's meaning that is particularly relevant to what is going on.

5. The acquisition of lexical meanings

People often do not know the meaning of a word in their language. Such ignorance may not matter. If someone says:

The explorers survived on pemmican and truffles

you may readily understand this remark, and only on being specifically questioned realize that you do not know exactly what pemmican and truffles are. The reason that an incomplete grasp of lexical meaning may be sufficient for comprehension is that you are nevertheless able to imagine the state of affairs described by the sentence. The evidence of the previous section shows that you do not necessarily retrieve all the semantic information that you possess about a word. If you lack some information, the gap may go unnoticed where it is not crucial to understanding the sentence.

Gaps in lexical knowledge are predictable. People are likely to be aware of what is important, and thus, for instance, if they know anything about the sense of a word they should know whether or not it means a substance fit for human consumption. They are similarly more likely to be aware of a perceptible property, such as whether a substance is solid or liquid, than of a more covert property, such as its provenance (whether it is natural or manmade). Graham Gibbs and I quizzed two groups of subjects about these three aspects of a set of rare words (see Johnson-Laird, 1975). Typically, our subjects knew for instance that "pemmican" was consumable and that "verdigris" was not, but their knowledge of the structure and provenance of these substances was less secure. Table 4 presents the mean numbers of errors that the subjects made on a set of 48 rare words. The trend was reliable for both groups. Of course, exceptions to the general trend are to be expected where a particular aspect of a substance is highly salient, and such exceptions have been demonstrated by Emma Coope (in an unpublished experiment).

Gaps in lexical knowledge point to the importance of the process of acquisition, since the way in which concepts are acquired will inevitably be reflected in the form and content of lexical entries. There are two obvious processes by which you can acquire the meaning of a word: you can be told what the word means or you can infer what it means from encountering it in use. To be told the meaning of a word presupposes that it is possible to frame a useful definition of its meaning. Jerry Fodor has often claimed that there are no good definitions (see e.g., Fodor, Garrett, Walker, & Parkes, 1980). The truth is—as many lexicographers would assert—there are no good definitions for *some* words. For other words, there are excellent definitions. Indeed the majority of words in the Oxford English Dictionary can only be acquired by definition because they hardly ever occur in actual discourse. Such words are in fact easy to define in a way that is genuinely informative, e.g. "an arblast

Table 4.   *The mean errors in categorizing 48 rare words on three semantic contrasts*

	Sample 1: University students (N = 24)	Sample 2: Technical college students (N = 12)
Consumable/Nonconsumable	4.7	5.0
Solid/Liquid	6.7	7.3
Natural/Manmade	9.1	10.0

is a cross-bow, consisting of a steel bow fitted to a wooden shaft, furnished with a special mechanism for drawing and letting slip the bowstring, and discharging arrows, bolts, stones, etc." Other words, however, are singularly difficult to define in a way that is useful. Dr. Johnson was perhaps satirizing the futility of definition in these cases when he defined a network as "anything reticulated or decussated, at equal distances, with interstices between the intersections". Anyone who does not know the meaning of the definiens is hardly likely to be helped by the definiendum.

Is there any way of predicting the difficulty of defining the meaning of a word? Gerry Quinn and I set out to answer this question in an experimental study of definitions. We asked our subjects to try to define a series of verbs in a way that would help children or foreigners whose grasp of English was insecure. We chose four levels of semantic complexity of the verbs following the analyses of Miller and Johnson-Laird (1976), and we predicted that semantically complex verbs, such as "watch" and "lend", would be easier to define than the semantically simplest verbs, such as "see" and "own". It should be easy to break down the meaning of a complex verb into simpler components for which there are corresponding words, but it should be hard to find such components for a simple verb. Our prediction was confirmed. For the simplest of the verbs, the subjects could at best offer only synonyms, which would not be very helpful to poor speakers of the language. As for the remaining verbs, the more complex they were, the easier the subjects found the task and the more accurate their definitions (see Johnson-Laird & Quinn, 1976).

The traditional account of lexical acquisition is that a child learns an association between a word and the thing that it denotes. There are many problems with this idea—establishing the set of referents for a word should not be confused with the mere conditioning of a stimulus (Harrison, 1972), the word could designate any of the manifold properties of the object rather than the object itself (Wittgenstein, 1953), and many words have either no perceptible referent or else are parts of speech for which the notion is irrelevant. Above all, however, children are no mere passive receivers of word-object associations: they entertain their own hypotheses about the meanings of words (Bowerman, 1977), and they coin their own words if no-one provides them with a suitable term (Clark, 1982). Hence, although children acquire words from observing them in use, a comprehensive theory of this process, such as might be modelled in a computer program, is a long way from being formulated. There are even theorists who are so perplexed by the process that they argue that learning has little role to play in it, and that concepts are innate and merely "triggered" by experience (Fodor, 1980). Although a native endowment is crucial, the phenomena above and some that I will describe in a moment imply that a form of learning does underlie the acquisition of lexical meanings.

Conservative estimates of the rate at which children acquire words suggest that at around the age of five they are adding to their vocabulary some 20 or more words per day (see e.g., Templin, 1957; Miller, 1977, 1986). So rapid a rate is hardly consistent with a theory that allows only for simple associative learning. One interesting conjecture is that children can pick up elements of the meaning of a word merely from hearing it used appropriately in constructions containing words that they already understand. Til Wykes and I confirmed this conjecture in an experiment with 3- and 4-year-olds. The children listened twice to a series of stories. Each story contained a novel word that the children had not heard before. For example, one story featured the novel verb, "mib", which was used transitively with a meaning resembling "soak" and intransitively with a meaning resembling "spill"—our idea was to inhibit the children from merely substituting a familiar synonym for the nonsense syllable. After they had heard the story twice, the children were able to pick out the one entity (orange juice) that could mib from a set of four alternatives. Their performance was similar for the other three nonsense verbs, and it remained above chance one week later when they had to carry out the same task with a new set of alternatives (see Wykes & Johnson-Laird, 1977). In an unpublished study, Jon Davies showed that children could also acquire elements of the meanings of nonsense *nouns* from hearing them used in constructions with verbs with which they were familiar.

There may be an analogy between acquiring a language and the implementation of a compiler for a new high level programming language. A compiler is a special program for taking programs written in the new language and translating them into the machine code that controls the actual operation of the computer. It is sensible to write part of the compiler in assembly language (which maps readily into machine code), and to write the rest of the compiler in the new language itself. The former translates the latter into machine code, and saves the designers from the chore of writing the whole of the compiler in assembly language. It is not too far-fetched to imagine that lexical learning lifts itself up by its own bootstraps in a similar way. Children first learn, or perhaps know innately, how to relate certain internal representations to states of affairs in the world. Once a fragment of the language has been mapped onto this knowledge, it becomes possible to acquire other words indirectly by inferring their meaning from the contexts in which they occur or by being given explicit definitions of them. Some words are likely to fall clearly into the category of those acquired by direct acquaintance, for example simple words like "see" and "own" that are so hard to define; other words are likely to fall clearly into the category of indirect acquisitions, for example "arblast" and "eleemosynary". Many words, however, will be of mixed acquisition; and different individuals will acquire a given word in different ways.

6. Meanings and prototypes

To understand an assertion is to know how the world would be if the assertion were true. This formula does not imply that when you understand an assertion you know how to verify it, or indeed that it is possible to verify it. It is one thing to know how the world should be and quite another to know how to find out whether the world is in that condition. However, if you have no idea what constraints an assertion implies about reality, then you have no idea what it means. One striking feature of natural language is that for the language community as a whole there are lexical items (within the same syntactic category) that vary in the completeness with which their semantics specifies this information. Consider the earlier example:

He sighted a herd of elephants on the plain.

The function words and the words "sighted", "herd", and "plain", have a complete semantics, because no conceivable advance in human knowledge can force us to add to our conception of their meaning or to cause us necessarily to modify it. The way we conceive the world given the truth of this utterance is, in principle, completely specified as far as the meanings of these words are concerned. The case is different for the word, "elephant". Most speakers of English have a good idea of what an elephant is—they have seen an elephant, or a picture of one, and they know something of the nature of the beast. Yet the term is a theoretical one. It designates a set of creatures within our categorization of animals. Our knowledge of such matters is far from complete, and we are committed to the existence of the category without knowing for certain what the essentials of elephanthood actually are—indeed without knowing incontrovertibly that the class is a truly unitary one. Such words notoriously give rise to the problem of demarcating what should go into the dictionary from what should go into the encyclopedia—a problem for which there appears to be no principled solution (see Gerrig, 1985). These words are "natural kind terms", and it is doubtful whether there are any necessary and sufficient conditions for defining them (Putnam, 1975).

The existence of natural kind terms has important implications for the contents of lexical entries. The entry for "elephant" is likely to include information that can be used for identifying elephants and for imagining them, as well as other conceptual information (Miller & Johnson-Laird, 1976). If I assert that I have sighted an elephant, then you will interpret my utterance to mean that I saw a large, four-legged mammal with tusks and a trunk. Such interpretations cannot be mediated by meaning postulates or any other form of lexical representation that implies that these attributes are necessary components of elephants. They are not; an elephant may lack any of them. They are not essential characteristics; and they are not mere inductions, since to check them inductively presupposes some independent method of first identifying elephants. In fact, they are part of our "theory" of elephants, which tells us that a prototypical member of the class has each of these attributes.

Eleanor Rosch and her colleagues have collected much evidence that is consistent with the existence of prototypes (e.g., Rosch, 1976). Real objects, unlike many of the concepts studied in the psychological laboratory, have features that are correlated—if an animal has a trunk, it tends to have tusks—and such correlations will be reflected in the prototype. Likewise, not all instances of a concept are equally representative, and the speed with which instances are categorized depends on how prototypical they are (Rosch, 1973). The major problem with prototypes is how they are represented in the mental lexicon. Rosch (1976) has suggested that a prototype is represented by a concrete image of an average category member. Ironically, Kant (1787) had already raised a decisive objection to this theory:

> In truth, it is not images of objects, but schemata, which lie at the foundation of our pure sensuous conceptions. No image could ever be adequate to our conception of triangles in general. For the generalness of the conception it could never attain to, as this includes under itself all triangles, whether right-angled, acute-angled, etc., whilst the image would always be limited to a single part of this sphere.

The lexical entry for "elephant" must therefore consist of a schema representing the prototypical animal, and perhaps the best way to think of a schema is in terms of a mental model defined in terms of an interrelated set of "default values" (Minsky, 1975), that is, specific values for variables that can be assumed in the absence of information to the contrary. Thus, default values have a different status to the normal representation of a word's contribution to the truth conditions of a sentence. Normal truth conditions support valid inferences since they are necessary components of a word's meaning. Default values place a weaker constraint on how the world should be: they hold only in the case that nothing is asserted to the contrary. Hence, your knowledge of the default values for "elephant" lead you to assume that I saw an animal with one trunk, two tusks, four legs, etc., unless you have evidence to the contrary.

Lexical entries containing default values still place constraints on the world, but they do so indirectly by way of the set of alternative prototypes governing a domain. You will not necessarily judge that I spoke falsely if the animal I saw had no trunk and one tusk. But, you will think me mistaken if, on inspection, the beast turns out to fit the prototype of a rhinoceros, or alternatively not to fit the prototype of an animal at all.

7. Towards a theory of the representation of lexical meanings

The clues of the five previous sections fit together to suggest a coherent picture of the meanings of words. This theory, which I will outline here, is intended to answer three central questions: What are the contents of lexical meanings? How are they mentally represented? And what is their role in speech and comprehension?

The evidence from the semantic search task implies that there are entries in the mental lexicon that allow ready access to the information that an individual has about the sense of a word. The contents of an entry may be incomplete in one of two distinct ways. First, the individual may have yet to acquire a complete semantics for the word; second, the word may be a theoretically based one for which there is only an incomplete semantics. There are other expressions and nonce words with meanings that depend essentially on the context in which they occur, for example, the verb "porched" as in "The newsboy porched the newspaper" (see Clark & Clark, 1979; Clark, 1983). Words that are acquired by direct acquaintance with their denotata are likely to have lexical entries that contain ineffable specifications of their truth conditions, that is, entries that specify how the world has to be for them to apply to it, and that are all but impossible to define. In the case of natural kind terms, a major component of the representation of sense will consist of default values.

Words with a more complex semantics may be acquired from verbal definitions, or from encountering their use in verbal expressions. Their lexical representation may accordingly relate them to other words. Most words in common usage are likely to possess elements of both sorts of information, for example, people have access to procedures for imagining elephants, and they have access to other conceptual information about elephants, which they may have acquired either from usage or from a definition, such as the fact that elephants are animals.

The theory therefore draws a basic distinction between ineffable truth conditions (akin to expressions in machine code) and verbal definitions (akin to expressions in a high level programming language). The distinction relates, of course, to the old arguments about the existence of semantic primitives. What it implies, however, is that although primitives exist they are remote from the directly expressible analyses of the meanings of words. They are unanalysable by normal cognitive mechanisms, outside conscious awareness, and presumably innate. One can advance plausible conjectures, however, about the functions that they are used to compute, for example, the perceptual representation of the world, the representation of discourse in the form of an imagined model of the state of affairs it describes, and the choice of appropriate words to describe a perceived or imaginary state of affairs. Likewise, one can begin to advance hypotheses about their role in the identification of objects (Marr, 1982) and in the construction of mental models of discourse (Johnson-Laird, 1983).

The specifications of verbal relations in the lexicon can be based on some mechanism akin to a semantic network or to meaning postulates, though the power of such theories is likely to make it difficult to test them empirically (see Johnson-Laird, Herrmann, & Chaffin, 1984).

The specifications of truth conditions in the lexicon can be thought of as the ingredients necessary for the procedures that construct, modify, and manipulate mental models. Thus, the representation of, say, "on the left of" calls for a specification that will enable a verification routine to scan a mental model in the appropriate direction to verify the relation, and that will enable a construction routine to scan a mental model in the appropriate direction before adding an element to the model, and so on.

The specification of default values can depend on similar procedures, but their results in models can be undone in the light of other information. Exactly such procedures are needed in any case whenever a model is based on information that is insufficiently determinate to specify a unique situation, that is whenever a model is based on virtually any piece of discourse. I describe my office, for instance, and you form a mental model of the arrangement of the furniture, but since my description is bound to be consistent with more than one possibility, you may have to revise your model in the light of subsequent information (see Johnson-Laird, 1983, for a description of computer programs using both truth conditions and default conditions of these sorts).

The dichotomy between ineffable truth conditions and verbal formulae has a number of repercussions. The logical properties of words, for instance, can arise in two distinct ways: from a representation of an explicit verbal relation ("elephants are animals") or from the consequences of the representations of their truth conditions. Hence, if you know what has to be the case for something to be an elephant, and you know what has to be the case for something to be an animal, then a simple thought experiment will lead you to the same conclusion that elephants are animals. There are a number of clear cases where the logical properties of words arise only from their truth conditions, because the vagaries of their logical behaviour are too great to be encompassed by simple verbal definitions, for example, natural language quantifiers, and spatial expressions such as "on the left of".

The contrast between verbal formulae and truth conditions also arises in the interpretation of discourse, which seems to call for a listener to construct an initial verbal representation close to the linguistic form of the utterance and then to use this representation, together with lexical entries, to construct a mental model of the discourse. Although the existence of these two levels of representation is a matter of controversy, they are borne out by the need for independent representations of sense and reference, by linguistic phenomena such as the two classes of anaphora (surface and deep), and by experimental results on the memory for discourse (see e.g. Mani & Johnson-Laird, 1982; Johnson-Laird, 1983).

A major problem confronting the present theory is to reconcile two important constraints on the process of comprehension. On the one hand, information from an utterance is integrated into the existing model as a function of the referential links, if any, between the utterance and the model; on the other hand, the interpretation of the sense of a sentence almost certainly depends on combining the senses of its constituent words according to the syntactic relations between them. No existing theory has yet shown how these two different demands can be met within a single unitary theory of comprehension.

One question remains: why do we lack a conscious access to the nature of lexical representations? The answer is that the truth conditions of words are intimately dependent on the mind's ability to relate representations to the world. There is a twofold evolutionary advantage in not having conscious access to such perceptual mechanisms: first, they can operate in parallel and therefore more efficiently; and, second, if you see a tiger, you take avoiding action rather than inspect the process of perception to ensure that it is operating correctly. The lexical system inherits the inaccessibility of this basic representational machinery. There is a further advantage in this lack of access: you do not become aware of a gap in lexical knowledge unless it is immediately germane to the interpretation of the discourse. If you had a conscious access to your lexical representations, then every time you encountered a word for which you possessed an incomplete semantics, you would be aware of it. You would be in a comparable state of mind to someone who looks up a word in a dictionary only to find that part of the relevant entry has been torn out. This intrusive awareness would occur even if the missing information were not actually required to construct a model of the discourse. Similarly, every time you encountered an ambiguous word, you would be aware of it—even if the ambiguity were resolved by the immediate context.

Since your aim is to grasp the significance of an utterance and perhaps to act upon it, your interpretative system has no need to present these details to consciousness, just as there is no need to make the details of the perceptual process accessible. The same consideration, of course, applies to the acquisition of meaning: children can acquire a new element of meaning *en passant* without becoming aware that they are so doing, and in this way they can attend primarily to the significance of the utterance rather than the process by which they are interpreting it.

8. Conclusions

The present theory of lexical meanings rests on seven principal assumptions:

(1) Comprehension requires the listener to construct a model of the state of affairs described by the discourse. Words contribute to the sense of utterances, but this model depends on inferences from context about the specific referents of expressions.

(2) There is a mental dictionary that contains entries in which the senses of words are represented.

(3) A lexical entry may be incomplete as a result of ignorance or because the word is a theoretical term with an intrinsically incomplete sense.

(4) The senses of words can be acquired from definitions or from encountering instances of the word in use. The former procedure can only work with words that contain a complex semantics.

(5) Corresponding to the method of acquisition, elements of a lexical representation can consist of (a) relations to other words, which could be represented by a mechanism akin to a semantic network, and (b) ineffable primitives that are used in constructing and manipulating mental models of the world.

(6) The primitive elements in a lexical representation may specify the word's contribution to the truth conditions of the expressions in which it occurs, or else the logically weaker default values of the word.

(7) The contrast between explicit verbal relations and ineffable truth conditions is related to the way in which discourse, in turn, is represented initially in a superficial linguistic form and subsequently in the form of a model of the state of affairs that it describes.

References

Anderson, A. (1983). *Semantic and social-pragmatic aspects of meaning in task-oriented dialogue.* Ph.D. Thesis, University of Glasgow.

Anderson, J.R. (1976). *Language, memory, and thought.* Hillsdale, NJ.: Erlbaum.

Anderson, J.R., & Bower, G.H. (1973). *Human associative memory.* Washington, D.C.: Winston.

Anderson, R.C., & Ortony, A. (1975). On putting apples into bottles—a problem of polysemy. *Cognitive Psychology, 7,* 167–180.

Anderson, R.C., Pichert, J.W., Goetz, E.T., Schallert, D.L., Stevens, K.V., & Trollip, S.R. (1976). Instantiation of general terms. *Journal of Verbal Learning and Verbal Behavior, 15,* 667–679.

Bowerman, M. (1977). The acquisition of word meaning: an investigation of some current concepts. In N. Waterson and C. Snow (Eds.) *Development of communication: Social and pragmatic factors in language acquisition.* New York: Wiley.

Cairns, H.S., & Kamerman, J. (1975). Lexical information processing during sentence comprehension. *Journal of Verbal Learning and Verbal Behavior, 14,* 170–179.

Clark, E.V. (1982). The young word-maker: a case study of innovation in the child's lexicon. In E. Wanner and L.R. Gleitman (Eds.) *Language acquisition: The state of the art.* Cambridge: Cambridge University Press.

Clark, E.V., & Clark, H.H. (1979). When nouns surface as verbs. *Language, 55,* 767–811.

Clark, H.H. (1983). Making sense of nonce sense. In G.B. Flores d'Arcais and R. Jarvella (Eds.) *The process of understanding language.* New York: Wiley.

Collins, A.M., & Quillian, M.R. (1969). Retrieval time from semantic memory. *Journal of Verbal Learning and Verbal Behavior, 8,* 240–247.

Conrad, C. (1974). Context effects in sentence comprehension: A study of the subjective lexicon. *Memory and Cognition, 2,* 130–138.

Fischler, I., & Bloom, P. (1979). Automatic and attentional process in the effects of sentence contexts on word recognition. *Journal of Verbal Learning and Verbal Behavior, 18,* 1–20.

Fodor, J.A. (1980). Fixation of belief and concept acquisition. In M. Piattelli-Palmarini (Ed.) *Language and learning: The debate between Jean Piaget and Noam Chomsky.* Cambridge, Mass.: Harvard University Press.

Fodor, J.A., Garrett, M.F., Walker, E.C.T., & Parkes, C.H. (1980). Against definitions. *Cognition, 8,* 263–367.

Fodor, J.D. (1977). *Semantics: Theories of meaning in generative grammar.* New York: Crowell.

Fodor, J.D., Fodor, J.A., & Garrett, M.F. (1975). The psychological unreality of semantic representations. *Linguistic Inquiry, 4,* 515–531.

Garnham, A. (1979). Instantiation of verbs. *Quarterly Journal of Experimental Psychology, 31,* 207–214.

Gerrig, R.J. (1985). Process and products of lexical access. Unpublished MS., Department of Psychology, Yale University.

Gibson, E.J. (1971). Perceptual learning and the theory of word perception. *Cognitive Psychology, 2,* 351–368.

Glass, A.L., & Holyoak, K.J. (1974/5). Alternative conceptions of semantic memory. *Cognition, 3,* 313–339.

Gumenik, W.E. (1979). The advantage of specific terms over general terms as cues for sentence recall: instantiation or retrieval? *Memory and Cognition, 7,* 240–244.

Halff, H.M., Ortony, A., & Anderson, R.C. (1976). A context-sensitive representation of word meanings. *Memory and Cognition, 4,* 378–383.

Harrison, B. (1972). *Meaning and structure.* New York: Harper & Row.

Hodgkin, D. (1977). *An experimental study of sentence comprehension and sentence meaning.* Ph.D. thesis, University of London.

Holmes, V.M., Arwas, R., & Garrett, M.F. (1977). Prior context and the perception of lexically ambiguous sentences. *Memory and Cognition, 5,* 103–110.

Johnson-Laird, P.N. (1975). In A. Kennedy & A. Wilkes (Eds.) *Studies in long term memory*. London: Wiley.

Johnson-Laird, P.N. (1981). Mental models of meaning. In A.K. Joshi, B.L. Webber, & I.A. Sag (Eds.) *Elements of discourse understanding*. Cambridge: Cambridge University Press.

Johnson-Laird, P.N. (1983). *Mental models: Towards a cognitive science of language, inference, and consciousness*. Cambridge: Cambridge University Press/Cambridge, Mass.: Harvard University Press.

Johnson-Laird, P.N., Gibbs, G., & de Mowbray, J. (1978). Meaning, amount of processing, and memory for words. *Memory and Cognition, 6*, 372–375.

Johnson-Laird, P.N., Herrmann, D., & Chaffin, R. (1984). Only connections: A critique of semantic networks. *Psychological Bulletin, 96*, 292–315.

Johnson-Laird, P.N., & Quinn, J.G. (1976). To define true meaning. *Nature, 264*, 635–636.

Kant, I. (1787). *The critique of pure reason*, Second edition, Translated by J.M.D. Meiklejohn, London: Dent (1934).

Katz, J.J., & Fodor, J.A. (1963). The structure of a semantic theory. *Language, 39*, 170–210.

Kintsch, W. (1974). *The representation of meaning in memory*. Hillsdale, N.J.: Erlbaum.

Mani, K., & Johnson-Laird, P.N. (1982). The mental representation of spatial descriptions. *Memory and Cognition, 10*, 181–187.

Marr, D. (1982). *Vision*, San Francisco: Freeman.

McClelland, A.G.R., Rawles, R.E., & Sinclair, F.E. (1981). The effects of search criteria and retrieval cue availability on memory for words. *Memory and Cognition, 9*, 164–168.

Meyer, D.E., & Schvaneveldt, R.W. (1971). Facilitation in recognizing pairs of words: evidence of a dependence between retrieval operations. *Journal of Experimental Psychology, 90*, 227–234.

Miller, G.A. (1977). *Spontaneous apprentices: Children and language*. New York: Seaburg Press.

Miller, G.A. (1986). Dictionaries in the mind. *Language and Cognitive Processes, 1*, 171–185.

Miller, G.A., & Johnson-Laird, P.N. (1976). *Language and perception*. Cambridge, MA: Harvard University Press/Cambridge: Cambridge University Press.

Minsky, M. (1975). Frame-system theory. In R.C. Schank & B.L. Nash-Webber (Eds.) *Theoretical issues in natural language processing*. Preprints of a conference at MIT, Reprinted in P.N. Johnson-Laird and P.C. Wason (Eds.) *Thinking: Readings in cognitive science*. Cambridge: Cambridge University Press (1977).

Putnam, H. (1975). The meaning of 'meaning'. In K. Gunderson (Ed.) *Language, mind and knowledge*. Minnesota Studies in the Philosophy of Science, Vol. 7. Minneapolis: University of Minnesota Press.

Rosch, E. (1973). On the internal structure of perceptual and semantic categories. In T.M. Moore (Ed.). *Cognitive development and the acquisition of language*. New York: Academic Press.

Rosch, E. (1976). Classification of real-world objects: origins and representations in cognition. In S. Ehrlich & E. Tulving (Eds.) La mémoire sémantique. *Bulletin de Pychologie*, Paris. Reprinted in P.N. Johnson-Laird & P.C. Wason (Eds.) *Thinking: Readings in cognitive science*. Cambridge: Cambridge University Press (1977).

Ross, B. (1981). The more, the better? Number of decisions as a determinant of memorability. *Memory and Cognition, 9*, 23–33.

Rumelhart, D.E., Lindsay, P.H., & Norman, D.A. (1972). A process model for long-term memory. In E. Tulving & W. Donaldson (Eds.) *Organization and memory*. New York: Academic Press.

Schaeffer, B., & Wallace, R. (1970). The comparison of word meanings. *Journal of Experimental Psychology, 86*, 144–152.

Schuberth, R.E., & Eimas, P.D. (1977). Effects of context in the classification of words and non-words. *Journal of Experimental Psychology: Human Perception and Performance, 3*, 27–36.

Smith, E.E., Shoben, E.J., & Rips, L.J. (1974). Structure and process in semantic memory: a featural model for semantic decisions. *Psychological Review, 81*, 214–241.

Swinney, D.A. (1979). Lexical access during sentence comprehension: (re)consideration of context effects. *Journal of Verbal Learning and Verbal Behavior, 6*, 645–659.

Swinney, D.A., Onifer, W., Prather, P., & Hirshkowitz, M. (1979). Semantic facilitation across sensory modalities in the processing of individual words and sentences. *Memory and Cognition, 7*, 159–165.

Tabossi, P. (1982). Sentential context and the interpretation of unambiguous words. *Quarterly Journal of Experimental Psychology, 34A*, 79–90.

Tabossi, P. (1983). *Interpreting words in context.* D.Phil. Thesis, University of Sussex.

Tabossi, P., & Johnson-Laird, P.N. (1980). Linguistic context and the priming of semantic information. *Quarterly Journal of Experimental Psychology, 32*, 595–603.

Tanenhaus, M.K., & Lucas, M.M. (1987). Context effects in lexical priming. *Cognition, 25*, this issue.

Templin, M.C. (1957). *Certain language skills in children: Their development and interrelationships.* Minneapolis: University of Minnesota Press.

Tweedy, J.R., Lapinksy, R.H., & Schvaneveldt, R.W. (1977). Semantic context effects on word recognition: Influence of varying the proportion of items presented in an appropriate context. *Memory and Cognition, 5*, 84–98.

Weinreich, U. (1966). Explorations in semantic theory. In T.A. Sebeok (Ed.) *Current Trends in Linguistics*, Vol. 3. The Hague: Mouton.

Wittgenstein, L. (1953). *Philosophical investigations.* New York: Macmillan.

Wykes, T., & Johnson-Laird, P.N. (1977). How do children learn the meanings of verbs? *Nature, 268*, 326–327.

Zwicky, A., & Sadock, J.M. (1973). Ambiguity tests and how to fail them. *Working Papers in Linguistics.* Ohio State University.

Résumé

Cet article présente cinq phénomènes concernant le sens des mots. Il s'agit de (1) notre accès introspectif. limité quant à la nature des représentations lexicales; (2) l'existence d'entrées lexicales qui rendent accessible le sens d'un mot; (3) les effets du contexte sur l'interprétation des mots; (4) les lacunes systématiques dans l'acquisition du savoir lexical; et (5) l'existence de différents types sémantiques de mots appartenant à la classe ouverte. Ces phénomènes servent de point de départ à une théorie psychologique du sens des mots.

9

Context effects in lexical processing

MICHAEL K. TANENHAUS*
MARGERY M. LUCAS
University of Rochester

Abstract

This article examines the extent to which word recognition is influenced by lexical, syntactic, and semantic contexts in order to contrast predictions made by modular and interactive theories of the architecture of the language comprehension system. We conclude that there is strong evidence for lexical context effects, mixed evidence for semantic context effects and little evidence for syntactic context effects. We suggest that top-down feedback effects in comprehension are primarily limited to situations in which there is a well-defined part-whole relationship between the two levels and the set of lower-level units that could receive feedback from a higher level is restricted.

1. Introduction

Linguists are in general agreement that language can be described in terms of a number of subsystems, such as phonology, morphology, syntax, and semantics. These systems appear to be fairly independent in that the rules and representations used to describe each are different. However, there has been considerable debate among psycholinguists about whether this structural autonomy translates into processing autonomy. According to one viewpoint, *the modularity hypothesis*, the language processing system is composed of a set of processing modules that are functionally autonomous in that a module will compute the same output given a particular input, regardless of the information being computed by other modules. Forster (1979) and Cairns

*This work was partially supported by grant BNS-8217378 from the National Science Foundation and by grants HD 10169 and HD 18944 from the National Institute of Child Health and Human Development. We are grateful to Gary Cottrell, Gary Dell, Jerry Feldman, Ken Forster, Don Foss, Lyn Frazier, Mary Hayhoe and Steve Lapointe for helpful suggestions and to the editors, Uli Frauenfelder and Lolly Tyler. Margery Lucas is now at the Department of Psychology, Wellesley College. Requests for reprints should be sent to Michael Tanenhaus, Department of Psychology, University of Rochester, Rochester, NY 14627, U.S.A.

(1984) have proposed modular theories about the organization of the language comprehension system, while Fodor (1983) has presented a modular theory for input processes in general. Modular theories can be contrasted with *interactive models* in which information from different domains is shared throughout the comprehension system. Interactive theories have been proposed by Marslen-Wilson and colleagues and others (Elman & McClelland, 1984; Marslen-Wilson & Welsh, 1978; Marslen-Wilson & Tyler, 1980; McClelland, & Rumelhart, 1981).

In the domain of lexical processing, the autonomy or modularity hypothesis makes two predictions: (1) the information accessed during each stage of lexical processing will be invariant across processing contexts and (2) the speed with which this information becomes available will not be influenced by context (Tanenhaus, Carlson, & Seidenberg, 1985). These predictions arise in a modular system because modules communicate only at the input and output ends. The output of one module may serve as the input to a second module; however, the internal operations of a module are blind to the status of processing in other modules. In contrast, interactive models predict that context can influence what information is accessed during lexical processing, as well as the speed with which the information becomes available. These predictions arise from the assumption that information is unrestricted in its flow through the system once lexical processing has been initiated by the appropriate sensory input.

In this article we examine to what extent lexical processes function as autonomous processing modules during language comprehension. We begin by characterizing the difference between modular and interactive models in terms of feedback: interactive models allow for feedback from higher-level representations to lower-level representations, whereas modular models deny the existence of such feedback. We then review evidence suggesting that feedback is found between certain levels in the processing system but not between others. These observations motivate several hypotheses about the scope of interactions between components of the comprehension system.

A potential problem with evaluating the claims of modular and interactive theories is that many models of the language comprehension system have been proposed and these vary a great deal in the assumptions made about the nature of representation and how information is transferred between levels of the system. Our solution is to adopt a framework in which we can talk explicitly about representations and communication among representations when making comparisons between theories and evaluating evidence. We have chosen the connectionist network (Dell, 1985; Feldman & Ballard, 1982; McClelland & Rumelhart, 1981) in which knowledge at each level is represented by nodes that communicate by passing activation. We find this framework useful because it is explicit and because it can be used to illustrate both interactive and modular systems.

The difference between an interactive and a modular system now can be illustrated by considering a simple example. Assume a model of lexical processing in which there are only three levels of representation: a feature level, a phoneme level, and a lexical level. In a modular system the information flow would be strictly bottom-up. Feature nodes, when activated, would send activation to phoneme nodes, which would in turn send activation to lexical nodes. Although there are dependencies between levels (e.g., processing at the phoneme level is dependent upon phoneme nodes receiving input from feature nodes), there is no reason to assume that processing at a higher level must await the completion of processing at a lower level upon which it is dependent (McClelland, 1979). Thus whether the system is serial or parallel has nothing to do with whether or not it is modular. The modularity of the system is determined solely by whether or not feedback is allowed between nodes at different levels: interactive models use feedback to provide a mechanism for higher-order knowledge to guide lower-level processing, whereas modular models do not allow it. From this perspective modularity can be viewed as a constraint on the scope of interactions with completely modular and interactive systems at different ends of a continuum. (See Fodor, 1983, and Seidenberg, 1985, for further discussion.)

As an illustration, consider the case of feedback between the lexical and phonemic levels. Assume that the input word is *bat*. As *bat* is being processed, the node representing the phoneme /b/ will become activated and it will begin activating all lexical nodes that represent words beginning with /b/. Thus far the system is operating in a manner consistent with both the modularity and interactive hypotheses. In an interactive model, however, lexical nodes might send activation back to their component phonemes. For example, the phoneme /b/ would activate the lexical nodes for *bat* and *bag*, which would in turn send activation to the phonemes /b/, /ae/, /t/, and /b/, /ae/ and /g/ respectively. As the activation of the word *bat* increased as a result of activation from /ae/ and /t/, more activation would be sent to the phonemes, /b/ /ae/, and /t/ further increasing their activation. Consider some of the consequences of word-phoneme feedback. Phonemes (or letters in visual word recognition) will be recognized faster when they are embedded in a word than a nonword because of greater positive feedback from the word level. Degraded or deleted phonemes will tend to be restored when enough lexical feedback is present, and these effects will tend to be greater towards the end of the word as lexical nodes begin to accrue more activation and thus send more feedback to their component phonemes. Feedback between higher-level nodes and lexical nodes could be provided in ways analogous to word-phoneme feedback. For example, verbs might activate syntactic subcategorization frames and thematic roles, which would in turn send feedback to nouns that might fill these frames. Similarly, activated knowledge-frames such as scripts might send feedback to lexical nodes corresponding to words that are likely to be encountered when that script is activated.

2. Terminological and methodological preliminaries

In order to assess the empirical evidence for feedback it is important to consider the loci of context effects. Unfortunately, terminology in this domain is often confusing and contradictory. Virtually all researchers agree that lexical processing can be divided into at least two stages. The first stage involves using sensory input to make contact with candidate lexical representations. Information stored with activated lexical candidates such as a word's pronunciation, spelling, syntactic category, and meaning is then made available to the language processing system. The second stage, often referred to as *post-lexical*, involves the selection, elaboration, and integration with context of the information made available during the first stage (Cairns, Cowart, & Jablon, 1981)—in other words those processes that Fodor (1983) has identified with the fixation of perceptual belief. The processes associated with activating lexical candidates and making available lexical codes are generally held to be the proper domain of *word recognition*, where word recognition is used as a general term for lexical processing, whereas post-lexical processes, as the term suggests, are associated with processes that occur after word recognition is complete.

Terminological difficulties arise because some researchers (e.g., Bradley & Forster, 1987, this issue) use *lexical access* to refer to first stage processes, whereas others (e.g., Pisoni, 1987, this issue) use word recognition to refer to activating lexical candidates and selecting the best fit, and lexical access to refer to the retrieval of lexical codes. These differences reflect different theoretical perspectives about the nature of lexical processing that are beyond the scope of this discussion. For the purposes of evaluating context effects, we will follow Seidenberg, Waters, Sanders, and Langer (1984) in dividing context effects into those with pre- and post-lexical loci. Pre-lexical context effects are those that influence the activation of lexical candidates or the access of lexical codes. These effects are considered pre-lexical because context has its effect before first stage lexical processes are complete. Post-lexical context effects are those that influence latter stages in processing, that is, the selection and integration of activated lexical representations.

Determining the loci of context effects on lexical processing is complicated by the difficulty in distinguishing between context effects that are due to feedback and those that are due to what we will refer to as *decision bias*. In order to clarify the distinction consider an experiment in which the listener's task is to monitor for the phoneme /b/ and the target phoneme can occur either early or late in a word or a nonword. An interactive model incorporating feedback between word and phoneme levels would make the following two predictions: (1) detection times will be faster when the phoneme is embedded in a word than in a nonword and (2) detection times will be faster when the target occurs late in a word. Both of these effects can be attributed to differences in the amount of word to phoneme feedback. Phonemes embedded in words will receive more lexical feedback than phonemes embedded in nonwords because word stimuli will activate a lexical node more than nonword stimuli. Phonemes occurring late in a word will receive more feedback than phonemes occurring early in a word because lexical activation will increase as bottom-up input consistent with the lexical node accumulates as the word is being processed. These same data can also be accounted for without postulating feedback by assuming that listeners can use information at higher levels to guide decisions about lower levels. Given the same sensory evidence that a phoneme has been presented the listener might be more inclined to respond "YES" given reason to believe that a word containing the phoneme was being processed. This situation might arise when both a phonemic representation and the lexical representation of a word containing the phoneme were partially activated, or alternatively, when the word was activated beyond threshold but the phoneme was not.

The crucial difference between a feedback explanation and a decision bias explanation is that in a feedback explanation the activation level of the phoneme node is increased when a lexical node containing that phoneme is activated. In contrast, in a decision bias explanation the criteria to decide that a phoneme was presented may be altered by the presence of an activated lexical node, but the activation level of the phoneme node itself is unaffected. Most, if not all, context effects that are explained by feedback within an interactive system have corresponding decision bias explanations within a modular system. Thus in order to identify the locus of a contextual effect on lexical processing it is necessary to determine whether the effect is best explained by feedback or decision bias. Context effects due to feedback will generally be pre-lexical, whereas context effects due to decision bias will generally be post-lexical.

We now turn to a brief review of contextual effects on lexical processing. Our goal is to develop some general principles about the organization of the language comprehension system by examining how different types of contextual information influence lexical processing.

3. Lexical effects on phonemic processing

A number of studies have investigated the effects of lexical context on phonemic processing. Warren (1970) found that listeners frequently fail to detect a distortion in a word introduced by excising a phoneme and replacing it with a cough or a buzz. This "phonemic restoration" effect has been studied extensively by Marslen-Wilson and Welsh (1978) and Cole and Jakimik (1980). In the Marslen-Wilson and Welsh experiments a word was distorted by replacing a phoneme occurring early or late in the word with a phonetically similar or dissimilar phoneme (where the number of different features was used to determine phonetic similarity). The resulting stimulus was not a word. In a shadowing task, more distorted words were restored when the distortion was small and when the distortion occurred late in the word. In a detection task, large distortions were detected more frequently than small distortions and early distortions were detected more frequently than late distortions. These detection results replicate earlier findings by Cole and Jakimik. Marslen-Wilson and Welsh (1978) also found sentential context effects. More distorted words were restored during shadowing when the distorted word was predictable given the preceding discourse context than when the distorted word was unpredictable.

As we have seen these effects can be naturally accounted for by feedback. The size and position of distortion effects are explained by lexical to phonemic feedback and the discourse context effects are explained by feedback between higher-level representations and lexical nodes. However, the same results can also be explained by decision bias without invoking feedback. The methodological challenge, then, is to distinguish between these two explanations. Perhaps the most promising approach is to use signal detection theory to determine whether contextual effects are due to changes in decision bias. This approach is exemplified by an important set of experiments by Samuel (1981a,b).

Samuel used a signal detection analysis in a paradigm in which a phoneme in a word or nonword was either replaced by noise (noise-replaced) or had noise added to it (noise-added). The subjects's task was to discriminate between noise-added and noise-replaced trials. Samuel reasoned that if feedback operated between the lexical and phonemic levels, then noise-replaced phonemes should often be restored in word stimuli making them perceptually similar to the noise-added trials. The result would be poorer discriminability for word stimuli than for nonword stimuli. If, on the other hand, lexical knowledge were influencing response bias, then the discriminability of word and nonword stimuli should be unaffected, but subjects should show a greater bias to label word stimuli as noise-added.

The results supported a feedback account. Discriminability, as measured by d′, was poorer when the altered phoneme occurred in a word than when it occurred in a nonword, indicating that lexical context was perceptually restoring the altered phoneme. Samuel also examined phoneme restorations in sentential contexts. Phonemes were altered in words which were either congruent or incongruent with the preceding context. Here the results supported a decision bias interpretation. Congruency had a large effect on response bias: congruous words were more likely to be judged as noise-added; however, congruency had no effect on discriminability.

Samuel's results suggest that feedback obtains between lexical and phonemic levels but not between sentential and lexical levels. At first blush both lexical-phonemic feedback and the absence of sentential-lexical feedback seem inconsistent with some results from the phoneme monitoring literature. Foss and Blank (1980) found that phoneme monitoring times to an initial phoneme were equivalent regardless of whether the target phoneme occurred in a carrier word or a nonword. While these data could be used to argue against lexical-phonemic feedback, a more likely explanation is that the subject's decision is made before the lexical node representing the carrier word has received enough bottom-up activation in order to begin sending feedback to the phonemic node. When the target phoneme occurs later in the word, feedback effects begin to emerge (Marslen-Wilson, 1984).

Two studies present possible counterexamples to the claim that sentential context does not affect phonemic processing. Morton and Long (1976) found that reaction time to detect a phoneme was faster when the carrier word had a high transitional probability in its context, a result that was partially replicated by Dell and Newman (1980) and by Foss and Blank (1980). These results were interpreted as evidence that a word—and consequently its component phonemes—is recognized more rapidly when it is predictable in context. However, Foss and Gernsbacher (1983) have demonstrated that Morton and Long's results were due to a subtle artifact in their materials. Foss and Gernsbacher found that phoneme detection times are correlated with the duration of the vowel following the target phoneme, with faster detection times preceding shorter duration vowels. Morton and Long's high transitional probability stimuli tended to have shorter vowels; post-hoc correlational analyses conducted by Foss and Gernsbacher demonstrated that vowel length was most probably accounting for the Morton and Long results. However, it should be noted that transitional probability was not confounded with vowel length in Dell and Newman's study. Their results are, of course, consistent with either a feedback or a decision bias interpretation.

On the basis of Samuel's results we will tentatively conclude that feedback effects exist between lexical and phonemic processing. However, Samuel's evidence for feedback between lexical and phonemic level processing is stronger than his evidence against feedback effects between higher-level and phonemic processing. While, in principle, feedback from syntactic or semantic levels to the lexical level should result in increased activation at the phonemic level (through word-phoneme feedback), these second-order effects are likely to be weak and slow. A more appropriate test would be an experiment in which subjects were forced to choose between two words that differed in only one phoneme (*bank* or *tank*) or between a word and a non-word (e.g., *bank* or *pank*), perhaps when the target stimuli were presented in a noise background following a biasing sentential context. Unlike the Samuel procedure which is designed to measure sensitivity at the phonemic level, this procedure would measure sensitivity at the lexical level and thus would enable a more direct test of whether or not there is sentential to lexical feedback. The experiments by Samuel are the only studies that to our knowledge attempt to parcel out effects of decision bias; however, enough indirect evidence about the locus of sentential context effects on lexical processing exists to motivate some reasonable hypotheses. We will consider, in order, syntactic, semantic, and lexical contexts.

4. Syntactic context

Several studies using visual presentation have reported weak syntactic context effects. Goodman, McClelland and Gibbs (1981) found that lexical decisions were faster to target words when they were syntactically appropriate continuations of a prime word (e.g., *they laugh*) than when they were syntactically inappropriate continuations (e.g., *it laugh*). Similarly Lukatela, Kostic, Feldman, and Turvey (1983), found that lexical decisions to nouns in Serbo-Croatian were faster when the target was preceded by an appropriate preposition than when preceded by an inappropriate preposition. However, there is reason to believe that the syntactic effects in these experiments are due to decision bias rather than to feedback. Goodman et al. also conducted an experiment in which syntactic contexts were intermixed with semantic contexts in which the prime word and the target word were semantically related. Under these circumstances, no effects of syntactic appropriateness obtained, leading the authors to conclude that the syntactic effects were strategic. Seidenberg et al. (1984) have confirmed Goodman et al.'s suggestion. They found a syntactic priming effect with Goodman et al.'s stimuli using the lexical decision task but not the naming task. This experiment was one of a series of experiments contrasting lexical decision and naming which were based on the hypothesis, developed by Forster (1979) and West and Stanovich

(1982), that lexical decision is more apt to be influenced by decision bias than naming. In most lexical decision experiments the subject's task is to discriminate between word and extremely wordlike nonword stimuli. When a word is placed in context, the subject has another source of information to use in making this discrimination. If a stimulus can be integrated with the context, it is likely to be a word; if it cannot be integrated with the context, it is likely to be a nonword. This strategy will only fail on the (usually) small proportion of trials in which a word is presented in an anomalous context. Another way of thinking about post-lexical effects in yes-no decision tasks like lexical decision is that they are a type of 'cognitive stroop' phenomenon (Seidenberg et al., 1984) in which the subject is required to say "Yes" when something is clearly wrong. If information about contextual congruity becomes available rapidly enough in processing, it might well influence lexical decisions without influencing lexical processing (Forster, 1979; West & Stanovich, 1982). In contrast the naming task seems less likely to be influenced by post-lexical processes because naming a word requires accessing phonological information that is specific to that lexical item. Knowing whether or not a word makes sense in a context provides no information about how to pronounce the word. Naming should be speeded, though, when pre-lexical processing is facilitated.

The syntactic contexts (one word) in the Goodman et al. (1981) and Seidenberg et al. (1984), studies may have been too impoverished to have activated normal syntactic processing mechanisms. Wright and Garrett (1984) found syntactic context effects in lexical decision using full sentential contexts. It could be argued that these effects are due to decision bias since the lexical decision task was used, however, Tyler (personal communication) and West and Stanovich (1986) have found similar effects with naming. These results might well be taken as evidence that syntactic context constrains initial lexical access, however, there is an alternative explanation. Motley, Baars, and Camden (1981) have demonstrated output editing effects in producing syntactically ill-formed phrases. If output editing is inhibiting the pronunciation of syntactically inappropriate words in the Tyler and West and Stanovich studies, then the loci of the syntactic context effect may be post-lexical.

Three empirical results suggest to us that the output editing explanation is likely to be correct. First, West and Stanovich (1986) found that their syntactic context effects were purely inhibitory, and inhibitory effects are generally associated with later processes than facilitatory effects (e.g., Neely, 1977). Secondly, Dell and Tanenhaus (1986) have recently provided direct evidence for non-lexical syntactic context effects using the naming task. They measured naming times to appropriately or inappropriately inflected target stimuli following contexts ending with a modal verb such as "They thought they might ..." Targets were either words (e.g., *compete* or *competes*) or nonwords (*con-

dete or *condetes*). Appropriately inflected targets were read aloud faster than inappropriately inflected targets, for both word and nonword targets, with no interaction between appropriateness and type of target. Generalizations from this study are limited to the loci of syntactic agreement effects, but these are clearly post-lexical.

Finally, Tyler and Wessels (1983) examined the effects of syntactic context on word recognition using the gating paradigm developed by Grosjean (1980). In this paradigm, the amount of sensory information necessary for listeners to recognize a word with a certain probability is measured. The sensory input needed to recognize a gated word was not significantly reduced when the context highly constrained its possible syntactic class. Although the gating paradigm does not distinguish between feedback and decision bias, it is a powerful global measure of context effects. Thus Tyler and Wessel's failure to observe syntactic context effects provides strong evidence that syntactic context is not guiding initial lexical access.

Studies of lexical ambiguity resolution also suggest that context does not influence pre-lexical processing. Tanenhaus, Leiman and Seidenberg (1979) and Seidenberg, Tanenhaus, Leiman and Bienkowski (1982) used a cross-modal naming task in which subjects listened to a sentence that ended in an ambiguous word and then named a visually presented target related to either the syntactically appropriate or inappropriate meaning of the ambiguous word (e.g., "They all rose" or "They bought a rose" followed by the target *flower* or *stood*). When targets were presented immediately after the ambiguous word, an equivalent amount of priming obtained to targets related to syntactically appropriate and inappropriate readings of ambiguous words, indicating that both readings of the ambiguous word were initially accessed. When a 200-ms delay was introduced prior to the presentation of the target, only targets related to the appropriate meaning were facilitated indicating that context had been used to select the syntactically appropriate reading. In an unpublished study, Prather and Swinney (1977) reported similar findings using a cross-modal lexical decision task.

Although these studies found no evidence that syntactic context affects lexical access, they are subject to at least two criticisms. The biasing contexts in the Tanenhaus et al. and Seidenberg et al. studies were extremely short, often only two or three words, and the ambiguous words were monosyllabic. As a result, listeners may not have had time to make use of the syntactic information prior to the ambiguous word, particularly if feedback takes time to develop. A second concern raised by Cowart (1983) is that many of the contexts used to create a verb bias used the infinitive *to*, which can be homophonous with the adjective *two* and thus compatible with either a following noun or verb. These criticisms were addressed by Tanenhaus and

Donnenwerth-Nolan (1984) in a study using a cross-modal lexical decision task. In this study, the infinitive *to* was pronounced with reduced stress (as "tuh"), eliminating the possibility that it could be interpreted as the adjective *two*. A condition was also included in which a 400-ms pause was introduced between the syntactic context and the ambiguous word. If context effects were not observed in previous studies because feedback did not have sufficient time to develop, then context effects should have obtained in the pause condition. Facilitation to targets related to syntactically appropriate and inappropriate meanings was observed in both the pause and no pause conditions.

Clearly more empirical work is necessary before a definitive conclusion can be reached about the effects of syntactic context on lexical access. On the basis of the evidence reviewed above, however, it seems likely that syntactic context does not influence pre-lexical processing.

Why should there be lexical-phonemic feedback but not syntactic-lexical feedback? There are important differences between the two cases that might account for why feedback obtains in one but not the other. Words and phonemes bear a *part-whole* relationship to one another in that a sequence of phonemes defines a word (ignoring for the sake of simplicity the complications introduced by syllabic and morphological structure) and vice versa, whereas the relationship between words and syntactic categories is one of *set membership*. The contrast between part-whole relationships and set membership relationships is interesting because part-whole relationships seem characteristic of arbitrary associations that must be stored, and set membership relationships seem characteristic of the interface between levels of representation that enter into rules (e.g., syntactic categories) and stored units that do not (e.g., words). Thus the relationship between the phoneme /b/ and the word *big* can simply be stored, whereas the relationship between a context and the word *big* must be computed.

It appears that feedback would be more useful in part-whole relationships than in set-membership relationships. For units that have a part-whole relationship, such as phonemes and words, the feedback set is highly restricted. An activated lexical candidate could send feedback only to those nodes representing phonemes that are contained in the activated word. An interesting property of feedback between units bearing a part-whole relationship is that the cost/benefit ratio is very low. To see this consider that the conditional probability that a phoneme was presented given the presence of a word containing the phoneme approaches 1.0 (e.g., the probability that the phoneme /d/ was presented given that the word *dog* has been activated is extremely high).[1] Thus the activation of a lexical node highly constrains the phoneme

---

[1]This observation is due to Gary Dell.

nodes that should be activated.

In contrast, the kinds of constraints that syntactic context can place on an incoming word are restrictions about which syntactic categories—not which lexical items—are grammatical continuations of a sentence. This follows from the fact that syntactic knowledge is expressed in terms of syntactic categories and that the relationship between a lexical item and a syntactic category is not a part-whole relationship, but rather a set membership relationship. Thus syntactic-lexical feedback must be mediated by syntactic categories. In contrast to part-whole feedback, set-membership feedback will be minimally useful. More than one syntactic category will usually be a grammatical continuation of any syntactic sequence and the number of lexical items that are members of the major syntactic categories is extremely large. The problem is further compounded because many lexical items can belong to more than one syntactic category. Thus feedback from a syntactic context to words that belong to possible or even expected syntactic categories will do little to reduce the potential number of lexical candidates. In other words, the conditional probability of a lexical item given a syntactic category will usually be quite low. Thus it would appear that syntactic to lexical feedback would generally be of limited utility (see Tanenhaus, Dell, & Carlson, in press, for further development of these ideas). However, there are two possible exceptions that should be mentioned. When the syntactic context activates a grammatical category that contains closed class words, the set of lexical candidates receiving feedback would be fairly restricted. Also, syntactic context might be useful in processing morphologically complex words, particularly if it turns out that these words are parsed rather than simply recognized as units.

5. Semantic context

In this section we will be using the term semantic context loosely, as it has often been used in psycholinguistic research, to refer to the conceptual model that the listener develops during a discourse (Johnson-Laird, 1983). This model includes a representation of the propositions introduced into the discourse as well as relevant knowledge about the world. We assume that this knowledge, in conjunction with the local context, can often be used to generate reasonable expectations about the incoming speech. The question at issue is whether these expectations generally influence pre-lexical processes.

5.1. Lexical priming

There is one type of context that clearly influences lexical processing. Recognition of a word is facilitated when the word is immediately preceded by a semantically related word (e.g., people are faster to respond to *pepper* when they have just seen or heard *salt*). Although the most robust semantic priming effects are found with the lexical decision task, which has a large post-lexical strategic component, small but reliable priming effects clearly obtain with both the color naming and naming tasks, both of which seem relatively free of strategic effects. An important unresolved question is what is the locus of these semantic priming effects. One possibility is that semantic priming effects are mediated by shared semantic features between words. Thus the word *boy* would prime the word *girl* because the semantic features activated when the meaning of *boy* is accessed would feedback to activate the word *girl*. We will consider this type of priming to be *conceptually-mediated*, on the assumption that the meaning of a word is not a specifically linguistic representation, but rather a general conceptual one. Conceptually-mediated priming clearly violates the modularity hypothesis. It should be noted, however, that the types of semantic-lexical connections needed to produce conceptually mediated semantic priming are independently required by the language production system because lexical retrieval must be guided by activated conceptual knowledge.

An alternative view of priming that preserves the modularity hypothesis is that priming is strictly intra-lexical (Fodor, 1983; Forster, 1979; Seidenberg & Tanenhaus, 1986). On one view (Fodor, 1983) the structure of the lexicon simply mirrors the structure of experience. Whatever is frequently connected in the real world is reflected in connections between corresponding nodes in the mental lexicon. By this account *salt* primes *pepper* because the frequent co-occurrence of the words and/or the objects referred to by the words has caused connections to be made between the nodes representing those words. This, in turn, means that when one word of the pair is activated, the recognition threshold of the other will be lowered. Fodor argues that intra-lexical associations have the virtue of increasing the efficiency of processing lexical items in context by causing the system to function *as if* expectations had been generated without bringing into play the expensive (in terms of time and capacity) central processes that usually generate expectations. However, their utility is limited because semantically related words do not often co-occur in sentences (Forster, 1979; Gough, Alford, & Holley-Wilcox, 1981).

Associations might also develop among words that become simultaneously activated during production because they share similar concepts. Priming is then due to these associative connections. On this view words that are related to concepts that are activated as a result of combining word meanings during production should not become activated during comprehension. Thus one would predict that the phrase "large dog" would be no more likely to prime "collie" than the phrase "dog large". Is there any reason to expect that priming is in fact due strictly to intra-lexical associations? Suggestive evidence comes from picture-word priming studies. Babbitt (1982) found that viewing a picture of a horse did not lead to color naming interference when the word *horse* was printed in colored ink, suggesting that a concept can be activated without priming its name. In contrast, semantically related word primes resulted in color naming interference. Similarly, word-word priming effects occur at shorter prime-target SOAs than picture-word priming effects even though semantic information can be retrieved more rapidly from pictures than from words (Carr, McCauley, Sperber, & Parmelee, 1982). These results suggest that at least some proportion of semantic priming effects is due to intra-lexical associations. However, this cannot be the whole story.

Several recent studies have examined whether conceptually, but not associatively related words, prime each other in the naming task, which, as we have seen, is less subject to strategic influences than lexical decision. Seidenberg et al. (1984) found small but significant priming effects in naming using stimuli developed by Fischler (1977). Lupker (1984) also found small priming effects using non-associated category members, although the effects were marginal. In several unpublished studies we have found clear priming effects using non-associated synonyms. On balance, these studies provide support for conceptually mediated priming. However, we should mention one caveat. Conceptual-priming effects in naming are small and the naming task is not completely immune from bias effects. Thus it will be important to determine whether or not conceptual priming obtains when paradigms that can factor out bias are used.

Another line of evidence suggesting that intra-lexical associations are not the sole mechanism for priming effects comes from studies of the time course of lexical ambiguity resolution. Recall that immediately following an ambiguous word, priming is obtained to targets related to contextually appropriate and inappropriate word senses (see also Merrill, Sperber, & McCauley, 1981), but once contextual integration is complete, priming is observed only to targets related to the contextually appropriate sense. The fact that contextual appropriateness modulates lexical priming is clear evidence that lexical priming can be conceptually mediated because there is no obvious mechanism that would enable contextual appropriateness to influence purely intra-lexical priming.

In summary, there are reliable lexical priming effects. Some proportion of these effects can probably be attributed to intra-lexical priming but some appear to be due to feedback from activated semantic representations. Thus the question shifts from are semantic feedback effects possible, to how extensive are the effects of semantic feedback? With this in mind we turn to semantically-based sentential context effects.

5.2. Sentential context

There are a number of clear demonstrations that semantic context influences lexical processing. What is not so clear, however, is the proper locus of these effects. The gating study by Tyler and Wessels (1983) described earlier also examined the effects of semantic contextual constraint on the amount of sensory input necessary for word recognition. Substantially less sensory input was required to recognize a word as semantic contextual constraint increased. Tyler (1984) has also used the gating paradigm to show that semantic constraints affect the rate at which lexical candidates are eliminated from an initial activated pool of "cohorts". As we pointed out earlier, however, while the gating paradigm can demonstrate global effects of context on lexical processing, it cannot be used to identify the locus of those effects.

Marslen-Wilson and Tyler (1980) examined category, rhyme, and word monitoring in normal prose, semantically anomalous prose, and random-word prose. Monitoring times decreased as contextual constraint increased, both among conditions and within sentences, leading the authors to conclude that contextual feedback can speed word recognition. There has been extensive discussion of this paper (see Norris, 1982, and Cowart, 1982, for critiques, and replies by Marslen-Wilson & Tyler, 1983, and Tyler & Marslen-Wilson, 1982); however, little attention has been focused on whether these effects are due to decision bias or to true feedback. The possibility for responses based upon guessing strategies seems particularly problematic in monitoring paradigms because contexts that are only moderately predictable become highly predictable when category and rhyme cues are provided (Tanenhaus et al., 1985). Distinguishing between feedback and guessing strategies should be relatively easy to accomplish using the monitoring paradigm. For example, on some proportion of trials, target words could be replaced by phonetically similar words. Thus either sentence (1a) or (1b) might be presented following the category cue *animal*.

(1a) At the zoo, we were surprised at how big the *lions* were.
(1b) At the zoo, we were surprised at how big the *lines* were.

The role of semantic context in lexical processing has also been addressed extensively in the lexical ambiguity literature. Swinney (1979) used a cross-modal lexical decision task in which a visual target word was presented either immediately or several syllables after an ambiguous word in a spoken sentence. For example, the word "bug" was presented in a sentence that biased its "insect" sense, and the visual targets were *ant*, *spy*, and an unrelated control word. Lexical decisions to targets related to both the contextually biased and unbiased meanings were facilitated when the target immediately followed the ambiguous word, but only targets related to contextually biased targets were facilitated when the targets were presented several syllables after the ambiguous word, suggesting that biasing context does not guide meaning access. These results have since been replicated and extended in a number of studies including Onifer and Swinney (1981) and Lucas (1983). These studies demonstrated that contextual bias does not interact with relative frequency in initial lexical access.[2] In only one study using a cross-modal paradigm was any evidence found for context biasing initial lexical access. Seidenberg et al. (1982) examined the effects of several different types of biasing contexts on ambiguity resolution for noun–noun and noun–verb ambiguous words using a cross-modal naming task. One type of context (pragmatic context) biased the interpretation of a noun–noun ambiguous word without including any strongly associated words (e.g., The man walked on the deck), while other contexts included both pragmatic and lexical bias (e.g., The *captain* walked on the deck). Visual targets followed immediately or 200 ms after the sentence-final ambiguous word. Priming to targets related to both biased and unbiased meanings were initially facilitated in pragmatic contexts, whereas only targets related to biased meanings were facilitated in contexts that included both pragmatic and lexical bias. Further research is needed to determine whether the contexts including lexical bias actually blocked initial access to the unbiased sense or merely speeded ambiguity resolution. Nonetheless, these results suggest an important difference between the effects of lexical and pragmatic context.

Although the lexical ambiguity studies present a compelling case for the modular nature of lexical access, it is important to consider a potentially serious problem that compromises their interpretation. The logic underlying lexical priming paradigms is that a word will activate related words and thus facilitate their recognition. The spread of activation is assumed to be in a forward direction, that is from the prime to the target. However, Koriat (1981) has demonstrated a "backward priming" effect in lexical decision in which facilitation is obtained to targets when the prime is an associate of the target but not vice versa. Thus it is possible to argue that access of contextually inappropriate meanings for ambiguous words occurs in cross-modal prim-

---

[2]Simpson (1981) found an interaction between contextual bias and frequency of meaning, with targets related to low frequency meanings being primed only when they were contextually biased. However, this result is difficult to interpret because the targets were presented at a brief delay (about 100 ms) after the end of the ambiguous word. In the studies finding multiple access, there was no delay between the end of the ambiguous word and the presentation of the target.

ing tasks, not because these meanings are initially accessed, but because the target acts as a context to cause the related meaning of the ambiguous word to become activated. Why then should backward priming affect the response to the target, if the meaning of the ambiguous word is not activated until the target has been processed? The likely answer rests in the sensitivity of the lexical decision task to decision biases. The subject's confidence that the target is a word may be increased when a relationship between the prime and the target is noticed, thus speeding the lexical decision. This logic led Seidenberg et al. (1984) to predict that backward priming should not be observed with the naming task, a prediction that was confirmed. Most of the results in the ambiguity literature—the exception being the studies varying frequency of meaning—have been replicated with both the naming and the lexical decision task. Thus we can tentatively conclude that backward priming does not compromise the basic finding that both contextually appropriate and inappropriate word senses are initially accessed.[3]

The literature on semantic context effects is extremely difficult to evaluate. Although there are a number of demonstrations that lexical processing is facilitated when a word is presented in a biasing context, it is unclear whether these effects are best attributed to feedback or to decision bias. The fact that lexical priming effects can be modulated by context suggests that feedback effects are possible between the conceptual representation being developed by the listener and lexical processing, but it is unclear whether the time course of these effects is rapid enough to influence pre-lexical processes.

The interpretation of semantic context effects is further clouded because few studies to date have attempted to factor out lexical context effects from context effects that arise from the discourse model that the listener is developing. The results obtained by Seidenberg et al. (1982) suggest that this might be an important consideration. This brings up a point that has been largely ignored in both the literature on semantic context effects in auditory word recognition, and the much larger companion literature in visual word recognition. In contrast to lexical and syntactic contexts where it is possible to

---

[3]Glucksberg, Kreuz, & Rho (1986) argue that context does constrain lexical access. They used Onifer and Swinney's (1981) sentences with wordlike nonwords (e.g., the target *petals* was changed to *petls*) and found that lexical decisions to the targets were slowed only when the target was related to the contextually biased sense of the ambiguous word. However, in several experiments conducted in collaboration with Curt Burgess and Mark Seidenberg we have found that lexical primes *do not* interfere with lexical decisions to related nonwords (e.g., the prime *flower* does not interfere with *petls*). Therefore, although the nonword interference task may be sensitive to sentential context, it is not sensitive to lexical priming. Thus the task is inappropriate for studying lexical ambiguity resolution.

define the notion of context precisely, semantic context is used as a general umbrella term (see Clark & Carlson, 1982, for discussion of this point). It seems unlikely that much progress will be made towards understanding context effects until the nature of the contextual constraint is specified more precisely.

6. Conclusions

In comparing lexical-phonemic context effects and syntactic-lexical context effects, we developed a contrast between levels of representation arranged in a part-whole and set-membership relationships. It is interesting to note that words and conceptual or semantic features also have a part-whole relationship, particularly in light of the emerging evidence for conceptually mediated lexical priming. Thus there appear to be at least three well-documented cases where context effects seem to have a pre-lexical locus: lexical effects on phonemic processing, associative or intra-lexical priming, and conceptually mediated priming. What these cases have in common is that the relationship between the context and the unit being affected by the context can be stored in memory and the set of items being activated by the context would be quite restricted. Some aspects of sentential contexts would appear to have these properties. For example, there is probably a part-whole relationship between words and formulaic phrases. Concepts that are activated as part of accessing stored representations such as scripts might well activate a limited set of words. However, to the extent that the relationship between a word and its context is mediated by categories that enter into rules (e.g., case or thematic roles), feedback seems less likely. A first reasonable hypothesis about the scope of interactions in word recognition is that context effects mediated by established relationships among stored representations will be due to feedback, whereas apparent interactions among computed and stored representations will turn out to be due to decision bias.

We conclude with a few remarks about the implications of the literature on context effects in lexical processing for the general architecture of the language processing system. Why has the question of whether language processing is interactive or modular been of such general interest? One answer has to do with fundamental disagreements about the nature of language. Proponents of a processing system divided into autonomous subsystems have often been driven by the pre-theoretic assumption that there are distinct levels of representation, some specifically linguistic, that are computed in language processing. In contrast, proponents of interactive models have tended to argue that comprehension is heavily contextualized and that it is difficult to draw boundaries between linguistic and non-linguistically based processing. Although these disagreements are important, they are basically orthogonal to the modularity issue. As we have seen, the same representations can be arranged in a modular or an interactive manner. The fundamental disagreement that does bear on the modularity issue is about the relative costs and benefits of an interactive versus a modular architecture. The strongest argument for interactive systems is that feedback provides a mechanism for higher-level constraints to guide lower-level processes and thus reduce the noise in the processing system. The cost associated with allowing these interactions is that the system loses some ability to discriminate the source of the input. The strongest arguments for modularity (e.g., those marshalled by Fodor, 1983) are that cognitively driven perception is both inefficient and potentially dangerous in that the cost of not being able to discriminate the source of the input is so great that input systems have evolved as modules. The tentative conclusion that emerges from our review is that modularity or interactiveness may not be built into the language processing system as a design characteristic, but rather that it may result from the relationship among representations. There are some cases, such as the part-whole example, where feedback reduces the perceptual noise with little cost. For other cases, feedback, even if unconstrained, would have little benefit. Thus we may well find that the language processing system has both modular and interactive properties.

References

Babbitt, B.C. (1982). Effect of task demands on dual coding of pictorial stimuli. *Journal of Experimental Psychology: Learning, Memory, and Cognition, 8*, 73–80.

Bradley, D.C., & Forster, K.I. (1987). A reader's view of listening. *Cognition, 25*, this issue.

Cairns, H.S. (1984). Current issues in language comprehension. In R. Naremore (Ed.), *Recent advances in language sciences*. San Diego: College Hill Press.

Cairns, H.S., Cowart, W., & Jablon, A.D. (1981). Effect of prior context upon the integration of lexical information during sentence processing. *Journal of Verbal Learning and Verbal Behavior, 20*, 445–453.

Carr, T.H., McCauley, C., Sperber, R.D., & Parmelee, C.M. (1982). Words, pictures, and priming: On semantic activation, conscious identification, and the automaticity of information processing. *Journal of Experimental Psychology: Human Perception and Performance, 8*, 757–777.

Clark, H.H., & Carlson, T.B. (1982). Context for comprehension. In J. Long & A. Baddeley (Eds.), *Attention and Performance IX*. Hillsdale, N.J.: Erlbaum.

Cole, R.A., & Jakimik, J. (1978). Understanding speech. How words are heard. In G. Underwood (Ed.)., *Strategies of Information Processing*. London: Academic Press.

Cole, R.A., & Jakimik, J. (1980). A model of speech perception. In R. Cole (Ed.), *Perception and production of fluent speech*. Hillsdale, N.J.: Erlbaum.

Cowart, W. (1982). Autonomy and interaction in the language processing system: A reply to Marslen-Wilson and Tyler. *Cognition, 12*, 109–117.

Cowart, W. (1983). Reference relations and syntactic processing. Evidence of a pronoun's influence on a syntactic decision that affects word naming. Distributed by Indiana University Linguistics Club.

Dell, G.S. (1984). Representation of serial order in speech: Evidence from the repeated phoneme effect in speech errors. *Journal of Experimental Psychology: Learning, Memory, and Cognition, 10*, 222–233.

Dell, G.S. (1985). Positive feedback in hierarchical connectionist models: Applications to language production. *Cognitive Science, 9*, 3–24.

Dell, G.S., & Newman, J.E. (1980). Detecting phonemes in fluent speech. *Journal of Verbal Learning and Verbal Behavior, 19*, 608–623.

Dell, G.S., & Tanenhaus, M.K. (1986). The loci of grammatical priming of inflected words. Manuscript in preparation.

Elman, J.L., & McClelland, J.L. (1984). Speech as a cognitive process: The interactive activation model. In N. Lass (Ed.), *Speech and Language* (Vol. 10). New York: Academic Press.

Feldman, J.A., & Ballard, D. (1982). Connectionist models and their properties. *Cognitive Science, 6*, 205–254.

Fischler, I. (1977). Semantic facilitation without association in a lexical decision task. *Memory & Cognition, 5*, 335–339.

Fodor, J.A. (1983). *The modularity of mind: An essay on faculty psychology.* Cambridge, Mass.: Bradford.

Forster, K.I. (1979). Levels of processing and the structure of the language processor. In W.E. Cooper and E.C.T. Walker (Eds.), *Sentence processing: Psycholinguistic studies presented to Merrill Garrett.* Cambridge, Mass.: MIT Press.

Foss, D.J., & Blank, M.A. (1980). Identifying the speech codes. *Cognitive Psychology, 12*, 1–31.

Foss, D.J., & Gernsbacher, M.A. (1983). Cracking the dual code: Toward a unitary model of phoneme identification. *Journal of Verbal Learning and Verbal Behavior, 22*, 609–632.

Glucksberg, S., Kreuz, R.J., & Rho, S. (1986). Context can constrain lexical access: Implications for models of language comprehension. *Journal of Experimental Psychology: Learning, Memory, and Cognition, 12*, 323–335.

Goodman, G.O., McClelland, J.L., & Gibbs, R.W., Jr. (1981). The role of syntactic context in word recognition. *Memory & Cognition, 9*, 580–586.

Gough, P.B., Alford, J.A., Jr., & Holley-Wilcox, P. (1981). Words and contexts. In O.J.L. Tzeng, & H. Singer (Eds.) *Perception of print: Reading research in experimental psychology.* Hillsdale, N.J.: Erlbaum.

Grosjean, F. (1980). Spoken word recognition processes and the gating paradigm. *Perception and Psychophysics, 28*, 267–283.

Johnson-Laird, P.N. (1983). *Mental models: Toward a cognitive science of language, inference, and consciousness.* Cambridge, Mass.: Harvard University Press.

Koriat, A. (1981). Semantic facilitation in lexical decision as a function of prime-target association. *Memory & Cognition, 9*, 587–598.

Lucas, M.M. (1983). *Lexical access during sentence comprehension: Context effects, frequency effects, and decision processes.* Unpublished Doctoral Dissertation, University of Rochester.

Lukatela, G., Kostic, A., Feldman, L.B., & Turvey, M.T. (1983). Grammatical priming of inflected nouns. *Memory & Cognition, 11*, 59–63.

Lupker, S.J. (1984). Semantic priming without association: a second look. *Journal of Verbal Learning and Verbal Behavior, 23*, 709–733.

McClelland, J.L. (1979). On the time relations of mental processes: An examination of systems of processes in cascade. *Psychological Review, 86*, 287–330.

McClelland, J.L., & Rumelhart, D.E. (1981). An interactive activation model of context effects in letter perception: Part I. An account of basic findings. *Psychological Review, 88*, 375–405.

Marlsen-Wilson, W.D. (1984). Function and process in spoken word-recognition. In H. Bouma & D.G. Bouwhuis (Eds.), *Attention and performance X: Control of language processes.* Hillsdale, N.J.: LEA.

Marslen-Wilson, W., & Tyler, L.K. (1980). The temporal structure of spoken language understanding. *Cognition, 8*, 1–71.

Marslen-Wilson, W.D., & Tyler, L.K. (1983). Reply to Cowart. *Cognition, 12*, 227–236.

Marslen-Wilson, W.D., & Welsh, A. (1978). Processing interactions and lexical access during word recognition in continuous speech. *Cognitive Psychology, 10*, 29–63.

Merrill, E., Sperber, R.D., & McCauley, C. (1981). Differences in semantic coding as a function of reading comprehension skill. *Memory & Cognition, 9*, 618–624.

Morton, J., & Long, J. (1976). Effect of word transitional probability on phoneme identification. *Journal of Verbal Learning and Verbal Behavior, 12*, 431–461.

Motley, M.T., Baars, B.J., & Camden, C.T. (1981). Syntactic criteria in pre-articulatory editing: Evidence from laboratory-induced slips of the tongue. *Journal of Psycholinguistic Research, 5*, 503–522.

Neely, J.H. (1977). Semantic priming and retrieval from lexical memory. Roles of inhibitionless spreading activation and limited-capacity attention. *Journal of Experimental Psychology: General, 106*, 226–254.

Norris, D. (1982). Autonomous processes in comprehension: A reply to Marslen-Wilson and Tyler. *Cognition, 11*, 97–101.

Onifer, W., & Swinney, D.A. (1981). Accessing lexical ambiguities during sentence comprehension: Effects of frequency of meaning and contextual bias. *Memory & Cognition, 9*, 225–236.

Pisoni, D.B., & Luce, P.A. (1987). Acoustic-phonetic representations in word recognition. *Cognition, 25*, this issue.

Prather, P., & Swinney, D. (1977). Some effects of syntactic context upon lexical access. Presented at the American Psychological Association Meetings, San Francisco, Ca.

Samuel, A.G. (1981a). Phonemic restoration: Insights from a new methodology. *Journal of Experimental Psychology: General, 110*, 474–494.

Samuel, A.G. (1981b). The role of bottom-up confirmation in the phonemic restoration illusion. *Journal of Experimental Psychology: Human Perception and Performance, 7*, 1124–1131.

Seidenberg, M.S. (1985). Constraining models of word recognition. *Cognition, 14*, 169–190.

Seidenberg, M.S., & Tanenhaus, M.K. (1986). Modularity and lexical access. In I. Gopnik (Ed.), *From models to modules: Proceedings of the McGill Cognitive Science Workshops*. N.J.: Ablex Press.

Seidenberg, M.S., Tanenhaus, M.K., Leiman, J.M., & Bienkowski, M. (1982). Automatic access of the meanings of ambiguous words in context: Some limitations of knowledge-based processing. *Cognitive Psychology, 14*, 489–537.

Seidenberg, M.S., Waters, G.S., Sanders, M., & Langer, P. (1984). Pre- and post-lexical loci of contextual effects on word recognition. *Memory & Cognition, 12*, 315–328.

Simpson, G.B. (1981). Meaning dominance and semantic context in the processing of lexical ambiguity. *Journal of Verbal Learning and Verbal Behavior, 20*, 120–136.

Simpson, G.B. (1984). Lexical ambiguity and its role in models of word recognition. *Psychological Bulletin, 96*, 316–340.

Swinney, D.A. (1979). Lexical access during sentence comprehension: (Re)consideration of context effects. *Journal of Verbal Learning and Verbal Behavior, 18*, 645–659.

Swinney, D.A. (1982). The structure and time-course of information interaction during speech comprehension: Lexical segmentation, access, and interpretation. In J. Mehler, E.C.T. Walker, & M. Garrett (Eds.), *Perspectives on mental representation*. Hillsdale, N.J.: Erlbaum.

Tanenhaus, M.K., Carlson, G.N., & Seidenberg, M.S. (1985). Do listeners compute linguistic representations? In D. Dowty, L. Kartunnen, & A. Zwicky (Eds.), *Natural language parsing: Psychological, theoretical, and computational perspectives*. New York: Cambridge University Press.

Tanenhaus, M.K., Dell, G.S., & Carlson, G. (in press). Context effects in lexical processing: A connectionist perspective on modularity. In J. Garfield (Ed.), *Modularity in knowledge representation and natural language understanding*. Cambridge, Mass.: MIT Press.

Tanenhaus, M.K., & Donnenwerth-Nolan, S. (1984). Syntactic context and lexical access. *Quarterly Journal of Experimental Psychology, 36A*, 649–661.

Tanenhaus, M.K., Leiman, J.M., & Seidenberg, M.S. (1979). Evidence for multiple stages in the processing of ambiguous words in syntactic contexts. *Journal of Verbal Learning and Verbal Behavior, 18*, 427–440.

Tyler, L.K. (1984). The structure of the initial cohort: Evidence from gating. *Perception and Psychophysics, 36*, 417–427.

Tyler, L.K., & Marslen-Wilson, W.D. (1982). Conjectures and refutations: A reply to Norris. *Cognition, 11*, 103–107.

Tyler, L.K., & Wessels, J. (1983). Quantifying contextual contributions to word-recognition processes. *Perception and Psychophysics, 34*, 409–420.

Warren, R.M. (1970). Perceptual restorations of missing speech sounds. *Science, 167*, 392–393.

West, R.F., & Stanovich, K.E. (1982). Source of inhibition in experiments on the effect of sentence context on word recognition. *Journal of Experimental Psychology: Learning, Memory, and Cognition, 8*, 385–399.

West, R.F., & Stanovich, K.E. (1986). Robust effects of syntactic structure on visual word processing. *Memory & Cognition, 14*, 104–113.

Wright, B., & Garrett, M. (1984). Lexical decision in sentences. *Memory & Cognition, 12*, 31–45.

Résumé

Cet article étudie dans quelle mesure la reconnaissance des mots est influencée par le contexte lexical, syntaxique et sémantique, cela afin de comparer les prédictions faites par des théories modulaires et interactives de l'architecture du système de compréhension du langage. Notre conclusion est que les données montrent clairement qu'il existe des effets du contexte lexical, moins clairement qu'il existe des effets du contexte sémantique, et qu'il y a peu de données en faveur d'effets du contexte syntaxique. Selon nous, les effets de feedback "de haut en bas" dans la compréhension apparaissent essentiellement dans des situations où il existe une relation partie-ensemble claire entre les deux niveaux, et où l'ensemble des unités de niveau inférieur qui peuvent recevoir un feedback du niveau supérieur est restreint.

Index